# Walter Piston

# Studies in Musicology

George Buelow, Series Editor

Professor of Musicology
Indiana University

## Other Titles in This Series

# Walter Piston

by
Howard Pollack

UMI RESEARCH PRESS
Ann Arbor, Michigan

Copyright © 1981, 1982
Howard Pollack

Produced and distributed by
UMI Research Press
an imprint of
University Microfilms International
Ann Arbor, Michigan 48106

Library of Congress Cataloging in Publication Data

**Pollack, Howard.**
Walter Piston.

(Studies in musicology ; no. 50)
Revision of thesis—Cornell University, 1981.
Catalog of Piston's works: p.
Discography: p.
Bibliography: p.
Includes index.
1. Piston, Walter, 1894-1976. 2. Composers—United
States—Biography. I. Title. II. Series.

ML410.P593P6 1982     780'.92'4 [B]        81-16364
ISBN 0-8357-1280-X                         AACR2

*To William W. Austin*

Walter Piston. (Piston Collection)

# Contents

# List of Music Examples

# List of Plates

# Acknowledgments

The generous and enthusiastic help I received on this book was often testimony to the deep respect and admiration with which so many people hold the memory of Walter Piston. This was especially true of my interviews and correspondences with Piston's friends, relatives, colleagues, and students. Their conversations and letters, listed in the bibliography, were an indispensable aid in better understanding this elusive and private man. I equally benefited from the tapes, records, music, and written material that were made available to me by a number of individuals and organizations: Anne Adams, Associated Music Publishers, Leonard Bernstein, the Boston Symphony Orchestra, Broadcast Music, Inc., Dartmouth's Hopkins Center, Robert Freeman, Robert Hampel, Brian Harden, John Hilliard, George Humphrey, Rebecca Kelly, Luis Leguia, the Library of Congress, Harris Lindenfeld, Steven Monder, the National Symphony Orchestra, the Portland [Maine] Symphony Orchestra, RCA Records, Chris Rouse, Harold Shapero, Rolfe and Tom Sokol, Ruth Sutro, Betty Thorndike, Charles Whitlock, Wayne Willis, and Neil Zaslaw. I would also like to thank the staffs of the Boston Public Library, Cornell's Music Library, the Library of Congress, the Music and Dance Divisions of the New York Public Library, the Rockland Public Library, and Eastman's Sibley Music Library for numerous courtesies. The Rochester Institute of Technology helped finance some research trips to Boston, where I found the kind support of Elliot Forbes and William Crook, and the warm hospitality of Carol Roth, Lenny Levine, Robert Hampel, and Parker Prindle.

I was fortunate to have, among my friends, musicians—Wayne Burak, Laura Carroll, Keith Conrad, Mary Hunter, Maggie Jackson, Howard Kilbury, Craig Purdy, Paul Rosenbloom, Ellen Sacher, and Roland Vazquez—with whom I could play some of Piston's music at the piano. This was an invaluable opportunity. Conversation with Linda Nagle helped me to better understand Piston's writings. Philip Greene gave careful readings of some early chapters, and Linda Kowitt helped edit the whole study.

I am also grateful for the advice and encouragement of my parents, Adele and Walter Pollack. And I am most indebted to Professors William Austin, Robert Palmer, and Cushing Strout of Cornell University for their teaching and guidance.

# Introduction

Walter Piston's music and books, admired around the world for their freshness, originality, and sophistication, signify the coming of age of musical America. With Michael Tilson Thomas's recording of the *Second Symphony*, and Mark DeVoto's revision of *Harmony*, Piston's work is making itself known to a fourth generation of listeners and students of classical music. The importance of his work is further enhanced by his teaching career at Harvard, where he personally supervised the education of scores of important scholars, performers, and composers. The study of Piston's influence on American music would indeed be a vast and complex task.

This book takes for its subject a smaller topic, namely, the life and work of this influential composer. The first two chapters are biographical, and draw upon personal interviews and correspondences, as well as on published articles and archival material (including the recent Piston Collection of the Boston Public Library). Chapter 1 discusses the friends and family of Piston's childhood and adult life, while Chapter 2 outlines the composer's musical and liberal education. The next seven chapters survey all of Piston's music, both published and unpublished, in chronological order. A final chapter addresses the subject of Piston's pedagogical and critical writings.

A comprehensive survey of Piston's music has not been undertaken since Elliott Carter's 1946 "Walter Piston" for *Musical Quarterly*. Although this article is still valuable and illuminating, the intervening years permit us to reexamine the early music in a new light and to consider the many works that Piston wrote from 1947 to his death in 1976. In the present study, each work is treated individually; and although these discussions often depend on, among other things, the information at hand, they usually involve circumstances concerning the work's composition, technical and aesthetic analyses, comparisons and evaluations. The musical illustrations are intended merely to highlight certain points, and it is desirable that readers consult scores and records whenever possible. Note, by the way, that transposing instruments are rewritten in C for the musical examples.

The scope of this work precludes the lengthy, detailed investigation of any single composition, but such criticism, where it is found, is duly noted in the course of the text. The analyses provided are traditional in method and terminology. This author could not help but be influenced by Piston's own critical and theoretical writings. However, even when discussing Piston's music at its most conservative, terms like sonata, fugue, scherzo, major, mixolydian, and twelve-tone must be regarded cautiously. These are not abstract ideas to which Piston dogmatically subscribes, but rather principles of common usage that provide the background for understanding his own individual expression. This, after all, is how Piston himself viewed the music of both past and present composers. This is not to say, however, that Piston's music could not be profitably studied from new perspectives, including those based on the work of Schenker and Forte. A master's thesis on Piston's symphonic slow movements by Gregory Danner already makes trenchant use of some recent theoretical writings by Wallace Berry.

General observations are found throughout the present study, but especially at the beginnings and ends of chapters, and, of course, in the conclusion. A principal consideration throughout the entire work is the subject of content (which Piston acknowledged to be elusive and subjective), form (which he thought neglected by many contemporary composers), and the interaction between content and form (which he aspired to have in perfect balance).

Few readers, the author believes, will care to read this critical reference work straight through. A basic introduction to Piston's life can be gained by reading Chapters 1 and 2. Those who are new to Piston should listen to *The Incredible Flutist* and the *Carnival Song*, of which there are many good recordings, and then read Capter 4. On the other hand, those readers already familiar with Piston might want to begin with Chapter 3 and the reassessment of the works upon which Piston's reputation as a "neoclassicist" rests. And for those who want to catch up on the little-known works of Piston's old age, Chapters 8 and 9 are recommended. Any work by Piston is better appreciated after some consideration of his writings, the subject of Chapter 10. A catalogue, discography, and bibliography are included to aid in all such investigations.

# 1

# Piston's Family and Friends

Walter Hamor Piston, Jr., was born on 20 January 1894, in Rockland, Maine. The family name was originally Pistone, but Walter's Italian grandfather changed his name from Antonio Pistone to Anthony Piston shortly after he settled in Maine. At the time of his birth, Walter's one Italian grandparent was long dead, and the family's Italian heritage, writes Elliott Carter, "had already been considerably erased."[1] The family was essentially "down East" Protestant; and years later, when Walter's brother, Anthony, married a woman of Italian background, a rift in the family ensued. But Piston was proud of his Italian origin, as any composer might reasonably be. A childhood friend, Elizabeth Carini, writes to the composer, "Indeed we do cherish the Italian blood we inherited from our parents."[2] At any rate, Piston learned to speak Italian fluently, cultivated a taste for Italian food and wines, and visited Italy during the two years (1924–1926) he spent in Europe. Virgil Thomson thought Piston's personality was shaped by his Italian background.[3] This Italian background at least provided the opportunity for good jokes, as when Piston's friend E. Power Biggs mockingly bemoaned the Americanization of Pistone into the unfortunately mechanical Piston, and suggested that the eighty-year-old composer change his name, to which Piston wryly retorted, "What do you suggest? Carboretta?"[4]

Grandfather Anthony E. Piston was born in Genoa in 1820 and died in Rockland in 1876. Family legend has it that Anthony, a sea captain, was shipwrecked off the coast of Maine sometime in the 1840s. He settled in East Thomaston at a time when there were only about twenty Italian immigrants in all of Maine, and moved to the nearby lime-boom town of Rockland soon after he had begun to buy land there in 1848. Shortly before his death, Captain Piston left the sea and took employment in a confectionary and shipping office.

Walter often quipped that his grandfather came to Maine to get Experience: in about 1854 Captain Piston married Experience Hamor, born in Vinalhaven in 1834, the daughter of Captain Ezra Hamor (a fellow master mariner), and Eliza (Higgins) Hamor of Eden, Maine. Anthony and Experience had ten children, though only Delia, Agnes, Victor, Annie, and Walter survived infancy. Walter Hamor, their youngest son, was born in 1870. He became a bookkeeper and, in 1890, married Leona Stover. Leona, born in 1872, was descended from the Stovers of Belfast, Maine, most of whom were seamen. (Her lineage is said to include some Indian ancestry as well.[5]) Walter and Leona had four boys: Anthony (b. 1891), Walter, Jr., (b. 1894), Donald (b. 1901), and Edward (b. 1907). Walter, Jr., was born in his grandmother Experience's saltbox home at 15 Ocean Street, where the family lived until Donald's birth prompted a move around the corner to 10 Fulton Street. In 1904, just before the Pistons left Rockland, they lived at 55 Broad Street, which was further away from the waterfront. Throughout these ten years, Walter, Sr., worked as a bookkeeper for the Fred R. Spear Company, a supplier of coal, wood, mason's supplies, and hardware items.

Walter, Jr.'s, childhood in Rockland revolved about his family: his parents and brothers, his grandmother, his uncle Victor Piston (a traveling salesman), and aunt Hattie, his uncle George Wardwell (a ship carpenter), and aunt Agnes, his uncle Richard Saville and his aunt Annie. The young Walter probably listened to his grandmother reminisce about her Italian husband, and to his uncle George tell tales of the sea. His uncle Victor could have speculated on those new inventions, the telephone and the automobile, while his father and aunt Annie discussed local artistic events. Walter, Jr.'s, quiet reserve and dry wit, which so delighted and sometimes exasperated his urban friends, was rooted in the daily life of this coastal community. And like his relatives, Walter learned a certain quiet from the town itself, with its surrounding mountains and Penobscot Bay, large homes and spacious roads, sailboats and schooners at rest in the harbor, and horses and buggies on Main Street. But by the 1890s Rockland was no longer a sleepy rural hamlet: it had over 8,000 persons, and was an industrial center with the production of lime its principal industry. One late nineteenth-century writer described the town as "canopied by day with terebinthine smoke and illuminated at night with the brilliant fires of innumerable lime-kilns."[6] The Limerock Railroad and the automobile (which made its first Rockland appearance in 1900) were bound to suggest new rhythms to Walter.

Piston vividly remembered these Rockland years, as the following letter to Betty Thorndike testifies:

March 31 [1976]

Dear Betty,

    I am having a great time with the sections of the map that Mr. Hadlock sent me. All of the names on Ocean Street were very familiar to me—except Higgins, which was really on the next street (Fulton) but curiously we had back yards together. Also it is G. Higgins, not Ezra. I just thought it a remarkable coincidence. Owl's Head is not exactly where I pictured it. I found the location of our second home to which we moved to be nearer the upper school, and had a bath tub, Broad Street, I think number 55.

Bien à vous,

Walter[7]

And when Elizabeth Carini sent him their second-grade picture and related pleasant afternoons in his house after school, he responded with interest. Publicly, Piston rarely spoke of his childhood. In one instance he told of picking out a chanty at the piano after hearing it sung by an uncle. This uncle (was it the sea carpenter George, or perhaps Richard, whose daughter Gertrude was to become a pianist?) laughed and said, "Well, you'll never have to work for a living."

In 1905, when Walter was eleven, the Pistons moved to Boston at the urging of one of Walter, Sr.'s, business acquaintances.[8] At this time, Rockland's lime industry was suffering from the fast-growing popularity of cement. The town's economic strength was dwindling, and business opportunities were to be found elsewhere. Other members of his family also seized this chance for betterment: the Wardwells left for Boston in 1904, and Victor and Hattie left for Bangor in 1905. Experience, who had lived through the rise and decline of the lime industry, remained in Rockland and died there in 1910. Among the papers Piston willed to the Boston Public Library was a photograph of this robust woman with the inscription, "my grandmother Experience."

Within his first four years in Boston Walter, Sr., was promoted a few modest ranks in the firm of Armor and Company, and in 1908 he was made "cashier" or comptroller. This was a well-paying, respectable position that comfortably placed the family in the middle class. Walter, Sr., worked for Armor until 1926, after which he worked a few years for H. V. Green Investments and Cities Service Oil Company. But despite Walter, Sr.'s, steady and lucrative employment, the Pistons never found a permanent residence. In the sixteen years Walter, Jr., resided with his family in Boston, the Pistons lived at eleven different locations. The youngest son, Edward, writes, "We moved often because my mother was not used to the city life, and being dissatisfied in one place, moved to another, thinking it would be better."[9] Except for one year's residence in Charlestown (probably in order for Walter, Sr., to be close to work), the family lived in Dorchester or the surrounding area of Roxbury or Mattapan. These were years of transition for Dorchester: while it was still predominantly old Yankee, thousands of Jewish and Irish immigrants were finding a home there. For the Piston boys, each move meant new neighborhood friends, but it usually did not involve a change in schools.

In a letter written to this author (15 October 1977), Edward Piston provides the best portrait we have of the Pistons in Boston:

> . . . My mother was the dominant parent as far as running the household went. My father worked long hours, leaving for work about 6 a.m. and returning as late as midnight. My mother was a strong personality, a typical Englishwoman. I remember she was responsible for buying a piano for the house, about the time I was old enough to start school. My father's role was basically that of breadwinner.
>
> I remember playing cribbage and chess with my father, and we played whist as a family. My brother Donald and I used to attend concerts and visit art museums, and I occasionally went with my father. I would meet him after work and we would go to a concert together, to the MacDowell Club or the Boston Symphony.
>
> My mother was a partial invalid and did not go much of anywhere. She still ran the household, although we had a housekeeper who came every day.
>
> The family did sometimes go on picnics to Revere Beach or Nantasket Beach on Sundays. My parents did not attend church.
>
> My mother was very proud of her sons. Donald's widow says she often remarked that no one in the world had four more brilliant sons than she did.

Donald's widow, Mrs. Ruth Naugler, also reported to me that Walter and Leona "were very different from most people. They were very kind, and very intelligent, but they didn't have many friends."[10] They were a strong and independent couple, although Leona was more critical and outspoken than her introspective husband who was so fond of chess and music. "We're living in the foolish age," Leona would often remark, finding consolation in the wisdom of the Bible, especially Matthew 5, 6, and 7. Walter, Sr., must have quietly followed the young Walter's checkered education with some concern. He lived until 1933, long enough to hear Koussevitzky play his son's music in Symphony Hall. After her husband's death, Leona left Boston with her son Edward for Fresno, California. She died there in 1937, one year before Walter's greatest triumph, *The Incredible Flutist*.[11]

All four boys learned a quiet resourcefulness and a gentle humor from their father. They also acquired his aptitude for mathematics: Tony became an insurance company statistician; Walter was trained as an engineer; and Donald, a Malcolm Cotton Brown fellow in physics at M.I.T., taught at the University of Maine, received a Ph.D. in physics at Stanford University, worked for Twining Laboratories in Fresno, California, and wrote two books on meteorology. (Edward, like Walter, received a Bachelor's degree in the fine arts, and worked as Director of Information and Printing for the Fresno State College Association.) Another legacy from Walter, Sr., was his love for music: Tony sang in the chorus of the Handel and Haydn Society of Boston until his death in 1966; Walter made music his profession; Donald played violin and later viola in the Fresno State College Symphony Orchestra until his death in 1956; and Edward played piano and composed. Despite all these similarities, Walter sustained no close friendship with any of his brothers. Although Tony lived in Cambridge, his wife, a devout Catholic, was hostile to the Protestant Pistons and severed Tony's relations with the family. Their seven children barely knew their famous uncle in neighboring Belmont. Donald and Edward's move to Fresno inhibited any intimate relationship with Walter. Actually Walter was closest with Donald, and when the two brothers got together, reports Mrs. Naugler, they had a grand time. These two Pistons were very alike: their looks, their wit, and even their handwriting were similar. But Kathryn's sister-in-law, Margaret Nason, informs this author that although Walter and Kathryn were hopeful about this relationship, in later years they grew disappointed. As for Edward, thirteen years separated him from Walter. He had a deep respect for the composer, but was too shy to show him any of his own compositions, or even to phone his condolences to Walter after his wife Kathryn's death.[12]

Walter met Kathryn at the Massachusetts Normal Art School, where they both entered as freshmen in 1912. He was eighteen and she, born 24 October 1892, was twenty. She had a merry disposition and strikingly beautiful red hair. During World War I, Margaret Warrein (Nason), on a visit to Kathryn's studio, found Walter lolling about in "bohemian" attire, with long hair and a flowing bowtie.[13] Margaret's impressions of him were disagreeable, and she voiced her concern in a letter to her boyfriend (Kathryn's brother Tom) who was then fighting in France. On his return, the veteran Tom met the young dandy and was not reassured. On 14 September 1920, he received a note from his sister that went something to this effect:

> Dear Tom,
>     I don't know whether you know what I'm doing this morning. I'm going to marry Walter Piston. It's easy to see that you don't think much of Walter. You're all wrong. I know as well as I know that this is a rainy day that I'm doing the right thing.[14]

Kathryn also asked her parents, William and Kate, to suspend judgment. William's father, the Reverend Elias Nason, was an eminent minister, a friend of Whittier, Emerson, and Howe, and an erudite man who knew twelve languages and who published a number of tracts, including studies on oratorios and American hymnody.[15] But while William also entered the ministry, he gained little success as a preacher; he preferred to write poetry in private journals. The Nasons's life in North Bellerica was a constant struggle eased by the pleasures of music and art. William and Kate wanted greater security for their daughter than a free-lance musician was likely to afford. As for Kathryn's sister Gertrude, who was also a painter, Walter's bohemianism was mild compared to the sort that eventually attracted her to New York City. It was there that she met and married William Donahue, an abstract expressionist painter.

Walter and Kathryn were married in the Unitarian Church on Beacon Street and moved into an apartment at 20 Queensberry Street in the Back Bay area. This was in close proximity to Symphony Hall but a considerable distance from Harvard, where Walter had just enrolled as a freshman. In the fall of 1921, the Pistons moved to 77½ Charles Street (at the foot of Beacon Hill between Pinckney and Mt. Vernon Streets), where the couple stayed for three years. The neighborhood was lively, with artists, small shops, and cafés. Around one corner was the Harvard Musical Association, with its fine library of scores, and around another corner lived Kathryn's brother Tom and his recent wife Margaret Nason. While Walter studied music and Tom learned wood engraving, their wives worked to make ends meet. Sometimes the two couples would have dinner at the Athens, with its home-styled Greek food, or an Italian restaurant in the North End. Afterward, they might go see a movie or play. Fifty cents bought a seat in the top balcony of Copley Theatre, where they saw memorable performances of Ibsen, Shaw, and Chekov; they also enjoyed the more popular theatre of Du Bose Heyward's *Porgy*. Tom and Margaret came to appreciate Walter, but they preferred Kathryn's good humor to her husband's brittle wit. When the Pistons returned from Paris in 1926, they saw less of the Nasons, especially after the Nasons moved to Lyme, Connecticut in 1938. But Kathryn kept close ties with Tom as she did with her other siblings, namely Gertrude (b. 1885), Walton (b. 1886), and Florence (b. 1896). Florence, the youngest, was a violinist and played in a quartet that included Boston Symphony musicians. After her mother's death she moved in with the Pistons in Belmont, where she died in 1940 of cancer.

The Pistons moved to Belmont after their return from Europe in 1926. Whereas Belmont might have been too rural for Gertrude and too urban for Tom, it suited Kathryn very well. There lived a circle of lively and sympathetic painters; indeed, some of the surrounding meadows had inspired some of Winslow Homer's landscapes. This circle included Charles and Alison Coolidge, Nelson and Betty Chase, and Lyman and Grace Reasoner.[16] The group pioneered what they called "the Hill," an undeveloped section of Belmont. They learned to avoid political discussion, but shared an intense interest in art. They met regularly to sketch nudes, after which they would drink and play music. These sketching parties were mild compared to the wild bashes Nelson would sometimes throw at which Walter would play any waltz or rag his friends might request. Inevitably the group would gather around the piano to sing their theme song, "Our Lady of the Telephone," and there was dancing as well; Grace Reasoner remembers that Kathryn danced well, but Walter danced "like a tame bear."

These artists admired Walter more than they did his music. According to Alison, she and her husband were "musically disinclined." Grace faithfully attended the Boston Symphony where she heard Piston's works performed, but only a relaxed hearing of a recording of the *Fourth Symphony* at the Piston home ever convinced her of the composer's spirituality. Nelson found Piston's music "too rare" for his taste, and thought that the music, like the man, was too "modernistic" for the Belmont circle. It is easy to see the gulf between the still lifes of the Belmont painters and the musical canvases by Piston, but what does Chase mean by the man being too "modernistic"? Chase evaded this question when it was put to him. Piston was more conservative than moderate Republicans like the Coolidges, not to mention Roosevelt liberals like the Reasoners. Was Piston's modernism related to his conservative politics? In any case, Nelson had great admiration for Walter, whom he remembers as "dirty as hell and reeking with fun." Both men loved to get drunk, and Nelson fondly remembers one Belmont morning when they staggered about in the snow at three A.M. swearing at the birds and laughing.

In her old age, Kathryn continued to befriend local painters such as her second cousin Ruth Sutro,[17] and her neighbor Helen Groden, who preferred, as did her husband John, Walter's company to Kathryn's.[18] John Groden kept his old neighbor well supplied with Perkins 36 smoking tobacco, and Piston, for his part, gave Groden a book of Vermont humor after the lawyer had successfully helped to reinstate Alger Hiss to the bar. Piston, however, made his own friends outside the circle of Belmont painters and the Nason family in which Kathryn felt most comfortable. One such friend was Amory Thorndike, whose friendship with Walter lasted from his years in Boston after he graduated Harvard in 1921 to his death in Maine in 1972. Walter and Amory shared a down-Eastern humor, a Bostonian elegance, and an active interest in Boston's musical affairs, especially those of the Flute Players' Club. They were also in Paris together in the mid-twenties, when Amory, an accomplished amateur pianist, studied with Robert Casadesus while Walter worked with Boulanger and others.[19] In later years, Piston wrote his *Oboe Suite* for Amory's father, Dr. Augustus Thorndike.

Aside from his student years in Europe, Piston never travelled very far, except for a trip to Aspen in 1959 and to Los Angeles in 1961. He did not accompany his wife to Munich in 1936, nor did he accept a government invitation to visit the Soviet Union in 1957. (Piston responded to this invitation by writing: "Personally I have little interest in a trip to Russia. If I were to consider it at all it would be solely as a patriotic duty."[20]) He feared and avoided airplanes. He once told Conrad Aiken that travel was "a waste of time."[21] In two letters that Aiken sent Piston in the early 1930s he tried coaxing the composer and his wife to vacation at their English home, but to no avail. One letter, dated "avril 25 31," is published in the *Selected Letters of Conrad Aiken*. The ensuing letter is unpublished:

Rye Feb. 13.32

Well, Walter, so you're still so's to be about! You could have knocked me down with a feather. And my delight at getting the Bach gavottes, in so beautiful a holograph, and arranged by W. Piston, was only marred by my own inability—alas—to read or play them. However, Jerry did so, and then my son John, who is a Bach enthusiast, and who was as delighted with them as myself—he proceeded forthwith to learn them by heart, and so carried them back to London. It's not impossible, incidentally, that you'll be having him as a pupil one of these days—he may go to Harvard next fall. . . . But how are you, anyway? You're a hell of a goddam correspondent, if I do say so. Now and then I hear faroff rumours of the life on the Hill,—mostly re the witch and her ex-husband, and mostly in fact gleaned from one or tother by Jake Wilbur,— though I did have a note or two from Bill himself. I've occasionally trembled to think of you and Catherine there exposed all alone to the solitary one—I can see the baleful eye that gleams out from the little window on the stair—the white and incandescent face—the pointed and gleaming teeth—the long stride of twilight which precedes the panther-spring—and it seems to me unfair that you should be so defenceless. But perhaps you've developed a technique of self-defense—a sort of psychological jujitsu? Or maybe Catherine is still, as she always was, capable of inspiring, in the breast of the night-haunter, a wholesome daylight respect. . . . Anyway, I hope neither of you has been irreparably injured, that there are no tooth-marks on your throats, or green lights in your eyes. . . . And what have you been writing this year? what performing? what hearing? what doing? I suppose I shall never know, unless I come back and take a bus one surprising afternoon and walk up the unholy hill itself. Which may be. Our affairs are pretty desperate—I've only just now decided to linger on here till the summer, having teased a thousand out of Scribners for a ¼ written novel, which I now hope to finish in the next few months. Meanwhile, we wait on events, and if they are propitious, we may try another winter here—or we may go back to Cambridge and try to pick up odd jobs for a living. . . . Have you any idea of coming abroad next summer? Would you consider spending some of it here? I think you'd both like it— it's a mecca for artists—you'd both like Paul Nash, whether or not you know or like his work, which I think very fine—and we have a freak artist named Burra an amusing creature whom I used to think was a fairy—now I think he's just one of nature's eunuchs, but he does highly entertaining stuff—and there's a chessboard—a piano— a studio which C could use—movies—tennis courts—the sea—2000 books. Think it over. And it would be cheap. If we shared expenses, it would probably cost you (for both of you) about six pounds, or perhaps a little under—which, at present exchange, would be $21., per week. Not so bad. . . . If you really considered coming, we'd of course plan definitely to stay here till autumn, and perhaps go back with you, and with son John. . . . I've had a lot of chess with son John, and in a year and a half won perhaps five games from him, usually when he makes a slip out of mere fatigue. He makes a fool of me. However, I even things up at pingpong, of which we also play a great deal, and which is really a swell game. . . . We enjoy life here increasingly— lots of fun—are meeting all the Lesbians, Radclyffe Hall (who took a fancy to Jerry!) and so on—there are two rival camps of Lesbians which have no use for each other. In fact, as Nash says, there is almost everything here except normalcy. Even incest. . . . Do write me the news—have you seen any of the poetry boys—how's Amory— how's your cellar—and speaking of that, I drink you health in ale.

as ever

Conrad[22]

The Bach gavotte arrived in time to be incorporated into Aiken's unfinished novel, *The Great Circle*, published in 1933. In that book the hero, Andrew Carter, plays the gavotte when conversation with his unfaithful wife fails him. Aiken's feeling for the gavotte is more overt in the letter than it is in the novel.[23] The "Bill" in the letter is probably the man who had introduced them to each other, William Taussig, Aiken's old Harvard roommate and Piston's neighbor on Somerset Street. (The proximity of the Pistons and the Taussigs would also explain why the "witch" is such a constant threat.) This circle of friends also included Jack Wheelwright, Gordon Bassett, and Ed Burrows. Aiken celebrated their drinking parties in an elegy to Gordon Bassett entitled "Another Lycidas."

> Where shall it be:
> tonight, tonight again, where shall it be?
> Down 'Mulberry' Street
> beckon the streetlights, and our feet
> through rain or snow or sleet
> once more in unison to eastward turn
> not to Priapus Garden or to view
> what the 'poast' says is 'plaid' today
> but if the burlesque be on
> to the Old Howard, or the Tam or Nip,
> the Oyster House or Silver Dollar Bar
> then to the Athens, there once more to meet
> with Piston's whole-tone wit or Wheelwright's neat
> while the martinis flow and clams are sweet
> and he himself our morning star
> until Apollo's taxi ploughs the dawn.[24]

The men in this group must have been both earthy and elegant in ways that this verse suggests. Mary Aiken's remembrances of Piston fit with images left by her husband's letters and poems. She described Piston as a man who smoked "Violettas," a Mexican cigarette, and who wore natty European shoes and expensive English tweeds. Mrs. Aiken thought that his wit was better than her husband's, and subtler than Louis Untermeyer's. His humor often carried with it sexual innuendos that caused her to assume that he had seduced the "spinsterish" Kathryn, and to wonder whether he ever pursued other women. She thought that he and her husband were the two most honest men she had ever met. We will learn more about their relationship when the memoirs of the poet's second wife, Clarissa Lorenz Aiken, are made available. Piston also befriended Archibald MacLeish when the latter became Boylston Professor at Harvard, though his friendship with Ada MacLeish went back to student days with Boulanger.

Social life on the Hill began to wane as careers and responsibilities became more important, and the Second World War, writes Alison Coolidge, "was the finishing blow to such easy going affairs." Walter avoided social activity more assiduously than anyone else; he would decline invitations with the simple response, "I'd rather be doing something else." Some of Walter's friends were offended by his unsociability, and Tom and Margaret Nason were concerned for Kathryn. But it seems that Kathryn was just as content to stay at home with her husband. The Pistons had lived in a studio home at 92 Somerset from 1927 to 1933, and in a larger studio next door at 94 Somerset from 1933 to 1936. In that year, Kathryn and Lyman Reasoner designed the house which was constructed at 127 Somerset and which was to be the Piston home for the rest of their lives. This lovely house, which resembles an English country house, was artfully conceived. Walter's studio, at one end of the house, had high, uneven ceilings for excellent acoustics and a beautiful view of the garden and its brook. Kathryn's studio, at the house's other end, was sunken below ground level but had good lighting. The living room, "neutral territory" or "the arena," as Piston would say, had exposed beams, stucco walls, a grand piano, and a fireplace which the Pistons used all winter. The house was a more elaborate version of their summer cottage in South Woodstock, Vermont. In 1933, Kathryn had bought some land on a hilltop from a farming family, the Cranes, and designed a house for summer residence there. Kathryn loved to sketch and paint in the Vermont countryside; Margaret Nason contends that Walter would just as well have stayed in Belmont. While Piston furnished his Belmont home with a Steinway grand piano, he acquired a Kranich and Bach for this Vermont place. The Cranes liked the Pistons better than they liked most of the vacationers who resorted in Woodstock.[25]

Kathryn was a good and serious artist and, although she modestly pursued her career, she retained her maiden name. After her graduation from Mass Art in 1916, Kathryn won a fellowship at the Museum of Fine Arts. She later studied in Paris, where Matisse and other Fauve artists left their marks. Kathryn rarely exhibited her paintings, although she was active in many art associations, including the Cambridge Art Association, the Manchester (Vermont) Art Center, the National Association of Women Artists, and the Belmont Arts and Crafts Association. Her most memorable exhibit was probably the 1945 three-man show with her brother Tom and her sister Gertrude. Dorothy Adlow reviewed this exhibit and wrote:

> Kathryn Nason seems happiest on a hill-top in Vermont recording with a swift brush her impression of the sprawling hills and open skies. She roughs out the masses and indicates the hollow spaces. The manner is summary and the effect is airy and decorative.[26]

Kathryn's favorite painters included Charles Burchfield, Isobel Bishop, and Yusao Kumiyoshi, American contemporaries whose distinctive realisms all owe something to Oriental art. The same might be said of Kathryn's vibrant paintings, most of which are still lifes and landscapes. Kathryn once said, "We [she and Walter] have the same slant on artistic things. We use different mediums to interpret the same point of view."[27] Would Kathryn have challenged Nelson Chase's statement that Walter was more "modernistic" than the Belmont painters?

Kathryn, like Tom and Gertrude, wanted no children; only her brother Walton had offspring. The Pistons lavished affection on their gardens ("Some of my best musical ideas," said Piston, "come to me while I'm spreading manure."[28]) They also took pleasure in their pets. In their early years they had cats, and throughout their lives they had a series of dogs: Bumble, half-chow, half-police dog, and three standard poodles, Inky, Cimmie, and Gina. There is no evidence that Kathryn shared Walter's enthusiasm for chess and martinis, Garbo and Bogart,[29] or French and Italian literature. Neither had much interest in their television, which they kept in a closet.

Piston's last years were plagued with difficulties. Diabetes and old age enfeebled his sight and his hearing.[30] Then, in the 1970s, came a series of traumatic events: a burglary, a broken hip, and, finally, Kathryn's death on 19 February 1976. An invalid for some time, Kathryn had refused any hospital care, even on the night of her death, when her husband pleaded that she reconsider. Walter phoned the news of Kathryn's death to Margaret Nason and wrote the following note to Betty Thorndike.

February 21 [1976]

Dear Betty,

I have to send you the sad news that Kathryn died on the early morning of Thursday February 19. She was not in pain and unbelievably weak. I know you will understand that I can't say more at this time.

Love,

Walter

Later letters to Betty Thorndike testify that in the some nine months in which Piston survived his wife, he was very much preoccupied with settling her estate. The longest such letter follows:

May 20 [1976]

Dear Betty,

A trip to Maine seems extremely remote. I feel as well as I can under the circumstances but I have not ventured to any social gatherings or concerts. I drive only short distances near home, but when walking I have to stop and rest often. The piece for the Portland Symphony Quartet is done but no date of performance is set, probably next season. It is doubtful that I shall go—the receptions, etc., are too much, as I know from other occasions. I had to decline the invitation to spend three days at College of the Atlantic.

I am living alone with my dog. Not exactly gay but the neighbors are nice. The executor's help is dealing with thousands of problems and occupying my mind all the time. You won't guess what I am doing about Vermont. I could not bear going there now, nor could I cope with it physically. If I sold it, whoever got it would ruin it. If I gave it to something like Audubon, they could not take care of it. So I am *giving* it to the farm next door. Don't faint.

The Townsend-Crane farm is a real Vermont farm, with cattle, etc. They are beset with offers to buy their land, and with taxes, etc. They have cared for our place for 42 years. It is a natural part of their farm. This was Kathryn's dream and I know she would like it that way. I feel very good about this. It does something for the farmer and saves the place, as they have three generations and really want to be farmers.

There was an exhibit of Kathryn's painting in the month of March, in Belmont, a great success.

I hope this letter sounds hopeful. Anyway the food is passable. Also Gina is a great consolation.

With affection,

Walter

Piston was cheered not only by his poodle Gina, but, as other letters show, by Norton's interest in a fourth edition of *Harmony* and by his relatively good health. He also managed to retain a fair degree of independence despite the concerns of Grace Clark, Helen Groden, and other friends.

Piston died at home of a heart attack on 12 November 1976, at age eighty-two. Like his wife, he was cremated, and his ashes were strewn in Mt. Auburn Cemetery rather than placed in the paper bag about which he used to joke. He willed his wife's paintings (those he had not given to friends) to the Farnsworth Gallery in Rockland, Maine, his money to the Boston Symphony and the Boston Public Library's Thomas Nason Memorial Fund, and his personal effects to the Boston Library, except for his tapes, which he gave to the Library of Congress. A member of the Portland Quartet volunteered to take charge of his dog.

The present author never knew, or even met, Piston. Some of the friends and family that survived Piston's death—Edward and Jean Piston, Ruth Naugler, Margaret Nason, Betty Thorndike, Grace Reasoner, Alison Coolidge, Nelson Chase, Mary Aiken, John and Helen Groden, Ruth Sutro, and Fidelia Crane—were instrumental in providing much of the information for this chapter. Only Nelson Chase, it seems, was truly intimate with Piston, and when this writer spoke with him, he was reluctant to reminisce. But even without the testimony of Donald Piston or Amory Thorndike or the composer's wife, a fair perspective of the composer's social world is possible. Nothing is known of Piston's relationship with his parents, but of his three brothers, he was close with only Donald, with whom he occasionally visited and corresponded. (This correspondence seems to be lost with the exception of a letter about acoustics from the physicist Donald to his composer-brother.) Because his wife Kathryn had close family ties, her family essentially became his family, especially Tom and Margaret Nason, and, until her early death, Florence Nason. As for Piston's friends, they may be placed into three groups. First, there were professional contacts—colleagues at Harvard, musicians in the Boston Symphony, fellow composers, and so forth. Second, there were Kathryn's artist friends (and which of her friends were not artists?), including the Belmont crowd, in which Piston found congenial neighbors like Nelson Chase and Charles Coolidge. Third, there were men like Amory Thorndike and Conrad Aiken who perhaps comprised Piston's most intimate circle. Naturally enough, the friends from all these groups were largely men and women of Piston's generation, Boston-bred, educated, and artistic. This generation combined a Boston hauteur with a distaste for snobbery and Puritanism, an old-world elegance with a New England simplicity, and a conservative restraint with an artistic bohemianism. Their world is reflected in the novels of Aiken, Marquand, and Cozzens, and finds its supreme musical expression in the music of Walter Piston.

# 2

# The Composer's Education

In 1908, far from becoming a composer, Piston entered Boston's Mechanic Arts High School which provided him with an education that emphasized scientific and vocational skills. Upon graduation in 1912, Piston worked one summer as a draftsman for the Boston Elevated Railway Company, participating in the development of the "articulated car," a trolley that could be linked up with other trolleys.[1] Piston decided to go on to college. Torn between music and art, he finally chose the Massachusetts Normal Art School over the New England Conservatory because tuition at Mass Art was free. Piston spent four years, from 1912 to 1916, at Mass Art, majoring in painting, but also studying architectural drawing, Greek, German, French, American history, and other subjects. Though Margaret Nason's remembrances help us to visualize the young bohemian painter in these decadent pre-War years, it is difficult to imagine Piston, the Harvard professor who neither spent time at an easel nor seemed particularly bohemian, as the young dandy she describes.[2] Piston eventually gave up painting and often said that he did so because his wife, Kathryn, painted so much better than he. Actually, Piston did all the illustrations for *Orchestration*, except for the violin, which was drawn by Kathryn.

Piston offers no self-criticism of his artistic abilities to Peter Westergaard, but says:

> I went to art school, and earned money on the side playing the violin and the piano. I kept getting more and more interested in music, and by the end of the senior year I was entirely devoted to it; but by then I was so near to graduation I decided to finish up school and I got my diploma as a painter.[3]

Piston's love for music was a legacy from his father and perhaps his grandfather as well. Grandfather Anthony surely sang chanties, and he may have also played the flute;[4] he must also have known that a fellow Genoese, Paganini, had set new standards of instrumental playing during his father's lifetime. Anthony died when his youngest child was only six, and Walter, Sr., might have learned more about music from his mother and his siblings, especially Annie, whose daughter Gertrude became a pianist. Rockland offered some public musical fare, mostly from dance orchestras, wind bands, and church choirs. But in the 1890s a number of musical organizations were created to promote more serious music; these included the Fletcher Club (founded in 1892), the Wight Philharmonic Club (1893), and the Beethoven Club (1899). Did Walter, Sr., attend any of their concerts? If so, did he ever take his sons Tony or Walter with him?

Equally uncertain is how and when the Piston boys acquired their musical skills. When did Tony study voice, and what might have he sung at home? The Pistons had no piano in Rockland,[5] and did not own one in Boston until around 1906.[6] Is this when Tony and Walter began piano lessons, at ages seventeen and fourteen respectively? We only know that Walter studied with Harris Shaw, who also taught piano to his brother Edward and organ to Virgil Thomson. As for Walter and the violin, our knowledge here is sketchy as well. His father brought home a violin when young Walter was in high school, and he soon played it well enough to join the high school orchestra. He practiced the violin so much that his mother was forced to complain, "Must you practice all day?"[7] But when did Piston begin violin lessons with Florence Jones, a violinist in the MacDowell Club, or, for that matter, with Felix Winternitz, the concert violinist, and Jules Theodorowicz and Placido Fiumara, both with the Boston Symphony?

In all probability, Piston studied with most of the forementioned teachers between 1916 and his admission to Harvard in 1920. He spent two of these four years in the Navy Band stationed at MIT, for, as Piston explains:

> . . . when the war came, the First World War, that is, and it became obvious that everybody had to go into the service, I wanted to go in as a musician. I couldn't play any band instrument, but I knew instruments and I knew that the saxophone was very easy. So I went down to Oliver Ditson's and bought a saxophone, and stopped by at the public library to get an instruction book. I learned enough to play by ear. In a very short time I was called and I tried out for the band. I didn't pretend to read the part but just played notes that went with the harmony, and I was accepted. That turned out to be a rather valuable experience for me, because we had all kinds of spare time; with instruments always available in the band room I picked up a moderate ability to play something on each of them. I was proficient enough to play the English horn solo in the *William Tell* Overture on the little soprano saxophone in Symphony Hall.[8]

Piston may have joined the Navy Band specifically in order to continue his study of piano and violin. Or did he actually disapprove of American involvement in the War? This is doubtful, for he tried at one point to become an ensign (the transfer was denied because the Navy thought him too valuable as a musician).[9] But in later years, his attitude towards the War, or, at any rate, towards his involvement in the War, was decidedly ironic, as the two following quips reveal: "The only battle I took part in was the 'Battle of the Charles River,' "[10] and "The Germans gave up because I was playing saxophone in the Navy Band."[11]

In 1917, while in the Navy, Piston joined the MacDowell Club as a first violinist; and in 1920, his last year with the Club, he was promoted to principal second violin. The Club was essentially a woman's string orchestra, and even when the ensemble was expanded into a full orchestra for special concerts, women still dominated the ranks, playing the trumpets, the horns, and the trombones. From 1916 to 1925, the Club was directed by Georges Longy, the distinguished French musician who was hired as principal oboist by the Boston Symphony in 1898. Longy programmed concerts that emphasized Baroque and French Romantic music: a Club concert in 1919, for instance, presented works by Witkowski, Franck, Ravel, Enescu, Gluck, Bizet, and Gédalge. Under Longy, the MacDowell Club specialized in French music, as did the Boston Symphony, during these years, under Rabaud and Monteux.

Longy was nonetheless interested in the music of his adopted homeland. In 1919 the indefatigable oboist, who had already started a woodwind club and a music school, founded the Boston Musical Association, whose orchestra and chamber concerts were specifically intended to promote American music. At each of its concerts, a new American work, chosen by a panel that included Longy and Harvard's E. B. Hill, was performed. Longy revealed a colonialist's temperament when he urged Americans to write works like *L'Apprenti sorcier* and *L'Après-midi d'un Faun*, and this bias doubtless determined the works, listed below, that the panel decided upon.

| | |
|---|---|
| F. Stuart Mason | Four Characteristic Pieces for Violoncelli |
| Richard Platt | Violin Sonata |
| Charles Griffes | Poem for Flute and Small Orchestra |
| John Beach | Naive Landscapes |
| Arthur Whiting | Fantasie for Piano and Full Orchestra |
| Robert Bennett | Quartette for Flutes |
| Blair Fairchild | Legende for Violin and Orchestra |
| Daniel Mason | Sonata for Clarinet and Piano, Op. 14 |
| Warren Storey-Smith | Song with Orchestra: A Caravan from China Comes |
| Reginald Sweet | Prelude: Riders to the Sea |

Piston played principal second violin in all of the Association's orchestra concerts, and participated in some chamber concerts as well, playing

Turina's *Scène Andalouse*, Ravel's *Introduction and Allegro*, and, for a concert sponsored by the MacDowell Club, Vaughan Williams's *On Wenlock Edge*. The Association had a short history, from January 1919 to April 1921, but it was a noble experiment which anticipated and perhaps paved the way for Koussevitzky's great adventure.

Piston inhabited a different world as a violinist and pianist in dance bands at local cafés, restaurants, and hotels. This was Piston's main source of income for at least the decade 1912 to 1922, during which time he worked at such places as the Parker House, the Marliave Café, Blatz's Palm Garden ("one colorful and earthy place")[12], and, during the summer, at resorts like the Block Island Hotel. Piston sometimes took charge of these orchestras, which typically consisted of two violins, viola, flute, clarinet, two cornets, trombone, piano, bass, and drums. Their musical fare, says Piston, was "the familiar, routine popular music, endlessly repeating the platitudes in fashion at the time, occasionally relieved a bit by excerpts from musical shows or even selections from opera."[13] This music was undoubtedly mostly dance music: polkas, waltzes, tangos, and trots. Long after he quit this profession, Piston continued to play such music to entertain his friends at private parties.

The young dance band musician learned enough theory from Harris Shaw, or perhaps on his own, to place out of Harvard's harmony courses and enter Archibald Davison's Counterpoint class in the fall of 1919 as a special student. By then, it seems, Piston had decided to become a composer. Had he entertained this "perfectly mad idea"[14] as early as 1912 when he opted for art over music? Did composing for the Navy Band or some dance orchestras awaken this interest? Or was his exposure to new American works in Longy's Association the deciding factor? An aspiring composer in Boston could no do better, in any case, than to turn to "Doc" Davison, who had also been Harvard-educated, earning his doctorate in music in 1908 for the dissertation, "Harmonic Contribution of Claude Debussy," and a symphonic poem, *Hero and Leander*. In 1919, the thirty-five-year-old Davison was an accomplished choral conductor, a Renaissance specialist, a progressive educator, and a distinguished theorist. In his counterpoint class, students first sang and studied folksongs, then the melodies of Schubert, Rossini, Brahms, and others, and then wrote their own; finally, his students considered the art of combining voices. Piston spoke well of Davison as did Sessions, who attended Harvard before the War.[15] Piston said, "I often thought that Doc didn't realize what a top-notch natural musician he was. He could improvise or write on the blackboard original examples of polyphony of the highest excellence and vitality."

By the end of counterpoint class, tells Piston, "Doc was all fired up about getting me to come to Harvard. I think he more or less arranged the whole thing." And so Piston entered Harvard as an undergraduate in the fall of 1920 at the age of twenty-six. In his sophomore year, Piston took another Davison class, the History and Development of Choral Music, a newly designed course that featured a singing laboratory. It was this class, along with Davison's performances with the chapel choir and the glee club, that (according to Thomson) indelibly marked "a long series of musicians" of whom Thomson claims to be the first.[16] Thomson doubtless has Thompson, Fine, and Carter, not Piston, in mind, although Piston did eventually write two choral works, one of which—*Carnival Song*—was written for the Harvard Glee Club.

With the exception of Edward Ballantine, the other members of the Harvard music department (Clifford Heilman, Walter Spalding, and E. B. Hill) shared with Davison a pedagogical lineage that, via Widor, dated back to J. S. Bach.[17] It was a friendly department, its members often team-teaching and dedicating music and books to one another. Heilman assumed sole responsibility for the teaching of canon and fugue, a class Piston took in his freshman year. Two years later Piston also studied composition with Heilman, who had just published his *Trio*, Op. 7, one of the few works to earn him even a modest success as a composer. Piston performed this *Trio* with George Brown, cello, and the composer, piano, at a twenty-fifth anniversary concert or the Harvard Musical Club in 1923. Piston may have learned something from the work's elegant craftsmanship, if not from its maudlin sentiment.

Edward Ballantine, Piston's teacher of advanced harmony during his sophomore year, may have been more influenced by his colleague's tastes than by his years in Berlin with Schnabel and Ganz, for he too wrote a refined and old-fashioned music of French extraction. He was most famous, however, not for any of his delicate songs, but rather for a delightful burlesque, *Variations in the Styles of Famous Composers on "Mary Had a Little Lamb"* for piano (1924), whose popularity inspired a sequel in 1943. The "famous composers" include Bach, Franck, Puccini, and Stravinsky, and Ballantine's program notes are as facetious as the variations themselves.

Mozart. The title of Agneletto led Koechel to assign the piece to the third Italian sojourn of Mozart and the number K.OX37/8. But according to Wyzewa and St. Foix it is actually the work of Michael Haydn of Salzburg, although the only Ms. is in Mozart's hand.

Wagner. An orchestral excerpt from the 10th act of Lammfell, presenting the leading motive, that of Mary leading the lamb, 17 times, often with tragic import, and closing with the trance-figuration of the lamb in arpeggio figures.[18]

Piston surely found the clever and ironic Ballantine a kindred spirit, closer, at any rate, than the somewhat stuffy and oratorical Walter Spalding. Although Piston never took any of Spalding's classes, classes that Thomson disdained,[19] he worked as an assistant for Spalding (something that he did, in one year or another, for the entire faculty). Actually, the harmony textbook that Spalding wrote with Arthur Foote, *Modern Harmony in its Theory and Practice* (1905, revised 1924), seems to have influenced Piston's *Harmony* of 1941, not only in format but in details as well.[20] And although Spalding's *Music: An Art and a Language* (1920) might have seemed overbearing and flowery to Piston, some of its observations prefigure some of Piston's own remarks:

> Our studies should have made plain two definite facts: first, that the real message of music is contained in its melody—that part of the fabric which we can carry with us and sing to ourselves. . . . But we must be judicious and fair in estimating exactly what constitutes a real melody. . . . New types of melody are continually being worked out; all we can say is that the creative composer hears sounds in his imagination, the result of his emotional and spiritual experiences and of his sympathy with the world. . . .
>
> The second fact concerns the structure of music; that is, the way in which the thought is presented. We have seen that music always has a carefully planned architecture—that being necessary by reason of the indefiniteness of the material. But let us always remember that without abandoning the fundamental principles of all organic life, form may be—and should be—free and elastic. Every work which lives reveals a perfect balance between the emotional and imaginative factors and their logical presentation.[21]

Would Piston have agreed with Spalding, though, that of all contemporary American composers in 1920, Loeffler had best succeeded in finding this balance between form and expression? Would Piston have sooner pointed to Griffes, Chadwick, Ives, Carpenter, or Hill?

When Piston entered Harvard, E. B. Hill was forty-eight years old and nationally renowned. His grandfather, Thomas Hill, helped create, as President of Harvard, the Department of Music (a controversial issue in the 1860s) and was responsible for the inclusion of Counterpoint and Fugue in the University curriculum of 1863. His father, Henry B. Hill, taught chemistry at Harvard, sang tenor, played piano, and was, according to Spalding, "the 'beau ideal' of what a musical amateur should be." He was also a friend to John Knowles Paine, who "was often encouraged by his enthusiasm and critical judgment."[22] His son, E. B., was also Boston's "beau ideal." Thomson writes:

> Aloof but not unfriendly, tall, fifty, athletic, well-to-do, and French-trained, he was a Bostonian's ideal of the gentleman-artist. But there was also in him a straightforwardness of statement not unlike my father's and a thoroughness of knowledge cer-

tainly related to that of his own father, a chemistry professor and a son of a Harvard president.[23]

As a student at Harvard, Hill ran track, wrote for the Hasty Pudding Club, and studied with Paine. He became devoted to modern French music, and he studied with Widor in France before he joined the Harvard faculty in 1908. William Austin writes, "His book on *Modern French Music* (1924) hails the French as conquerors (more than liberators) so that a proper Bostonian can maintain an attitude of dignified provincialism."[24] His course on the subject, which Piston took in his junior year, emphasized d'Indy, Fauré, and Debussy, though he writes in his book, "d'Indy, also possessing distinct power for self-development of a progressive type, suffered from one point of view in the inheritance of a belief in the limitless potentiality of academic forms," whereas Debussy ". . . realized that the way to the future lay in the inherent expressiveness of music apart from academic concepts."[25] Hill nonetheless admired Dukas and Ravel for their classical ideals, and he encouraged his students to study with them. He also liked "Les Six," but he was suspicious of Stravinsky and Schoenberg, or at least of their influence on young American composers.

Thomson aptly alludes to Hill's New England sobriety and his French taste when he calls the composer "a sound impressionist."[26] Hill is often grouped with Carpenter and Loeffler, but his aesthetic is different from theirs and more like that of the poet Stevenson, most obviously in his *Stevensonia, Op. 24, Four Pieces for Orchestra after the Poems of R. L. Stevenson's "A Child's Garden of Verses"* (1915) and his second *Stevensonia Suite* (1924). In these works, Hill uses sensuous Franco-Russian techniques to create a world of courageous, innocent, and well-behaved children: Rimsky-Korsakov's massive frigate becomes a toy sailboat, and Debussy's faun becomes "the unseen playmate of happy children." C. T. Copeland, writing on Stevenson in 1895, discusses the Puritan background of this aesthetic:

No one, in these days, except a Scotchman or a New Englander, we must believe, could be so exquisite an artist and have at the same time so large a fund of ethical attention. The incongruity of the union in Stevenson, the like and unlike incongruity in Hawthorne, are to be explained, in the slight and tentative degree to which such mysteries can ever be shown, by the long persistance of the straiter sort of Puritanism in the two countries.[27]

Hill also admired that other "sound impressionist," John Singer Sargeant, whom he advised his students to study.[28] After the War, Hill took a fashionable interest in jazz and neoclassicism, although his *Jazz Study for*

*2 Pianos* (1922) is "a simple fox-trot,"[29] and his *Sinfonietta* (1932) hasn't much bite. The charming *Sextet* of 1934, is, like *Stevensonia*, stylish family entertainment.

Besides modern French music, Piston also studied composition, music history, and two years of instrumentation with Hill. The instrumentation classes must have been most helpful, for Hill was an exquisite orchestrator, and (according to Thomson, who orchestrated piano works by Schumann, Fauré, and Debussy for him) a superb teacher of orchestration.[30] Rimsky-Korsakov's *Scheherazade* and *Spanish Caprice* were known to Hill's classes as the "Bible" and the "Book of Common Prayer;"[31] and an anonymous writer says, "His classes in orchestration were celebrated for his vocal imitations of instruments and comparisons between musical and extra-musical sounds such as the 'crunching of snow.' "[32] Piston may have learned not only a skilled and subtle handling of the orchestra from Hill, but a certain elegant expressiveness as well. Hill's aesthetic, however, could not have impressed Piston very much. For one thing, Piston was not especially interested in children; and he was so improper a Bostonian as to have said to Aiken on the subject of abortions, "little foeti [feet I] didn't want."[33]

Piston naturally took courses outside his field: he studied English with Greenough, Greek with Jackson, French with Raiche and Mercier, Italian with Weston, European history with Haskins, cultural history with Babbitt, aesthetics with Langfeld, logic with Sheffer, zoology with Brues, and astronomy with Stetson. Piston found these courses "especially rewarding" and "intensely fascinating."[34] Irving Babbitt's course, The Romantic Movement in the Nineteenth Century, which the Harvard catalogue recommended to its music students, might have been the most fascinating of them all. Babbitt, a respected and controversial scholar, was turning many an American head (including that of Piston's aesthetics professor, Langfeld) with his knowledge of Western and Eastern culture, and his arguments against romanticism, naturalism, and religion as put forth in his most famous book, *Rousseau and Romanticism* (1919). Babbitt inspired, however, mostly protest, especially from Leftists and Christians who found his humanism a Boston Brahmin's pipe dream. Actually, Piston was something of a humanist himself, and kept up with the writings of Corliss Lamont and Lin Yu-tang. But Piston viewed humanism, it seems, in a more traditional sense, as ancillary, and not opposed, to social reform and religious belief.

Harvard also offered valuable opportunities outside the classroom, such as the free concerts of old and new music in Paine Hall, where Thomson performed Lili Boulanger's *Pour les funerailles d'un soldat* and

Satie's *Socrate* in 1923 after his first trip to Paris. In addition, there was a series of distinguished lectures during these years: d'Indy on "César Franck and his School," Arthur Bliss on "Contemporary English Composers," Landowska on "Les Précurseurs français de Sébastien Bach," and Milhaud on "The Evolution of Contemporary Music in Paris and Vienna." And then there was Harvard's school orchestra, the Pierian Sodality, which Piston directed from 1921 to 1924. Piston chose works that best suited the capability of the group, which consisted of about forty Harvard students and a few members of the Boston Symphony. The basic program for their first year was as follows.

| Harvard Marches | |
|---|---|
| a) Up the Street | Morse |
| b) Harvardiana | Williams |
| Overture, *Fingal's Cave* | Mendelssohn |
| Waltz, *Les Patineurs* | Waldteufel |
| Ballet Suite | Gluck |
| a)Aria from *Orpheus* | |
| b) Musette from *Armide* | |
| Selection from *The Rose Girl* | Goetzl |
| Valse Triste | Sibelius |
| Hungarian March from | |
| *The Damnation of Faust* | Berlioz |

The Pierian sometimes floundered,[35] but often did very well, as testified by Philip Hale's reviews for the *Boston Herald*, or by this anonymous review for the *Boston Evening Transcript*, dated 26 April 1922:

> The orchestra proved itself a plastic, responsive, finished body of players. Unstinted praise must fall to its conductor, Mr. Walter Piston, himself an undergraduate, for the high standard for performance the band has reached.

When the Pierian went on tour to New York and Washington in December of 1921, they featured Schubert's *"Unfinished" Symphony*. The Washington Star reported:

> At the conclusion of the concert the audience did an unusual thing. It remained seated and called back Walter Piston, the conductor, three times. Apparently they were satisfied that under the continued masterful leadership of Mr. Piston, the present Harvard Orchestra bids fair to secure a place in the exclusive small circle of distinguished amateurs.[36]

In 1935, Spalding singled out Piston's tenure with the orchestra as one of four periods of special attainment for the Pierian.[37] Piston earned eight dollars for each rehearsal and concert with the Pierian; the experience itself was invaluable.

Piston distinguished himself at Harvard. He was awarded a Juilliard Scholarship in his senior year, and he graduated "summa cum laude" and Phi Beta Kappa, with a John Knowles Paine Traveling Fellowship. Some of his student work is found in the Piston Collection, namely, three papers for "Doc" Davison: "Changes in Style of Choral Music from the XVIth to the XVIIth century," "A Comparison of the Choral Music of Mendelssohn and Brahms," and "National Characteristics as Represented in Folksong." The papers are all elegant, sensitive, and surprisingly assured for an undergraduate. "Changes in Style" reveals Piston's close familiarity with Renaissance and early Baroque music, a repertory not usually associated with him. We learn from this paper of his special admiration for Palestrina ("the greatest of all geniuses in choral music. In him we find surprising unworldly qualities attained with the slightest musical substance"), Lassus ("He had immense learning and a fine sense of humor"), the chorale ("It was a melody of dignified movement and strongly marked rhythm, with holds at periods"), the English madrigal ("The madrigal 'Fire, fire, my heart,' by Thomas Morley is fascinating, spontaneous, melodious and contrapuntal. It has great rhythmic vigor"), and Purcell ("the greatest composer of the English nation. He had a dramatic and religious gift and at this time we notice a rise of the dramatic, personal element in the religious as well as the secular field"). In the second paper, Piston sympathetically and insightfully compares the choral music of Bach, Mendelssohn, and Brahms, rating Bach higher than Mendelssohn, but lower than Brahms. The nations discussed in "National Characteristics" include: Austria, England, Scotland, Ireland, France, Germany, Russia, Italy, Holland, and (as one unit) Denmark, Norway, and Sweden. Piston ostensibly knows other folk musics as well; he writes, "Many smaller nations have folksongs of extreme beauty which are identified with the people, i.e. Wales, Lithuania, Finland. Bohemian folk-songs are among the most beautiful in existence." Piston's musical examples perfectly illustrate his observations, which are often delightfully aphoristic.

> The English folk-songs are direct, positive and unromantic, in fact they have a sort of "roastbeef" quality.

> Whatever may be the explanation, many of the Irish songs represent perfection of melodic curve, so that they have been used to a great extent in art music—even appropriated bodily as in the case of the "Last Rose of Summer" in the opera "Martha."

> The French folk-songs are, as we might expect, gay and often quite childlike, with a very marked feeling for design.

Nationalism and pompousness are characteristic of many German folk-songs.

The Russian folk-songs are unmistakably the expression of despair and a feeling of oppression direct from the common people.

In Italy it is difficult to distinguish the folk song from the art song. . . . These are questionable advantages, however, for in Italy we look in vain for the naive, natural, and spontaneous tunes which abound throughout the greater part of Europe.

Piston concludes this paper with the following paragraph:

It is to be regretted that the American people have not this traditional expression to call their own. We are not old enough and indeed it is doubtful if we ever shall be. Modern civilization has brought with it conditions and methods contrary to and quite incompatible with the modes of thought and communication which have been so important a factor in the evolution of these priceless treasures of musical expression.

The Paine Fellowship awarded its recipients $1500 a year for two or three years of study abroad. This was a great opportunity for Piston, who thought his undergraduate education insufficient, as Harvard frowned on "a real professional training such as would be needed to be the kind of composer I wanted to become."[38] He and Kathryn naturally chose Paris, where they stayed from 1924 to 1926, residing at 52 Rue Broca and traveling to Italy in the fall of 1925. Hill might have encouraged Piston to study with Dukas, while Thomson, back from Paris, might have also suggested Boulanger. Piston studied with both, not at the Paris Conservatory, as he had hoped, but at the Ecole Normale de Musique, which accepted students over thirty years old. The school had been founded a few years earlier, in 1919, by Cortot and Mangeot, and was then located on the Rue Jouffrey. Piston studied composition with Dukas, composition and counterpoint with Boulanger, and violin with Enescu, and he played viola in the orchestra, which "was conducted by the cellist Diran Alexanian, who was Casals' chief assistant in Paris and a very fine musician."[39] Piston impressed his teachers, as their evaluations of him indicate: "Remarquable artiste hors de pair," "Excellent musicien et habile contrepointiste," and "Nature sérieuse et bien équilibrée."[40]

By 1924, Paul Dukas, who had scored some triumphs at the turn of the century, had renounced composition in order to devote most of his time to teaching. William Austin notes the influence of Dukas on Enescu, Falla, Messiaen, Piston, Roussel, and Turina; and cites Messiaen's acknowledged debt to Dukas "for the techniques of motivic development and orchestration and 'the sense of artistic probity.' "[41] Thomson similarly found Dukas a superb teacher of orchestration,[42] and recommended him to Paul Bowles.[43] Dukas was also a shrewd and cautious critic of contemporary music, the subject of a 1924 article for *Courrier Musical*, "Les Tendences de la musique contemporaine," in which Dukas states, "Today's tendencies are so diverse, so tangled and finally so uncertain in many of their manifestations—despite the well-advertised assurance of some, in theory—that any judgment of the works reflecting them must appear conditional and tentative."[44] These tangled tendencies, Dukas continues, reflect the modern industrial state and its disrupted social environment. Piston perceived a mixed reaction from Dukas when he called the 1925 *Three Pieces*, "Stravinskique."[45] Was Dukas the model for Piston's elusive openmindedness?

The Stravinsky enthusiast Nadia Boulanger lived downstairs from Dukas at 36 Rue Ballu. She was much closer in age to their students at the Normale, only seven years Piston's senior. When Westergaard brought up the subject of Boulanger with Piston, the following discussion ensued:

> WP: I joined her counterpoint class (she wouldn't let me come to the harmony class; said it would be a waste of time for me). We started right at the beginning of the strictest kind of counterpoint, two voices, note against note.
>
> PW: Species counterpoint?
>
> WP: Yes, right up to eight parts. Of course none of that was what I'd ever write in a composition, but I believe it's because of having done it that I have been able to write my music.[46]

Some of these exercises survive among Piston's papers in the Library of Congress and the Boston Library. In one such study, Piston composed four lively counterpoints above a cantus firmus bass. One anonymous Boulanger student (could it be Piston?) wrote to Davison:

> Here the work done and the method of approach are similar to that at X, but, having twice as much time and picked pupils with longer preparation, the discipline is more rigorous and the course more complete. For example, in two part writing, you compose six different counterpoints to every cantus firmus (three above and three below), in three part writing, nine combinations are required, etc. The course carries you through eight part counterpoint.
>
> It is quite normal to remain in the theory courses at least two years and often much longer, for your training is considered adequate only when you can sit down at the piano and "realize" your exercises at sight, without hesitation and with a fair degree of certainty and polish.[47]

Douglas Moore similarly wrote to Daniel Mason in 1926, "I am doing strict counterpoint with Nadia Boulanger—stricter than I ever knew anything could be."[48]

Piston also studied composition with Boulanger, a lesson of which is described by Virgil Thomson as follows.

> The lessons take place with the teacher at the piano, the student in a chair at her right. She reads the score before her silently at first, then little by little begins to comment, spontaneously admiring here and there a detail of musical syntax or sound, expressing temporary reservations about another. Suddenly she will start playing (and perfectly, for she is a fabulous sight-reader) some passage that she needs to hear out loud or that she wishes the student to hear as illustration to her remarks.[49]

Boulanger's attributes as a teacher of composition have been cited so often as to have become legendary: her confidence that American music was about to "take off," her intense love for music, her ability to connect music with everything from Scripture to swimming pools, and her sensitivity to the needs of the individual student. According to Piston:

> Her faculty to perceive what a person was at, or wanted to be at, was nothing less than uncanny. I can remember showing up one time with a page of stems and rests and beams and clefs but no noteheads. She didn't show the slightest hesitation in entering into a discussion of the pros and cons. Now that's a stage in one's groping that one can discuss with oneself, but it's pretty hard for another mind to come into it.[50]

Boulanger was also admired for her Wednesday afternoon gatherings, at which, writes Thomson, "the most modern scores of the time (by Stravinsky and Schönberg and Mahler) were analyzed and played on the pianoforte, and the rarest madrigals of the Renaissance (by Monteverdi, Luca Marenzio and Gesualdo di Venosa) were sung in class."[51] "We'd run through all kinds of things," remembered Piston.

> She would suddenly name five people to do the Franck Quintet the next week. I recall digging into the piano part of that. Also I can remember going down to Fontainebleau to conduct a chorus of her students in *Les Noces*, with her at the piano.[52]

Paris had more than excellent schooling to offer young student composers. Its finest musicians performed the music of Stravinsky, Bartók, Falla, Ravel, Hindemith, Prokofiev, Szymanowski, Malipiero, Kodály, and many others, including, occasionally, Schoenberg and Berg. Even more music was available in score; and during his two years in Paris, Piston acquired the new scores not only of the acknowledged masters, but also of Conrad Beck, Theodor Blumer, Sam Dresden, Philipp Jarnach, Sandor Jemnitz, Karel Jirák, Heinrich Kaminski, Hugo Kauder, Egon Kornauth, Mario Labroca, Vittorio Rieti, Knudage Rüsager, Heinrich

Schmid, and Erwin Schulhoff. The diversity was, as Dukas noted, amazing. Thomson writes:

> A Dada tone was then the stylish tone for advanced artists and for the art-minded. Even the well-established Pablo Picasso, whom I first encounted at this time, had adopted Dada's debunking attitudes. As explained to me by Emmanuel Faÿ, the Dada principles were simply that all is convention, that all conventions have equal value (or none) and that an artist is therefore free to work in (or invent, if he can) any convention whatsoever that may please him. And Tristan Tzara, the Dada spokesman, had defined all art a "private bell for inexplicable needs."[53]

Amid the hubbub and clangor, Piston found his own, distinctive voice.

# 3

# Piston, Surrealist:
# From the *Three Pieces* (1925)
# to the *First Symphony* (1937)

Piston's first published work, the *Three Pieces for Flute, Clarinet and Bassoon*, was written while the composer was a student in Paris, and premiered by Blanquart, Coste, and Dhérin on May 8, 1925, at a Société Nationale concert. He dedicated the work to his wife. All earlier compositions appear to be lost, with the exception of a *Fanfare*, which now resides in the Piston Collection. This *Fanfare* is written out in an unrefined hand, and probably dates from World War I. It is a conventional fanfare, but one that already reveals Piston's fondness for chromatic lines, contrapuntal textures, and quartal harmonies. There were other early works as well, including a march written for the National Hotel. This youthful preoccupation with fanfares and marches is often reflected in Piston's more mature works, especially in his symphonic finales, but also in so unlikely a movement as the scherzo of the 1935 *Trio*. Moreover, marches and fanfares may have more obliquely, and more profoundly, shaped Piston's musicianship, so full of color and vitality. But this early period is obscure, and by the time the thirty-one-year-old Piston wrote the *Three Pieces*, his musical style had become distinctive and sophisticated. In fact the *Three Pieces* were immediately hailed by lovers of new music in France, Germany, and the United States, and it became a great favorite with Henry Cowell's New Music Society. It also became Piston's only work from the 1920s to achieve repertory status.

Piston rarely spoke of his early influences, and the rare occasions come only in his old age. In response to Westergaard's questions about the *Three Pieces*, he said:

> Certainly Hindemith had something to do with it . . . , but no, it may sound corny, but Bach had a great deal more to do with it. More than that I would say it was in the air.[1]

Piston also admitted a closeness to Stravinsky's *Octet*. In another interview, Piston stated, "I went through a stage of admiring people like Stravinsky, Hindemith, Schoenberg, Webern, and it's not possible for anybody not to be affected by men like that, you know, because I really believed I should know them. . . ."[2] Piston was clearly reticent, even apologetic, about the whole question of his early influences.

Dukas called the *Three Pieces*, "Stravinskique," and this is especially true of the work's slow movement, which closely resembles passages in the introduction to the second part of *The Rite*. Also "Stravinskique" are the opening movement's bassoon ostinato, and the third movement's cadenza for flute. The work's entire conception—its mood and instrumentation—is inconceivable without the *Octet*, and there are the same rich conflicts of dark and light. But the *Three Pieces* owe something to Hindemith and Schoenberg as well. Hindemith's influence is most strongly felt in the work's clever and lively invertible counterpoints and melodic inversions. The connection with Schoenberg is less obvious, and involves the use of short chromatic motives to construct larger melodies. The assimilation of such disparate influences gives the *Three Pieces* a character all its own. Stravinskian cross rhythms do not offset a Hindemithian steadfastness, and Schoenbergian chromaticism does not preclude a Stravinskian vitality. The work's tonal language is broad, encompassing Stravinskian ostinati and Schoenbergian atonality, although Piston's chromatic tonality most closely resembles Hindemith. The tonal meaning of any single voice is apt to be ambiguous or misleading, so that the issue of bitonality is irrelevant here. When considered together, however, the lines often form tonal patterns that are colorful and ultrarefined. The beautifully scored opening of the second movement is one such example (ex. 1). Although Dukas rightly found this passage "Stravinskique," he nonetheless may have found something of his own harmonic language therein.

The extreme reserve of the *Three Pieces* is what truly distinguishes it from Stravinsky, Hindemith, and Schoenberg. The proportions are sleek and modest, and the melodies are restrained and graceful. The more fantastic elements are carefully contained in the middle sections of the outer movements. This restraint is exceptional even in the context of Piston's oeuvre, and the composer himself writes that the *Three Pieces*:

> . . . are intended simply as pleasant and mildly diverting pieces to play and listen to. The first playful, the second nostalgic, and the third more dance-like. To the composer they seem like concise pencil drawings.[3]

But the lucid ordering of complex ideas becomes an important feature of Piston's aesthetic, one that is ultimately derived from Bach.

Ex. 1. Piston, "Lento," *Three Pieces for Flute, Clarinet and Bassoon* (San Francisco: New Music, 1933; New York: AMP), p. 6. Used by permission.

In the same year, 1925, Piston composed an *Orchestra Piece*, which was neither performed nor published. Piston did not even include the work in his catalogue, though he gave the score to the Library of Congress. In 1926, Piston wrote a *Piano Sonata,* which was also never published, but which was premiered in Paris at the Salle Gaveau by Marcel Ciampi on 5 May 1926 as part of a program of American music sponsored by the Société Musicale Independente. Thomson writes:

> . . . Boulanger, a member of the program committee (and with Walter Damrosch, her colleague at Fontainebleau, available for bringing in Americans to subsidize it), had conceived the idea of a special concert, outside the regular subscription, devoted to young American composers. On the program were to be my Sonata da Chiesa, for five instruments, piano pieces by Herbert Elwell, a song with flute and clarinet and two pieces for violin and piano by Aaron Copland, a piano sonata by Walter Piston, and a violin-piano sonata by Theodore Chanler. All the works except one of Copland's violin pieces were receiving their first performance anywhere; all were to be played by first-class artists; and all were the work of Boulanger's pupils. Adding the Antheil String Quartet was my idea; and that too was to be a first public performance.

Thomson continues:

> All these pieces were characteristic of the newest in American talent, as well as of postwar Parisian ways, which is to say that they applied old-master layouts to contemporary melodic inspirations and harmonic concepts. My way of doing this, also Antheil's, was derived from the latest works of Igor Stravinsky; the others had theirs more in Boulanger, who was both an organist conditioned to Bach and a pupil of Gabriel Fauré. A certain unity of musical method, nevertheless, underlay personal variations and gave to the concert a recognizable impact, just as fine executions gave it brilliance.[4]

On the other hand Roger Sessions, reviewing the concert for *Modern Music*, wrote, "The evening of American music . . . brought together six young composers who, although anything but a homogeneous group, unquestionably form the most promising array of young American musicians yet presented in public."[5] "Piston's piano sonata," says Sessions, "romantic and grandiose in mood, has excellent technical mastery, especially in the closing fugue." The French critic Raymond Petit found the first movement "a bit empty ('creux')" and the second movement, an "Andante," monotonous, though he liked the third movement, a fugue, and admired the piano writing.[6] While Piston did include this *Piano Sonata* in his catalogue, the manuscript appears to be lost, though there are sketches of the work in the Piston Collection.

Upon his return to the States, Piston was asked by Koussevitzky to write a work for the Boston Symphony, and the composer completed a *Symphonic Piece* in 1927. Koussevitzky had taken over the leadership of the Boston Symphony in 1924 and was busy commissioning works, playing new music, and improving the quality of the orchestra. Thus, the Boston Symphony was becoming a focal point for new orchestral music during these years. Piston premiered the *Symphonic Piece* with this virtuoso ensemble on 23 March 1928, on a program that also featured a new work by the Rumanian-American, Filip Lazar. The reviewer for the Boston Globe wrote:

> Both were too modern to win the favor of an audience still overwhelmingly conservative in its musical taste . . . Mr. Piston's musical ideas, though influenced by such composers as Prokofieff, Stravinsky and Ravel, do not lack individuality. He states them pungently, with a keen feeling for the use of contrast in music. There are some highly effective bits of orchestration, as for instance the beautiful shimmer of tone at the beginning. In other passages one felt that the scoring could be made more sonorous and less confused to advantage.

And writing for the *Christian Science Monitor*, L. A. Sloper stated:

> [The *Symphonic Piece*] proves that he has profited much by his excellent instruction and by observation of the styles of his day. But in following the fashion of polytonality and complicated rhythmic patterns he has not forsaken form or melody. Or shall we say that while respecting the older grammar he has employed a modern idiom?

Piston chose not to publish the *Symphonic Piece*, and the score is in the Library of Congress. Another unpublished work from 1927 is the *Minuetto in Stile Vecchio* for string quartet, which Piston wrote for a special concert given on 12 April 1927 by the Radcliffe Music Club. Piston's minuet was paired with one by Boccherini, and E. B. Hill wrote, ". . . both Minuets showed the results of intelligent practice, and the possession of musical sensibilities."[7] The score of this work appears to be lost.

Piston's first published orchestral score, the *Suite for Orchestra*, written in 1929, is a delightful three-movement work, an orchestral companion to the *Three Pieces*. Its opening "Allegro" has lively ostinati and snappy melodies similar to the outer movements of the *Three Pieces*, although here a connection with jazz, or, at any rate, popular music, is more obvious. This is especially true of the middle section, with its "torchy" melody for solo cello and an accompaniment that includes a piano and a snare drum with wire brushes. The movement has mixed meters and dissonant harmonies, but the aesthetic is somewhat old-fashioned, falling somewhere between Ravel, Hill, and Carpenter on the one hand, and Stravinsky, Milhaud, and Copland on the other. Piston's relationship to popular American music is more subtle, but then, perhaps, more integral than that of any of these other composers (though rags and trots left a

deeper impression, it seems, than any real jazz). Piston knew what the
"blues" were (he wondered whether Tippett did), and the *Suite*'s second
movement theme may owe something to the rhythm and modality of that
tradition. But like the middle movement of the *Three Pieces*, the mood is
tender, nostalgic, and romantic.

The "Allegro" fugue that concludes the *Suite* has a long, chromatic
subject that is treated to a four-voice exposition by the strings (p. 48), a
two-voice exposition by the winds (p. 49), inversion (p. 52), stretto (p. 58),
diminution in stretto (p. 62), and augmentation in stretto (p. 63). The episodes show off the winds, and include a fanfare for brass (p. 50) and a
nine-voice canon for woodwinds in which the nine entrances are staggered until the distance between the entrances reaches the eighth-note
(p. 60). These textures suggest that Piston has Bach's orchestral fugues
in mind, and when one considers the snappy dotted rhythms of the first
movement and the songful lyricism of the "Andante," one suspects that
the *Suite* was intentionally modelled after the Bach orchestral suites.

Piston conducted the work's premiere on 28 March 1930. Writing
again for the *Monitor*, Sloper thought the *Suite* a "marked advance" upon
the *Symphonic Piece*: "It is less obviously derivative, possesses a more
individual flavor." The *Suite* soon won a small following. Stokowski played
it with the Philadelphia Orchestra in April of 1931, and chose it as the
final selection of an all-American radio broadcast in the spring of 1933.
The *Suite* was also performed by Rodzinski and the Los Angeles Orchestra in March, 1933, and by Hans Lange and the New York Philharmonic in February, 1934. The New York reviews were mixed: "at best
it is adroit celebration," said the *Times*, while the *Herald Tribune* wrote,
"Mr. Piston's Suite, in three movements, is at times delicatedly tinctured
with jazz, is serene and lyrical in the slow movement, and ends with a
deftly written fugue."

Piston's *Flute Sonata* of 1930 deserves to rank with two other works
written in that year: Copland's *Piano Variations* and Sessions's *Piano
Sonata*. More than Copland, or even Sessions, Piston is a composer who
comes of age in the 1930s, for it is with this work that he bids our attention
as a serious, mature composer. By the end of the gay and experimental
twenties, Piston had published only the *Three Pieces* and the *Suite for
Orchestra*, a minor accomplishment when one considers the music that
Copland, Sessions, Harris, Thomson, Varèse, and other Americans of his
generation composed in the 1920s. But with the *Flute Sonata* begins a
decade of achievement that places Piston in the forefront of American
composers. In an article for *Modern Music* entitled, "1936: America's

Young Men—Ten Years Later," Copland apologizes for overlooking Piston in 1926.

It is significant that the *Flute Sonata*'s three-movement structure becomes characteristic of much of Piston's later music: a sonata movement, a slow ABA movement, and a sonata-rondo finale. In the first movement, Piston not only writes a well-defined sonata, but also explores the traditional conflict between tonic and dominant, though Piston's modal-chromatic language shows this conflict in a new light: the flute's arrival on the dominant A at m. 8 is as bold and exciting as the piano's ensuing chromatic descent back to D. According to sketches in the Library of Congress, this whirlwind piano accompaniment was based on Schoenbergian manipulations of a basic set, and the end result is nicely surreal, if somewhat heavy-handedly impetuous. The second theme fuses elements of ragtime and fanfare with the macabre, and creates a peculiar blend of whimsy and eeriness. The "Adagio" movement, for all its chic neo-Baroque suggestions, is an ardent contrapuntal fantasy, and while pianists would do well to heed Piston's "sempre legato," they should be warned against harmonic pedalling at the "poco mosso" section. Flutists, for their part, should carefully consider the many dynamic swellings. The movement's ending is an unusually mystical moment for Piston.

Unlike the ponderous first two movements, the finale is light and graceful, and is the work's most successful movement by far. Here is an early demonstration of one of Piston's great abilities: to create delightful, even hilarious, music in an advanced chromatic idiom. The rhythms are those of the tango, the march, and the polka, but the melodies and textures are delicate, subtle: anything but banal. The movement is best played crisply and "vivace," as it certainly was by flutist Georges Laurent, the work's dedicatee, and pianist Jesus Sanromá at the work's premiere on 15 February 1931, at a concert of the Boston Flute Players' Club. Laurent and Sanromá, both members of the Boston Symphony, were the first in a long series of notable artists to perform the work (which has become the most established Piston in the repertory). Rampal, Baker, Dwyer, Bryan, Padorr, and other flutists have recorded the *Sonata*. Rampal's recording has unfortunately been long out-of-print and is difficult to find, at least in the States. Dwyer's sensitive interpretation of the slow movement is definitely worth a hearing, as is the fiery piano playing of Karen Keys that accompanies Keith Bryan's performance.

The *Suite for Oboe and Piano* of 1931 was premiered by another first chair of the Boston Symphony, oboist Fernand Gillet, with Sanromá once again at the piano. The score, however, is dedicated to Dr. Augustus Thorndike, the father of Piston's good friend Amory and an amateur oboist. Was this work intended as a refined treat for a sophisticated amateur? The *Suite* is unusually romantic for Piston, a "fin de siècle" delicacy for the 1930s. The more decadent features of Piston's early style—whole-tone melodies, sixth and ninth chords, and harmonic motion by major thirds—are boldly indulged, creating a misty atmosphere that is both exquisite and suffocating. The *Suite* is intentionally nostalgic; four of its five movements are inspired by works of French Impressionism. The opening of the "Sarabande," for instance, echoes the beginning of Satie's *Second Sarabande*, though Piston's harmonies are stranger. There are closer connections between the "Minuetto" and Ravel's "Menuet" from *Tombeau de Couperin*, and Piston's "Nocturne" and "Gigue" make reference, respectively, to Debussy's "Clair de Lune" and Roussel's "Gigue" from the *Suite in F*.

Piston's *Suite*, however, is not as good as any of its models, but is rather an overripe piece of "art nouveau." The "Sarabande" begins well enough, though the last phrase, an inversion of the opening melody, sounds contrived. The "Minuetto" is a pretty waltz, but sometimes cloys. The "Nocturne" is probably the best piece of the set, with a really fine "lontano" melody for oboe that is fortunately left unaltered at its reprise except for a surprising and sumptuous cadence in G minor. The "Gigue" finale has a pleasant canon at its midsection, and a squeaky, funny final cadence, but the humor, on the whole, seems forced. Even less appealing is the work's opening "Prelude," an austere and thickly chromatic, almost atonal, contrapuntal study.

For a subtle listener like Israel Citkowitz, however, the *Suite* was worth at least a rehearing. In a review of Carlos Mullenix's performance in 1935, Citkowitz also wrote:

> It is such unassuming and self-contained music that we are apt at first to overlook its qualities. If by reason of this reticence it seems to lack a certain profile, none the less it is a music that proceeds on solid ground. This may be negative praise, but Piston's work, with its sure craftsmanship, and its fine sense of proportion gains continually on further acquaintance. It has more qualities than just his craftsmanship. For all its sobriety of manner it is curiously personal, with its dry wit, simplicity of mood, its unassuming decisiveness. His music may not seize us by its sheer force of expression, but it speaks for Piston the individual.[8]

The *Suite*'s sensitive and brilliant writing for oboe has also earned it the admiration of many oboists, not least of which is Louis Speyer, who recorded the work in 1940 with Piston at the piano. More recently, in 1975, a young dancer in New York, Rebecca Kelly, listened to Wayne Rapier's recording of the *Suite* in the Lincoln Center Library and decided to choreograph it for Paul Wilson's Theatre Dance Asylum. Unable to acquire a recording, she wrote to Piston, who subsequently offered to subsidize a tape ("I am thinking of normal charges," wrote Piston to Kelly, "but I would not like to be taken for a ride by high priced virtuosi"). In another letter, Piston agreed to Kelly's request to repeat the "Prelude" after the "Minuetto" for her dance, entitled *Pursuits* ("After all, it is not a concert," wrote Piston). After the tape was made by Vance Reger, oboe, and Zita Carno, piano, Kelly sent Piston the tape and a letter, which included the following remarks:

> I am beginning to know the piece (from a non-musician's point of view, of course) so that the notes are becoming a language to me and tell me what their (dance) movement should be. This is always an exciting stage in choreography, when the music begins to speak. I am about to start working with the "Minuetto" which is such a tender, lyric section. In the dance, it must be the most beautiful; it is about the pursuit of things loved.[9]

Although Piston conducted the premiere of the 1933 *Concerto for Orchestra* with the Boston Symphony on 6 March 1934, Koussevitzky performed the work quite often himself. In 1936, he brought the work to New York, where Colin McPhee heard it and wrote:

> The workmanship is sure and distinguished; logic prevails and the musical idea is always developed with a clear realization of its intrinsic possibilities. A remarkable energy pervades the work, an energy which is not only the result of rhythm and tempo, but it is also due to the directness with which each movement, like an arrow released from a bow, proceeds without hindrance to its ultimate note. The peculiar incisivness and brilliance of the orchestra owe much to the clarity of the contrapuntal texture of the music. The symphony [*sic*] was beautifully played, a musical event to which I keep looking back with pleasure.[10]

The *Concerto*, however, was a "succès d'estime," a work the cognoscenti (Henry Pleasants in 1939, Copland, in 1943, and Ingolf Dahl in 1946[11]) thought regrettably neglected. This neglect has worsened since the death of Koussevitzky, though the work remains compelling, even monumental, one of Piston's boldest creations.

The *Concerto for Orchestra* is closely modelled after Hindemith's 1925 work of the same name. Both first movements are in ritornello form and are full of lively counterpoint and soloistic writing for the instruments, including the principal strings. Piston's chromatic counterpoint works much better here than in the "Prelude" of the *Oboe Suite*: the lines have a surer tonal direction, especially in the powerful ritornello sections, which are offset by brilliant episodes for the different orchestral families. Piston's second movement scherzo, like Hindemith's, features perpetual motion in the strings, though its elegant and playful "razz-matazz" is closer to Copland than to Hindemith. The trio's woodwind fugato is another bow to Hindemith, although the surreal solo cello-bass clarinet melody that precedes it is Piston's own idea. Finally, the scherzo returns in retrograde, sounding emphatically backwards, and none the less funny for this. It is perhaps the most famous example of Piston's brilliant craftsmanship.

Whereas Hindemith writes two movements, a march and a passacaglia, to conclude his *Concerto*, Piston writes one "Adagio-Allegro moderato" passacaglia movement. The modal-chromatic passacaglia theme (ex. 2) is set forth by a solo tuba (this is, after all, a concerto for orchestra), who repeats it another three times as the other brass instruments gradually, organically enter, growing to a "forte" climax. Following this is a dreamy section for woodwinds, which is like a bizarre organ improvisation: a long, graceful melody for flute is accompanied by the inverted passacaglia theme in the bassoon and the English horn. The strings enter, "Allegro moderato," with a fugue on the passacaglia theme, which is also found in the double basses as a "basso ostinato." The entire orchestra joins in for a fugal episode, a gigue-like fantasy, and, finally, a huge return of the brass choir "Adagio" climax accompanied by wild and frenzied activity in the strings and woodwinds.

In the Claire Reis correspondence at the New York Public Library, there are letters from Piston to Reis, chairman of the League of Composers during these years, that outline the unfortunate history of Piston's next orchestral work, *Prelude and Fugue for Orchestra*. In the first letter, dated 3 December 1933, Piston wrote, "I am pleased and honored to accept the commission which the League so kindly offers me—to write something for Bruno Walter and the Philharmonic. Your plan is most encouraging and stimulating, and I hope will bring some worthwhile results." This plan called for eight works, commissioned by the League, to be performed during the 1934–1935 season by eight organizations, as follows:

| Works by | Directed by | Organization |
|---|---|---|
| Roger Sessions | Leopold Stokowski | Philadelphia Orchestra |
| Walter Piston | Bruno Walter | Philharmonic Orchestra |
| Louis Gruenberg | Frederick Stock | Chicago Orchestra |
| Roy Harris | Artur Rodzinski | Cleveland Orchestra |
| Randall Thompson | Dr. Archibald Davison | Harvard Glee Club |
| Virgil Thomson | Margaret Dessoff | Adesi Chorus |
| Nicolai Berezowsky | | Stradivarius Quartet |
| Israel Citkowitz | | Pro Arte Quartet |

Ex. 2.   Piston, "Adagio," *Concerto for Orchestra* (New York: Cos Cob Press, 1934; New York: AMP), p. 51. Used by permission.

Ex. 2 (continued)

On 31 August 1934, Piston apologized for a delay detailing that he had had to wait until the end of the school term before he could begin work, and that he was "a very slow composer." On 19 September, Piston informed Reis that the score, *Prelude and Fugue for Orchestra,* was completed. Then on January 9, 1935, Piston wrote the following to Reis:

> I am naturally disappointed that Bruno Walter did not find my work interesting enough for a performance but on the other hand I would have been surprised if it had turned out otherwise. I must confess I had misgivings from the start and only agreed to do it for the sake of supporting the League's plan. I felt my position to be quite false as I knew that Mr. Walter would not be sympathetic to my musical idiom and I likewise knew that he would not play it if it were distasteful to him.

Piston's misgivings were soundly based: Walter did not like modern music, and in his memoirs of 1955, the conductor says, "I have attempted to understand what is happening in my time . . . The fact that in this endeavor I have had not only to disappoint the expectations of others, but also to leave my own intentions unfulfilled, has caused me to examine my conscience again and again—with unvarying result, however."[12] How could such a fiasco, undoubtedly embarassing to Walter and Reis as well as to Piston, have occurred? Did Piston's academic post and conservative demeanor blind the League to the sort of music he was writing? The *Prelude and Fugue* was finally premiered on 12 March 1936, by the Cleveland Orchestra and Rudolf Ringwall, its assistant conductor. Herbert Elwell, critic for the *Cleveland Plain Dealer*, thought it one of the season's highlights.

The *Prelude and Fugue* is indeed in Piston's prickly thirties idiom, and makes no concessions to Walter's taste (whose outer limit was late Mahler or possibly early Schoenberg). The "Prelude" is chromatically sinuous and rhythmically elusive. The "Fugue" is formally adventurous. as the following outline suggests:

A.  Exposition
1.  A four-voice exposition of the main subject for winds. The voices enter on a series of ascending major thirds.
2.  A two-voice exposition of a subsidiary subject for strings.
3.  A two-voice exposition of a shortened version of the main subject for brass.

B.  Episode/Development
1.  A slow-moving, minor theme in winds is decorated by figuration in strings and other winds.
2.  A canon for strings is juxtaposed against a restatement of the slow-moving theme.

C.  Recapitulation
1.  The main subject, transformed, is stated by the strings.
2.  The climax: the main subject is played by the brass in augmentation and in canon; a variant of the subsidiary subject is counterpointed against this.

Piston's fugues are never very strict, and in this case, Piston molds his fugue into a sonata with a separate secondary theme (A2). For Piston, fugue is not a rigid form, but rather a means of exploring new orchestral textures and advanced contrapuntal ideas. When he was asked, years later, to comment on A. E. F. Dickinson's 1956 statement, "As a creative stimulus, fugue is now dead. The final stages of the Bach era show the wearing out of the time-honored vehicle, and the exceptional and always qualified fugal achievements of Beethoven and after confirm beyond doubt an impression of exhaustion and emergency," Piston answered:

> The vast literature of music of the nineteenth and twentieth centuries is adequate refutation of Dickinson's sweeping statement. Unless we grant him a most limited and superficial definition of the fugue. It is questionable whether or not we can say that

the fugue is a form. It is rather a principle of growth which has had tremendous significance since Bach's time, and especially in the twentieth century.[13]

Piston's three chamber works from these years, the *First String Quartet* of 1933, and the *Second Quartet* and the *Piano Trio*, both written in 1935 on a Guggenheim Fellowship, are contrapuntal with a vengeance. The *First Quartet* is dedicated to the Chardon Quartet, who premiered the work on 7 March 1933, the day after the premiere of the *Concerto for Orchestra*. Theodore Chanler heard the New World Quartet play it at the 1933 Yaddo Festival, and it inspired the following remarks:

> An example of the kind of thing he had in mind [Nietzche's attack on hope as "the most mischievous of all evils"] is a certain attitude current in America towards our composers, an attitude of hopefulness which tends to look for potentialities rather than accomplishments, to yearn over the half-hatched, rather than try to estimate soberly what has fully emerged. This was well illustrated at the Yaddo festival last September by the reactions of certain hearers to the Harris *Sextet* and the Piston *Quartet*. The former, by far the more imperfectly realized work of the two, had a kind of urgency which to many people expressed itself no less appealingly by what it stammered than by what it managed to say. Walter Piston's exceptionally fine quartet, on the other hand—a work which is far superior to his recently heard orchestral suite—had that aloofness of music which does exactly what it sets out to do, without tentativeness or strain of any kind. It had, properly speaking, no potentialities, since everything was cast in its definitive form. People were inclined to find it uninteresting on that account. They didn't feel "needed"[14]

Chanler's statements are well taken, and the *Quartet* is a compact, unpretentious composition, one that became—and remains—a favorite of the Juilliard Quartet. The work is agreeable and charming, but by no means bland. The opening "Allegro's" first theme group, for instance, is all tension and anguish within a hypnotic 3/4 meter, while the second theme, an eerie F minor waltzlike theme, is dreamily approached by way of C-sharp minor. The whole thing is nightmarish. The ensuing "Adagio" contrasts a brooding solo cello with soft, nostalgic ripples in the upper strings, like a sorrowful man in a peaceful country setting. This movement, which is centered by an intense fugue, is an admirable showpiece for a quartet's cellist. Piston concludes the *Quartet* with a deliciously whimsical finale with spectacular string writing that is sure to win a good quartet lots of applause. There are, nonetheless, some disorienting twists here, such as the cello cadence on E at letter A that is sustained as the violin begins its theme in C. Although this is not exactly bitonality, the moment this C tonality usurps the cello's E is fuzzy, producing a dreamlike effect.

In 1941, Copland, discussing Piston's music, wrote, "Among his chamber works my preference goes to the two string quartets. A work like the First String Quartet, with its acidulous opening movement, the poetic mood painting of its second, and its breezy finale, sets a superb standard of taste and of expert string writing."[15] In 1946, Elliott Carter also expressed his admiration for these two quartets, but stated a preference for the *Second*.[16] The *Second Quartet*, premiered by the Chardon on 16 March 1935, is a bolder, more ambitious work, disturbing but not shocking. Despite motivic unity, smooth rhythms, and, at one point, a double canon, the 9/8 "Lento" introduction to the 6/8 "Allegro" ambles through wildly restless chromatics. Its profile is dim: it is more than a tension builder, and yet how much more is difficult to assess. The principal motive, A-C-D$^b$, a prominent motive, by the way, in many other of Piston's works, is basic to the ensuing "Allegro" as well as to the work's "Adagio" and finale. This first movement "Allegro" is violent and breathless, with dramatic changes of texture, including a mystical "sur la touche" passage that precedes the haunting canon that is the movement's second theme. This canon's soulful "blues" notes are even more unusual when placed against a bizarre and distant accompaniment in the recapitulation. Finally, all four voices take part in the canon, "pianissimo," creating the movement's most eerie moment.

The second movement is also intense, with strenuously independent lines, although Piston manages here to evoke a deep sorrow unencumbered by nostalgia. A detailed analysis of this movement's phrase structure is found in a 1964 D.M.A. thesis by Robert Donahue, who discusses the movement's carefully balanced design. Although Donahue states, "The classicism of Piston's phrase structure is not particularly reenforced by the other elements of the music . . ." he nonetheless describes Piston as "classical" as opposed to the "romantic" Bartók.[17] Actually, Piston and Bartók are hardly diametric opposites, and in fact have real affinities, as noted by Virgil Thomson, who points "to the sophisticated and hermetic way that Piston expresses private meanings by developing analytically, much as Bartók was doing, materials based on intervalic contradictions."[18] In the final "Allegro giusto," Piston unfurls his dissonant counterpoint within a mixed meter, with somewhat tentative results. The finale's second theme, however, is elegant fun, and though diatonic, or "pandiatonic," its G major and, even moreso, its E-flat major tonalities make the theme sparkle in this A minor movement. The movement's tonal conflict between A minor and C major is battled out in the coda, which first swings to C, then cadences in A minor, and finally concludes with a single, surprising A major chord.

The *Trio for Violin, Violoncello and Piano*, commissioned by the Elizabeth Sprague Coolidge Foundation and dedicated to Mrs. Coolidge, was premiered by William Kroll, violin, Horace Brett, cello, and Frank Sheridan, piano, at a Founder's Day Concert at the Library of Congress on 30 October 1935. It is a better work than the two early quartets, less "sophisticated and hermetic," but more direct in its emotional appeal. Whereas the *Quartets* develop arguments based on small motives, the *Trio* unfolds relaxed, nicely shaped melodies that are unified not so much by intervalic or rhythmic details as by the use of a scale that emphasizes the major and minor third, the tritone, and the flatted seventh. In the sonata first movement, the piano accompaniment, as in the *Flute Sonata*, adds chromatic interest to the modal melodies, although roots on powerful downbeats give a firmer sense of harmonic rhythm. In the second theme group, the accompaniment, shared alternately by the piano and strings, provides a macabre background to a comical, carefree tune.

The *Trio*'s "Adagio" is straight from the heart, with tender melodies and beautiful modulations. Like the slow movement of Ravel's *Trio*, which it resembles, the "Adagio" is a passacaglia-variation movement. The cello states the theme (mm. 1–9), and then repeats it against a counter-melody in the violin (10–21). The piano then plays the theme in canon while the strings, also "pianissimo," play the countermelody in unison (22–28). The next variation (29–34), contrapuntal and ornate, leads to a climactic, passionate variation (35–45) in which the piano's running sixteenth-note ostinato is the theme in diminution. The movement concludes with a restatement of the theme for cello, and there is a final cadence, almost medieval in tone, based on the opening of the violin's countermelody (46–56).

The scherzo pits modal melodies in the strings against chromatic acrobatics in the piano. Piston's string melodies, in mirror canon, resemble Copland in their syncopated 6/8 rhythms, although their origin is clearly in the fanfare. The trio section is completely diatonic, and uses a device associated with Harris during these years, namely, the "autogenetic" melody, or a melody that adds a new note with each successive repetition. Piston's manipulations, including invertible counterpoint and diminution, get quite complex; and while the diatonicism is refreshing, the artifice is extreme. The finale is also contrapuntally intricate. At its start, the violin theme is accompanied by its inversion in canon in the cello, and its augmentation, in the dominant in the piano. The counterpoint is vigorous and spiky, like the first movement of the *Concerto for Orchestra*. In fact, the *Trio*, with its passacaglia, its lighthearted scherzo, and its contrapuntal finale, is the chamber work by Piston that comes closest to the spirit of that orchestral work.

In 1936, the Columbia Compositions Commission, headed by Deems Taylor, commissioned Copland, Gruenberg, Hanson, Harris, Piston, and Still, "on the basis of ability and variety," to write a work for the Columbia Broadcasting System.[19] All six works, Copland's *A Saga for the Prairie*, Gruenberg's *Green Mansions*, Hanson's *Third Symphony*, Harris's *Time Suite*, Piston's *Concertino for Piano and Chamber Orchestra*, and Still's *Lenox Avenue*, were premiered on the radio. Piston wrote for a chamber orchestra because he wanted to avoid, or at least minimize, interference from the control room engineer, and because he found Mozart and Haydn to sound better over the air than big orchestral works.[20] The *Concertino* was premiered on 20 June 1937, with Howard Barlow conducting Sanromà and the Columbia Symphony Orchestra. The first concert performance of the work took place on 24 February, 1938, with Sanromà once again at the piano and Bernard Zighera conducting the Boston Symphony Chamber Orchestra.

The *Concertino* is a one-movement, multisectional work, somewhat like an extended sonata, with two main themes, a scherzo and an "Adagio" in place of a development, a toccata-like cadenza to link the "development" with the recapitulation, and a final coda the size of the scherzo to balance the whole. The piano is clearly the star, with marvelous passagework that endlessly teases the listener (and performer) with its chromatic, contrapuntal, and rhythmic subtleties. The orchestra, for the most part, takes a back seat, offering a broad tonal and rhythmic scope for the piano's details (although there are exceptions, such as the instrumental fugatos in the scherzo and the coda). Furthermore, in the course of the beautiful "Adagio," Piston makes stunning use of a solo cello, a clarinet and oboe duo, a string quartet, and a flute and horn duo, not to mention the rich sonorities of the piano.

As for the themes, they are relaxed and eminently vocal, with the perfect fourth much more important than Piston's favored intervals, the minor second and the tritone. The real gem is the cellist's "Adagio" 5/4 theme, one of Piston's great melodies (ex. 3). This tune, which wins for itself some lovely variations, is undeniably French in tone, as are other moments of the *Concertino* (such as the first sprightly pages, which pop open like a bottle of champagne, and the sentimental interpolation at mm. 309–18). The French touch is handled much better here than in the *Oboe Suite*; the *Concertino* is less derivative and nostalgic, and more elegant in its wit.

Piston's *First Symphony* is the culminating achievement of his early period. He wrote the work in 1937 at age forty-three, the age at which Brahms wrote his *First Symphony*. It is a grand and complex composition, somewhat in the tradition of Brahms but even more in the tradition of Franck and Roussel. One of its most intriguing features, especially in thinly scored passages, is its piquant and fantastic orchestration. Consider, for instance, the work's very opening: first, a solo "pianissimo" timpani roll, then a chromatic ostinato for cellos and basses, "pizzicato" and "pianissimo," then the bassoon's entrance with the motto theme, "pianissimo ma espressive," which is soon taken up by the violas, then the entrance of flutes, clarinets, and bassoons in unison, and so forth— a palette reminiscent of Sibelius, but more delicate. The colors are more mutable here than in the *Concerto for Orchestra*; and for sheer sensuality of sound, this work has few equals in the orchestral literature. For all its beauty of sound, however, the lyricism of the introductory "Andantino quasi Adagio" is ponderous, like the introduction to the *Second Quartet*. The ensuing sonata "Allegro" is, on the other hand, very dramatic, with an unsettling conflict between a taut and powerful first theme, reminiscent of Roussel, and a second theme of indescribable sweetness. The move-

Ex. 3.    Piston, *Concertino* (New York: AMP, 1939), p. 13. Used
          by permission.

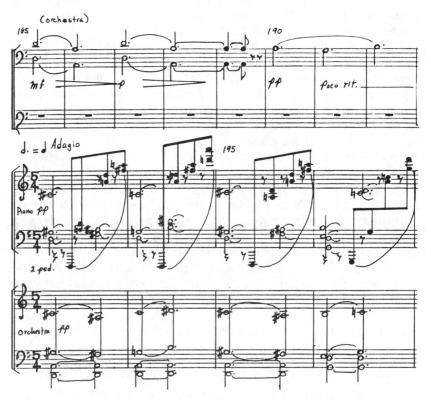

Ex. 3 (continued)

ment concludes, surprisingly, with the dreamy second theme, though the final "pizzicato" statement of the opening ostinato offers at least a passive and resigned reconciliation.

The ABA slow movement, one of Piston's longest, is a contrapuntal fantasy on a melody for English horn. Rich, ornate ideas, gorgeously orchestrated, float by like a dream, and cover a large emotional range—from the melodramatic climaxes in the A sections to the curiously exotic and static B section. There is also an exotic quality to the finale's first theme, though it is full of incredible nervous tension. The gravity of this finale is emphasized by the return of the bassoon's motto theme as a second theme, scored darkly in the exposition, and as an ornamented chorale theme in the recapitulation. This climactic return, however, has none of the heroic grandeur of Franck's *Symphony* nor the religious affirmation of Hindemith's *Mathis der Maler Symphony*. Rather, it has an atmosphere of anguish and urgency, although the final major triad holds out some hope for victory and is more positive than the major/minor clash that concludes the *Concerto for Orchestra*.

Piston conducted the first performance of the *First Symphony* with the Boston Symphony on 8 April 1938. After this performance, Piston rarely premiered an orchestral work, a decision that may have been influenced by Sloper's review of the *First Symphony* for the *Monitor*:

> When a symphonic conductor, at a concert which he is directing, turns over the first performance of a new work to its composer, the public suspects that the conductor doesn't think much of the work. . . . Mr. Piston apparently secured a satisfactory performance, but it is possible that if Dr. Koussevitzky had chosen to conduct it, the symphony might have been presented in an even more favorable light.[21]

Some of the critical reaction to the *First Symphony* was positive in the extreme. Geroge Smith wrote, "Certainly there is no American work in the same form equal to it,"[22] and Moses Smith asserted that Piston's *First Symphony* ". . . exhibited him as technically the most masterly of his generation of American composers."[23] Elliott Carter regretted that the *Concertino* rather than the *Symphony* was selected for a 1939 all-American concert at Carnegie Hall: ". . . its elegance and craftsmanship and distinction would have added much to the program."[24] The work, however, had none of the success of a Hanson *Second*, a Copland *First*, or a Harris *Third*, let alone a Shostakovich *First* or a Roussel *Third*, and Leonard Bernstein's review alludes to what must have been an unenthusiastic, if not disastrous, reception to the work's premiere:

> A very important premiere was the *Symphony* of Walter Piston, a composer who can always be depended upon for the best in workmanship. Adverse criticisms were profuse and diverse: some thought the Largo unduly long and uninteresting: others found the work lacked emotional appeal. Whatever the case, (for opinions at a time as transitional as this must be considered as personal) no one could deny the expert handling of the orchestra, the innovations in instrumental tone-color, the never-failing good taste, the masterly proportioning of the structure, and the fine lyrical sense which Mr. Piston has not often betrayed in the past.[25]

With the publication of the *Symphony* ten years later, Arthur Berger could offer a more accurate, though still tentative, assessment of the work.

Walter Piston's *First Symphony* is a solid work with many fascinating elements that do not easily give up their secret. It is a joy to discover how everything fits into place in this elaborate constellation of tones. Piston is not, like other native composers, discouraged by complexities. If he ventures at times almost as far into atonal realms as is possible within a tonal idiom, he does not commit the atonalist heresy of allowing the large form to reflect the obscurity of the material. The form is that of the traditional symphony and fine rhythmic continuity holds everything together. Highly chromatic episodes flow smoothly into such completely diatonic passages as the second theme of the first movement. There is terrific power in the main subject of the first allegro, with its nervous tension, range and impressive extension, but some other themes, while they seem quite motory, do not always move in the most interesting directions. I suspect, however, that the total effect of a performance may make them seem more convincing.[26]

Even with the first recording of the work in 1979 critical reaction was positive, but still cautious. Peter Davis of the *New York Times*, for instance, wrote, "this score is a luminously textured, elegantly crafted and intensely lyrical statement by a man who will most likely be regarded as the country's most important exponent of the symphonic form."[27]

This sort of uncertain grappling is endemic to Piston criticism, especially in the 1930s, when composers like Copland, Elwell, Chanler, McPhee, Carter, Berger, and Bernstein took Piston's work very seriously. Copland showed himself a stout supporter when he chose Piston along with Sessions, Thomson, Harris, and himself for a series of one-man concerts at the New School in 1935, which helped center attention on Piston. But it was Israel Citkowitz, in a 1936 article for *Modern Music* entitled, "Walter Piston—Classicist," who most thoroughly and insightfully probed Piston's problematic art. In the article's first pages, Citkowitz enumerates Piston's virtues, including his "singularly refined conception of the exact limits of a given medium," his contrapuntal skill, and his successful conjunction of diatonic and chromatic lines. Citkowitz also points to defects, "instances where the contrapuntal design seems crowded, and where a simpler, more anonymous voice-leading would have given more transparent results" and other instances where the chromatic element "tends to congest the contrapuntal design, producing an effect of turgidity and strain." But Citkowitz's most interesting remarks are addressed to "the whole creative drama" of Piston's music.

I might define this drama as the struggle between the abstract demands of pure architectonics, and the actual content of musical feeling and expression which the artistic sensibilities dispose. I have mentioned above that Piston's orientation to the problem of form was conditioned to some extent by neo-classic criteria. The sum of musical creation, according to these criteria, resolves itself into a sheer problem of architectonics. All considerations but those of pure design are excluded. While Piston does not subscribe in whole to these ideas he does tend to plan his form on this exclusive basis. As a result, the actual content will often lag behind the structural proportions. While the architectonic scheme is carried out with admirable skill, a divergence between form and content becomes a formidable problem. It may be stretching the point rather finely, but it does seem as if the congestion and strain of some of this music occurs in the attempt to fill these lacunae. Stravinsky's music, in its later aspects, presents so smooth and impeccable a surface, just because the perfect neutrality of content permits him to spin out his design with all the precision of an engineer. But Piston has two forces to reconcile and adjust: on the one hand, the impulses of emotion and expression which furnish the very marrow of musical content; on the other, the intellectual demands for design and cogency, for a demonstrable and well-ordered form.[28]

In a recent work like the 1935 *Trio*, Citkowitz argues, "there is a marked advance in the flexibility of adjustment between the form and animating idea." While Citkowitz probably found the *Concertino* another step closer to a "living classicism," he might have reasonably been disappointed, as so many were, in the *First Symphony*.

Citkowitz's discussion best explains the mixed reaction a listener is likely to have on hearing one of Piston's early works. But it also raises some questions: did Piston aspire to be a classicist? Was such a classicism possible in the 1930s? Would our reactions be less confused if we can shake off the label, "classicist"? As for the first question, it seems that Piston did indeed strive to create a classic statement. At Harvard, he studied, like T. S. Eliot, with Babbitt, and he wrote appreciatively of Brahms's ability to unite the heart and the mind. In later years, he expressed the desire to find the "perfect balance between expression and form," and thought he first approached this ideal with the *Fourth Symphony* of 1950. Was this "balance" possible for an interbellum composer? As Citkowitz notes, Stravinsky comes closer to it than Piston does (and so does Hindemith, for that matter). But Piston is more than a failed classicist, or a minor Stravinsky. His music contains something that is very distinctive, and which may be profitably discussed in contexts other than classicism, namely, mannerism and surrealism.

Piston was acquainted with sixteenth-century mannerist art. He sang "the rarest of madrigals" with Boulanger, he collected reproductions of El Greco and Brueghel, and he set to music a poem by Lorenzo de Medici in 1938. Given Piston's broad interests, this involvement with mannerism seems casual; but coincidental or not, there are profound similarities between Piston's music and the mannerist aesthetic as interpreted by an advocate like Arnold Hauser.[29] Especially relevant in the light of Citkowitz's discussion is the conflict in mannerist art between abstract formalism and irrational passion, for this conflict need not be viewed as an unsuccessful classicism, but rather as part of a particular aesthetic that is ambiguous in its relationship to classicism. Hauser writes, "It is impossible to understand mannerism if one does not grasp the fact that its imitation of classical models is an escape from the threatening chaos, and that the subjective overstraining of its forms is the expression of the fear that form might fail in the struggle with life and art fade into soulless beauty.''[30] If the sixteenth-century artist was torn between the spirituality of the Middle Ages and the naturalism of the Renaissance, Piston was similarly divided between the spiritualism of the eighteenth century and the naturalism of the nineteenth century. The result of this conflict is, in Piston's music as well as in mannerist art, an international and aristocratic art which is elegant, intellectual, and lacking in popular appeal. Consider, too, the background of political and economic turmoil against which the mannerists and Piston quietly practiced their art.[31]

Some of these generalizations hold true for twentieth-century surrealism as well, and Hauser writes, "The quasi-mannerist trends of modern art appear in their purest form in surrealism. . . . As so often in the history of ideas, we are obviously confronted here with a case, not of direct derivation, of straightforward causality, but of interdependence and synchronism of meaningfully connected phenomena.''[32] Surrealism is, of course, the more accurate historical context for Piston, although his conservative, traditional art might be closer to the mannerists after all. If Piston avoided a doctrinaire and radical surrealist like André Breton, which seems probable, he nonetheless had some concrete, if peripheral, connections with surrealism: while in Paris he attended the lectures of Henri Bergson;[33] in later years, he read Pirandello and Gide, and he was good friends with Conrad Aiken, whose surrealist poems and "stream-of-consciousness" novels stressed the erotic and the psychoanalytical. More to the point, Piston's music, with its extremely independent lines that seem to defy any unity of tonality, pulse, or even mood, can often be described as dreamlike or surreal. Or consider the use of the same line unfolding at different rates as in the *Trio*. Sometimes Piston's formal sense is surreal as well, whether it be, as in the *First Symphony*, the exaggerated contrasts of the opening movement, or the complex collage of the slow movement. Even Piston's melodies, such as the solo cello melodies in the *Suite* and the *Concerto*, take twisted shapes. All this creates a misty and murky atmosphere that Citkowitz found at once evocative and turgid.

With Piston, then, we have an art in which classical form is rigorously imposed upon romantic expression. Classic and romantic elements are not smoothly integrated as they are in Mozart, but, on the contrary, are in violent opposition. The music is poised and refined on the outside, as it were, and brooding and passionate on the inside. This is a feature common to many artists who worked in the interbellum period between the two World Wars: the same disruptive forces that inspired such artists to create a classical art ironically undermined all such aspirations. While the term neoclassical is misleading in this regard, the term surrealism, coined by artists during these years, seems more accurate; the "realism" of surrealism suggests its classical intentions, while the "sur" of surrealism denotes the fantastic, dreamlike quality of its content. Perhaps it would do better to call Piston a surrealist than a neo-classicist.[34] In any case, the tension between form and content that we find in Piston is a moving struggle. And if the struggle is not always satisfactorily resolved by the standards of classicism, Piston is never too far off the mark and can certainly win our interest and compassion, and sometimes our awe.

# 4

## Music for Song and Dance:
## *The Incredible Flutist* and the *Carnival Song* (1938)

In 1938, Piston ventured out of the realm of abstract instrumental music with the ballet *The Incredible Flutist* and a choral work, the *Carnival Song*. The ballet was written for Hans Wiener and the Boston Pops Orchestra at the invitation of Arthur Fiedler, who had been collaborating with Wiener and his dance troupe since 1931. "To have the Boston Symphony Orchestra sitting in the pit, on the floor, was enough intriguing for me to want to do it," said Piston, "because ordinarily you have a ballet, they'll have, I don't know, a few instruments and a piano."[1] One assumes that Piston also welcomed the chance to work with Hans Wiener. In fact, an undated brochure about Wiener quotes Piston as follows: "Your approach to the Modern Dance gives such stimulating possibilities that it has been a great pleasure to collaborate with you in writing 'The Incredible Flutist.' Your dancing of the title role was most impressive and brilliant."

Hans Wiener was born Johann Maria David Wiener in Vienna in 1908 and changed his name, for a second time, to Jan Veen in 1942. After music studies at the Vienna Conservatory, and dance studies with Rudolf van Laban, Mary Wigman, and Jaques Dalcroze, Wiener toured the Orient, and started a school in Shanghai.[2] In 1929, he settled in Boston, where he served the artistic community in many capacities. His dancing, which combined elements of post-War Viennese dance with classical Chinese dance, won friends and critics alike. In 1941, Grant Code wrote that Wiener had managed to keep his "Viennese wit and theatrical effectiveness, his somewhat puckish and unearthly youth . . . his emphasis on wit, humor, sentiment, and color"[3] while in the same year John Martin stated that Wiener was theatrical "only in the rather derogatory use of that term to mean superficial and slightly flamboyant. The style of dancing stems from what has been aptly called the 'German phantasmagoria school.' "[4] Wiener died in 1967.

Copland, who wrote *Billy the Kid* in 1938, suggests that good opportunities and economic motivations explain the numerous collaborative efforts undertaken during these years.

> Motion-picture and ballet companies, radio stations and schools, film and theater producers discovered us. The music appropriate for the different kinds of cooperative ventures undertaken by these people had to be simpler and more direct. There was a "market" especially for music evocative of the American scene—industrial backgrounds, landscapes of the Far West, and so forth. This kind of role for music, so new then, is now taken for granted by both entrepreneurs and composers. But in the late '30s and early '40s it was almost without precedent, and moreover, it developed at just the time when the economic pinch of the Depression had really reached us. No wonder we were pleased to find ourselves sought after and were ready to compose in a manner that would satisfy both our collaborators and ourselves.[5]

In Piston's case, a light ballet score may also have been an agreeable change of pace from works like the just completed *First Symphony*. Actually, the collaborators worked very hard to have the ballet ready for its premiere on 30 May 1938. Piston composed the work section by section, making arrangements for piano four-hands, and recording them with Fiedler for Wiener's use in rehearsal. In the meantime, Marco Montedoro prepared the sets and the costumes.

Piston, Wiener, and Fiedler all participated in designing the ballet's scenario. The story was briefly outlined in the concert program, and a fuller synopsis was printed in the August 1938 issue of *Dance Magazine*:

> The siesta is over. With a hearty yawn and a wide stretch the village shakes off its drowsiness. First to wake up, the Apprentice opens the shop, and life begins its uneventful flow. The Merchant's Daughters demonstrate their father's wares to Shoppers. The Busybody and the Crank have their argument. But what is this? . . . A march is heard! The Band, the Circus Band, marches in, followed by the people of the circus. They're all here: the Barker, the Jugglers, the Snake Dancer, the Monkey Trainer and her Monkeys, the Crystal Gazer, and, of course, the main attraction, the Flutist. The Flutist is a remarkable fellow, an incredible fellow. He not only charms snakes; he also charms, believe it or not, the Snake Dancer. He is so romantic, the Incredible Flutist, and perhaps just a bit promiscuous, for he also charms the Merchant's Daughter, and they meet at eight o'clock that very evening.

> When the clock strikes eight, young couples are all over the place, and love is in the air. Even the prudish, rich widow cannot resist the charged atmosphere and grants the Merchant the kiss he's been begging for well nigh two years. But they don't fare so well. Their sustained embrace is discovered, and the poor rich Widow faints right into the arms of her bewhiskered boy friend. But the Incredible Flutist hies to the rescue. A little dancing, a little fluting and the Widow comes out of her swoon, none the worse for wear. And then . . . the Band strikes up, the spell is broken, the Circus, Incredible Flutist and all, leave the village.

A worksheet from the Piston collection offers an even more extensive outline of the ballet (the rehearsal letters and the page measure numbers refer to the four-hands reduction, copies of which reside in the Library of Congress and the Sibley Library at the Eastman School).

slow curtain: p. 1, m. 3.
apprentice naps in front of shop, hot lazy siesta hour
a fruit vendor with a big basket of fruit on head crosses stage sluggishly and yawning: m. 8.
fruit vendor sits on edge of stage: m. 13.
wine vendor enters, swinging two bottles roped on a yoke: m. 14.
wine vendor sits down: p. 2, m. 3.
picture peddlar bounces in: p. 2, A.
dance of the vendors—trio: p. 3, B.
picture peddlar exits: p. 7, m. 15.
wine vendor exits: p. 8, E.
fruit vendor exits: p. 8, m. 5.

apprentice comes to life, opens shop briskly: p. 8, F.
discovers merchant snoozing in shop: 4 before G.
wakes merchant with feather duster: p. 9, m. 11.
dance of the merchant's apprentice: p. 9, G.
great ado of pushing small platform in front of shop: p. 10, m. 21.
arrival of customers: p. 10, H.
merchant and apprentice make them sit down: p. 11, m. 11.
fashion show: p. 12, m. 3.
first daughter dances: p. 12, I.
second daughter dances: p. 12, m. 11.
third daughter dances: p. 13, m. 1.
fourth daughter dances: p. 13, m. 8.
four daughters dance together: p. 13, last measure.
daughters mingle with customers examining fashions: p. 15, J.

sound of circus band in distance: p. 16, m. 15.
band approaching: p. 16, m. 15 to p. 17, m. 1.
band with band leader and side show, parade arrives: p. 17, m. 1.
crowd noises made by orchestra members who do not play in the circus march
ringmaster at intervals introduces jugglers, monkey trainer with monkeys carrying box marked "Snake," crystal gazer, snake charmer, and the flutist: during repeat of the circus march.
imitation dog bark, made by a member of the orchestra: p. 18, m. 12.
dance of the trainer and monkeys: p. 18, L.
crystal gazer: p. 21, m. 19.
pulls out woman from crowd and foretells that she will have six children, she retreats angrily: p. 22, m. 5.
dance of the jugglers: p. 22, M.
trembling monkeys carry snake box to center of stage—flutist opens it cautiously: p. 24, m. 9.
solo of the flutist, charming snake in box: p. 24, N.
customers applaud: p. 25, m. 18.

flutist encores with snake charmer's dance: p. 25, O.
onlookers are hypnotized, and gradually join the dance: p. 27, m. 14.
dancers crowd nearer to the flutist: p. 29, top.
the spell is broken when the first daughter steps on the flutist's toe, "Ow": p. 29, m. 13.
he looks at her: p. 29, m. 15.
flutist makes date with first daughter for eight o'clock, counting on his fingers: p. 29, m. 15.
daughter agrees: p. 30, m. 3.
departure of side-show and customers: p. 30, m. 6.
daughters exit through shop: p. 31, m. 4.

entry of widow and two sons: p. 31, m. 14.
merchant servile and friendly to widow: p. 32, m. 7.
merchant claps hands—widow and sons sit down: p. 33, last measure.
four daughters in Spanish capes: p. 34, m. 1.
daughters' dance of display: p. 34, R.
dance of the widow and merchant: p. 37, S.
eight o'clock date by merchant and widow, also sons with third and fourth daughters: p. 38, m. 2.
everybody exits, stage darkens: p. 38, m. 7.

peddlars cross the stage sluggishly and empty-handed: p. 38, last measure.
empty stage—moonlight: p. 39, m. 6.
flutist tiptoes in, first daughter tiptoes out of house: p. 39, N.
love duet: p. 39, next to last measure.
flutist and first daughter hide in proscenium—apprentice and second daughter enter from shop, and hide in the other corner of proscenium: p. 41, V.
two sons enter, third and fourth daughter come from shop: p. 41, m. 24.
dance of sons and daughters—quartet: p. 42, m. 21.
hidden four come out to join in: p. 42, m. 21.
octet: p. 43, m. 3.
all hide—widow tiptoes in: p. 44, W.
merchant tiptoes in through shop: p. 44, m. 17.
widow and merchant, coy lovemaking: p. 45, m. 2.
"boo!" the eight hidden jump out making masks of their hands: p. 45, X.
widow swoons: p. 45, m. 20.
the eight point accusingly at the horrified merchant: p. 45, m. 22.
attempts to revive the widow fail: p. 46, top.
flutist offers to try: p. 46, m. 8.
merchant pleads and offers daughter's hand: p. 46, m. 11.
flutist tries: p. 46, m. 13.
widow revives slowly, falls into merchant's arms: p. 47, Y.
general dance of joy: p. 47, m. 6.
merchant and widow in center, octet in circle: p. 47, m. 14.
side-show and customers enter: p. 49, last measure.
daughters with capes: p. 50, m. 15.
couples embrace: p. 51, m. 5 to m. 11.
ensemble: p. 51, Z.
curtain: p. 52, m. 22

This delightful and silly scenario was sure to amuse even the most frivolous of the "frivolously disposed"[6] attendants at the Boston Pops. But the story is more than a convenient vehicle for staging some dances. Its theme, the transformation of life through art and imagination, is a serious one. The juxtaposition of the mundane town with the fairy-tale circus gives the work a surrealist tone that is reenforced by some other of the ballet's features, such as the consoling eroticism of the fashion shows and the hypnotic eroticism of the snake-charmer, a favorite surrealist motif. The flow of time, as represented by the "fade-in" and "fade-out" of the circus band and the sudden shift from day to night, is likewise surreal and reminiscent of film time. Finally, the opening "siesta" suggests, perhaps, that the whole ballet is a dream. Some of Piston's admirers regretted that he settled upon this trivial scenario,[7] though in fact, its exoticism and color, its cool romanticism, and its mild surrealism perfectly complement his early idiom.

It is the music, of course, that gives the story its richness and depth. The ballet opens with dreamy and fanciful "siesta" music, so quiet you can hear the beating of time. It is somewhat exotic in tone: is this Spain, North Africa, or some magical land even further east? When the lively picture peddlar "bounces in" to join the hot and tired fruit and wine vendors, the music, in fact, is quasi-Oriental. Furthermore, their trio evokes a grand bazaar, full of hawking, commotion, and exotic displays, though it is not known to this writer how Piston and Wiener visualized this dance. The "siesta" music rounds out this opening section, which serves as a prologue, and to set a mood of the *Arabian Nights*.

As if a soldier, the apprentice wakes up to a trumpet call and his dance is a spirited, fairy-tale march (the second phrase of which inverts the first phrase, and one wonders if Wiener interpreted this choreographically). Was the grand bazaar nothing but the dream of the poor beleaguered apprentice? The mock military atmosphere is sustained as the customers rush onto the stage. Their music is like a volley of gunfire and is counterpointed above by the apprentice's march and below by the merchant's leitmotif, which comically refers to an appropriate Pops favorite, Tchaikowsky's *1812 Overture*. The customers are momentarily appeased by the merchant's four daughters, who exhibit their father's wares in a suave and sensuous 5/4 tango; but at the dance's conclusion, the confusion and the haggling begin once more. With the arrival of the circus, however, the town again forgets its bickering.

The circus march is magical, despite its simplicity and its purposeful "wrong" notes, because of its wonderful associations. When Wiener's troupe first heard it played by the Boston Symphony, remembers Piston, "they all broke into cheers, because they'd been hearing little plinks on a disc. And Arthur said, 'What am I going to do, I can't stop them,' and I said, 'Don't stop 'em. This is going to be the best part of the ballet.' "[8] Similarly, Piston persuaded the hesitant Fiedler to allow the Orchestra's contra-bassoonist, Boaz Pillar, to "woof-woof" at the end of the march. Both the yelling and whistling during the march, and the barking at its conclusion, have since become traditional. A fanfare announces that the side-show attractions are about to commence. The first dance, the dance of the trainer and monkeys, is a "presto" tarantella with a repeated A and an ostinato pattern marking time. The tonality is D minor, though the whimsical ending implies D major. The dance of the crystal gazer, for trombones, "glissandi," bassoons, and solo cello, is only ten measures long, a mysterious and avant-garde miniature, while the dance of the jugglers is bright and flippant. The central dance (and the only circus dance Piston included in the ballet *Suite*) is the dance of the flutist, Hans Wiener's solo. The flute melody is exotic and rhapsodic, while the accompanying string harmonies are lush and poignantly dissonant, with a descending chromatic bass line. It is a miniature ABA design, with B involving a remarkable melodic inversion of A. In the next dance, the snake charmer, depicted by the oboe, joins the flutist in more conventional snake charming music.[9]

Piston uses fanfare and flourish to depict the pompous and fussy rich widow. In the minuet she dances with the merchant, however, her haughty contralto trills are transformed into coy soprano flutterings, one of the ballet's most brilliant comic touches. Like the customers, the widow must be appeased by the fashionable daughters, who dance for her not a sultry tango but rather a brilliant Spanish waltz with castanets. As the merchant closes shop, thoughts of the widow and their anticipated rendezvous transform the widow's theme into something tender and dreamy.

Even in this lighthearted score, Piston's music is rich and sensual, whether it be the elegant diatonicism of the "tango," the chromatic triads of the "Spanish waltz," or the more thoroughly chromatic tiptoe music for the clandestine lovers. The chromaticism of the beautiful siciliana for the flutist and the first daughter, however, is particularly restrained. The siciliana's 6/8 meter, D tonality, and pedal point all point back to the monkeys' tarantella, as if to suggest the heights to which man can evolve. Its form is an artful and dramatic AABA. The first A presents a long melody for clarinet that cadences in A minor, while the second A repeats the same melody a step higher, but for oboe and with different harmonies to bring it to F major. The B section uses canon and parallel thirds, while the last A unites the first half of the clarinet's A with the last half of the oboe's A, and returns to the opening D tonality. All in all, it is a beautiful metaphor for love. The final polka has some nice exotic touches in keeping with the rest of the ballet. It is somewhat derived, in fact, from the "siesta" music, while its climactic three notes, A-B-C, twelve measures from the end, look back to the weary fruit vendor (m. 8). This polka is occasionally interrupted with reminiscences of other dances, and the result is a medley-finale that is somewhat flat and contrived. The structure of the entire ballet, however, is carefully conceived, especially its tonal movement from D (the vendors) to G (the customers) to F (the circus) to C (the merchant and the widow) and back to D (the finale).

This tonal structure was retained for the *Suite* that Piston extracted from the ballet in 1939. Premiered by Fritz Reiner and the Pittsburgh Symphony on 22 November 1940, the *Suite* soon became a great success. The Cleveland Orchestra alone played the *Suite* twenty-five times in their 1940–41 season. The *Suite* was chosen, along with works by Harris, Barber, and Gershwin, for performance at the Moscow Conservatory on 4 July 1943. First recorded by Fiedler and the Boston Pops on 29 June 1939, the *Suite* was subsequently recorded by a number of other orchestras. Piston doubtless enjoyed the work's popularity, but though fond of its "tunes,"[10] he was slightly irked when people assumed that it was his best work. (This was even the judgment of Howard Hanson in an interview with this author in September 1979.)

The *Suite* was the inspiration for a poem, "The Incredible Flutist," by Philip Booth written in 1957 or 1958 when the poet taught at Wellesley.[11]

> The music does not begin,
> it sounds before we learn
> to hear it.
>     Newly we wake
> to the circus, to the clown
> who plays tunes. The snake
> is charmed, we are undone
> in our village square.
> The sudden dance is here
> where unknown to ourselves,
> our hearts, from the trance
> they fall out of, enlarge
> to the stranger's embrace.
>
> We wake from slow lives,
> cooks, milkmen, and bakers,
> young girls and old housewives,
> made one by this rake
> of a flutist. We waltz
> blindly on perfect feet,
> whirling until our tuned hearts
> take time by the surge

of his flute.

Incredibly we revive,
no worse for first love,
alive to the flutist's thin
tune, to the new tune
of the circus marching away.
Stay!
   Stay!
      Stay!
we call, but he has an elsewhere
to go. And we are left here
to sink back toward sleep.
Farmhand and teacher, we
dream of the hill girls, who slowly
approach our new hope.
But no, our stolid brains
prevent us. Halfway awake,
we turn cold, puritans
with more science than love.
The music is lost.
         We dream
again, the long flute tune
rising like morning before us.
We cannot, will not, believe
it. But loud as a circus
the circus returns to stay.
Stray dogs leap to tumble,
the weathercock spins, and today
for forever and one day longer,
we're joined by the flutist,
we dance, dance, and kiss,
we dance to the tune of the stranger.

In a letter to this author dated 19 February 1980, Booth recalled the origins of the poem.

> Whether the record was new to me at the time I cannot remember; I do know that I felt an implied narrative within the piece as I heard it, and I recall wondering what narrative I could make from/with/for the piece that might speak my joy in it yet not distort it. It was for me, I suppose, a labor of translation: I know that I listened over and over to Mr. Piston's music, taking notes to myself, jotting fragments, finally beginning to feel the poem happen as the poem it came to be. I believe I sent the poem to Mr. Piston, and I think that he wrote me a kind note.

Piston's other work from 1938, the *Carnival Song* for three-part chorus of men's voices and brass instruments, is dedicated to G. Wallace Woodworth and the Harvard Glee Club, who premiered the work on 7 March 1940. It is a setting of Lorenzo de Medici's "Trionfo d'Arianna e Bacco," a poem written for carnival time in Renaissance Florence. Here is the poem and a translation by Robert Hall, Jr.[12]

| | |
|---|---|
| Quant' è bella giovinezza<br>Che si fugge tuttavia!<br>Chi vuol esser lieto sia:<br>Di doman non c'è certezza. | How beautiful is youth,<br>Which is constantly fleeting.<br>Whoever wishes to be happy, be so;<br>Of tomorrow there is no certainty. |
| Quest' è Bacco e Arianna,<br>Belli, e l'un dell'altro ardenti:<br><br>Perche 'l tempo fugge e 'nganna,<br>Sempre insieme stan contenti.<br><br>Queste ninfe e altre genti<br>sono allegre tuttavia.<br>Chi vuol esser lieto, sia:<br>Di doman non c'è certezza. | These are Bacchus and Ariadne,<br>Handsome, and each in love with the other:<br>Because time flies and deceives,<br>They are always together in happiness.<br>These nymphs and other people<br>Are constantly merry.<br>Whoever wishes to be happy, be so;<br>Of tomorrow there is no certainty. |
| Questi lieti satiretti<br>Delle ninfe innamorati<br>Per caverne e per boschetti<br>Han lor posto cento aguati:<br><br>Or da Bacco riscaldati,<br>Ballan, saltan tuttavia<br><br>Chi vuol esser lieto, sia:<br>Di doman non c'è certezza. | These cheerful little satyrs,<br>Enamored of the nymphs,<br>In caves and groves<br>Have set a hundred ambushes for them;<br>Now excited by Bacchus<br>They are constantly dancing and leaping.<br>Whoever wishes to be happy, be so;<br>Of tomorrow there is no certainty. |
| Queste ninfe hanno anco caro<br>Da loro essere ingannate;<br>Non puon far a Amor riparo<br>Se non genti rozze e 'ngrate:<br>Ora insieme mescolate<br>Suonan, cantan tuttavia<br>Chi vuol esser lieto, sia:<br>Di doman non c'è certezza. | These nymphs are, in their turn, glad<br>To be deceived by them;<br>Love can be rejected<br>Only by uncouth and graceless people;<br>Now all mixed together<br>They are constantly making merry.<br>Whoever wishes to be happy, be so;<br>Of tomorrow there is no certainty. |
| Questa some che vien dreto<br>Sopra l'asino, è Silento:<br>Così vecchio e ebbro e lieto,<br>Già di carne e d'anni pieno;<br>Se non può star ritto, almeno<br>Ride e gode tuttavia.<br>Chi vuol esser lieto, sia:<br>Di doman non c'è certezza. | This heavy body which comes next<br>On the donkey, is Silenus;<br>So old, he is drunk and happy<br>In the fullness of flesh and of years;<br>If he cannot sit upright, at least<br>He is constantly laughing and joyful.<br>Whoever wishes to be happy, be so;<br>Of tomorrow there is no certainty. |
| Mida vien dopo costoro:<br>Ciò che tocca, oro diventa. | Midas comes after them;<br>Whatever he touches, becomes gold. |

| | |
|---|---|
| E che giova aver tesoro, | And what use is it to have treasure |
| Poiche l'uom non si contenta? | If a man is not content? |
| Che dolcezza vuoi che senta | What sweetness do you expect him to know |
| | |
| Chi ha sete tuttavia? | Who constantly feels thirst? |
| Chi vuol esser lieto, sia: | Whoever wishes to be happy, be so; |
| Di doman non c'è certezza. | Of tomorrow there is no certainty. |
| | |
| Ciascum apra ben gli orecchi: | Let everyone open their ears well: |
| Di doman nessun si paschi; | No one should feed his hopes on tomorrow; |
| | |
| Oggi siam, giovani e vecchi, | Today let us, young and old, |
| Lieti ognun, femmine e maschi; | Each one be happy, male and female: |
| Ogni tristo pensier caschi; | Let every sad thought be discarded; |
| Facciam festa tuttavia. | Let's constantly make merry. |
| Chi vuol esser lieto, sia: | Whoever wishes to be happy, be so; |
| Di doman non c'è certezza. | Of tomorrow there is no certainty. |
| | |
| Donne e giovanetti amanti, | Ladies and youths in love, |
| Viva Bacco e viva Amore! | Hurrah for Bacchus and hurrah for love! |
| | |
| Ciascun suoni, balli e canti! | Let everyone play, dance, and sing! |
| Arda di dolcezza il core! | Let our hearts be aflame with sweetness! |
| | |
| Non fatica, non dolore! | No toil, no sorrow! |
| Quel c'ha esser, convien sia. | Whatever has to be, must be. |
| Chi vuol esser lieto, sia: | Whoever wishes to be happy, be so; |
| Di doman non c'è certezza. | Of tomorrow there is no certainty. |
| | |
| Quant è bella giovinezza | How beautiful is youth, |
| Che si fugge tuttavia! | Which is constantly fleeting. |

Like *The Incredible Flutist*, the *Carnival Song* contrasts the beauty of love (the flutist and the daughter; the satyrs and the nymphs) with the sterility of materialism (the rich widow; Midas), though its ominous refrain, "Di doman non c'è certezza," lends a desperate intensity to the merrymaking. And whereas the circus in the *Flutist* transforms the entire village, this carnival processional merely extends an invitation, "Chi vuol esser lieto, sia," one that is so frenzied as to be at once delightfully infectious and poignantly reckless. Piston saw the poem's fraternal exaltation of youth and vigor as particularly apposite for a college glee club.

The work's introduction, for three trumpets, four horns, three trombones, and tuba, combines fanfare with Italian street song; and the mixolydian modality gives it a delicately antique flavor. A basic sonority in this introduction, and in the work as a whole, is an open fifth filled in either above or below by a major second, such as F-G-C or G-C-D. The chorus enters on such a chord, in this case F-B$^b$-C, and such close choral writing is typical of the entire work. The opening stanza is of impressive power and virility, to be topped only by the work's last pages and the final, climactic, "che si fugge tuttavia." When Bacchus and Ariadne make their entrance, the melodic contour becomes gentler and the modality shifts to D aeolian, but the brilliant F mixolydian fanfare returns at the refrain.

The four middle stanzas (those depicting, respectively, the satyrs, the nymphs, Silenus, and Midas) are distinct in mood, though they are suffused with the same delicate lightheartedness. The satyr santza possesses the satiric mischief that is so characteristic of Piston's humor, although its modulation from C major to E minor at the refrain is surprisingly forboding. The beautiful nymph stanza, with its trumpet-horn duet, its tenor solo, its aeolian modality, and its long lines with drooping fifths, is as exquisite a representation of love as is the siciliana from the *Flutist*. Even the line beginning, "Non poun far a Amor riparo," with its protruding G-sharps, is extremely elegant in its indignation. The final wavering major-minor cadence offers a certain emotional dimension not to be found in the secure D major resolution of the siciliana. In the next stanza, the drunken Silenus is depicted by an unsteady, chromatic ostinato in the tuba. The chorus mocks Silenus, but good-naturedly, and imitates him gladly. The basses sing a drunken low D on "pieno," while the tenors tipsily reach for a high A on "chi." All voices comically clash on "sia," while the ensuing bass line staggers home to D. Midas, too, is mocked by the chorus with music that suggests the clinking of coins, though Piston sets the stanza's rhetorical questions to forceful and contrapuntal music of burning intensity.

At this point, the fanfare in F returns to round out the whole. A preliminary sketch for the *Carnival Song* in the Library of Congress reveals the careful tonal symmetry of the work, as well as Piston's precompositional concern for dynamics, color, and attack.

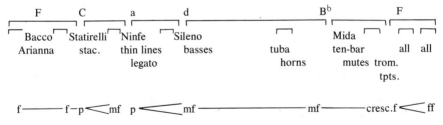

The final section, however, has some exciting tonal motion, for after the reestablishment of F, there is movement to V ("Ciascun apra"), then, suddenly, to V/vi ("certezza"), to vi ("cuore"), to the dominant again ("Non fatica"), and finally back to F ("Chi vuol esser lieto").

The exoticism and internationalism of both *The Incredible Flutist* and the *Carnival Song* can be explained, in part, by local associations. Hans Wiener, after all, had grown up in Austria and had travelled throughout Asia, so the fact that the ballet has him polka as well as snakecharm should not surprise us. In addition, the Wiener troupe often programmed Spanish ballets, including a 1934 *El Amor Brujo* with the Pops audience in costume, and this might have suggested the score's Spanish features: the "siesta" music, the tango, and the Spanish waltz. Similarly, the *Carnival Song* seems to have been inspired by Glee Club performances of Gabrieli with the Boston Symphony brass section. But both works have connections with international trends as well. Stravinsky's *Petrouchka*, Satie's *Parade*, and Prokofiev's *Love for Three Oranges* feature the sort of juxtaposition of audience and entertainers that one finds in the *Flutist*; while the work's exotic circus atmosphere suggests the work of a contemporary Soviet composer like Kabalevsky, who, in fact, wrote in 1956, "[Piston] is familiar to us through many successful performances of *The Incredible Flutist*."[13] As for the *Carnival Song*, its use of an old text in its original language, and its choral and brass writing, suggest the influence of *Oedipus Rex*, though it is closer to Respighi than to Stravinsky. Indeed, in both works, Piston's elegant poise, fatalistic hedonism, and tender romance give an old-fashioned sheen and serenity to the music.

At any rate, these two works of 1938 made explicit something that was only implied in the music Piston had written up until then, namely, that he was uninterested in the "American 'market' " that appealed to Copland and others. He rather preferred, on the one hand, a Boston elite that attended Symphony Hall to hear Falla and Gabrieli, and, on the other, a potentially international audience fond of Satie and Stravinsky. At the time, this internationalism distinguished Piston from most of his compatriots. In 1941, Copland wrote:

> If you had asked visiting foreign composers like Stravinsky and Hindemith, when first they arrived on these shores, which American composer they had found to admire, the answer would very probably have been Walter Piston. This response might be interpreted in two ways: either the music Piston writes is of so high a standard in taste and excellence as far to outdistance any other American's work, or it is couched in an idiom so little American as to seem quite familiar to the musician from overseas. There is a certain amount of truth in both these views . . . Neoclassicism, because of its internationalist aesthetic, is equally serviceable in any country anywhere. Piston's frank adoption of the international style makes his pieces easily negotiable in all countries and therefore quickly assimilable by the visiting foreigner.[14]

While Copland's remarks on Piston's "serviceable" and "negotiable" music are friendly, or at least discreet, Thomson is critical and sarcastic.

"I am not even certain," he writes in 1939, "that the international neo-classic style was not worked out as a stylistic medium for privately commissioned works, as a sort of 'lingua franca' that could be addressed to any possible patroness anywhere in the Western world."[15] Thomson goes on to define this style:

> It is a dissonant contrapuntal manner welded out of the following heterogeneous elements, all chosen for their prestige value:
> A.   The animated contrapuntalism of J. S. Bach
> B.   The unresolved dissonance of Debussy and Richard Strauss, and
> C.   The Berlioz tradition of instrumentation
> D.   To these elements were added frequently a fourth, the reconstructed or modern French sonata-form—a device practiced originally by the pupils of César Franck and expounded at Vincent d'Indy's Schola Cantorum.

Thomson also comments:

> For the bright young composers of the world, who knew all this long ago [the incompatibility of A and B with D], to have gone in as thoroughly as they did, between the years of 1920 and 1935, for such an indigestible mixture, such a cocktail of culture as the international neo-classic style, leaves us no out but to ascribe to them a strong non-musical motivation. The sharing of the available private commissions of the Western world among a smallish but well-united group of these composers I maintain to have been the motivation. That and the corollary activities of winning prizes and foundation awards and eventually, when all the prizes and all the possible commissions have been had, of grabbing off one of the fancier institutional teaching jobs.[16]

Although Thomson speaks of a style, he seems to have Piston, "one of the movement's chief survivors," uppermost in mind.

Thomson's criticism contains a good deal of insight, and his discussion of the incompatibility of "animated contrapuntalism" and "unresolved dissonance" with sonata form is as telling as Citkowitz's similar remarks about content and form in Piston's music. But although this incongruity admittedly prevents a classical style, Thomson does not allow that its mannerist aesthetic is sincere, let alone profound. At any rate, his conclusion that greed and ambition are at the root of this style is terribly exaggerated. The "American 'market' " was surely more profitable than the commissions of Koussevitzky and Coolidge, who, by the way, patronized Copland and Harris as much as they did Piston. Furthermore, Piston won no private commissions from Europe, nor did he need any such awards to secure his post at Harvard.

Piston's internationalism is undeniable, however, and is evident by the fact that his huge library of scores contained few works by Americans. Similarly, his collection of books included Italian, German, French, and

Spanish novels in their original languages, Greek, Latin, Portuguese, Russian, Hungarian, Chinese, and Japanese grammar books and dictionaries, and, again, few American works. But Piston was neither an expatriate nor even a traveler. And what Copland and Thomson both overlook is the fact that Piston's internationalism, whether idealistic or self-serving, was not shaped abroad, but in a cosmopolitan American city whose musical community was very European, especially in the thirties. In 1940, Piston suggested that his musical personality was American in the sense that it was Bostonian and New England.

> "Is the Dust Bowl more American than, say, a corner in the Boston Athenaeum?" he asks? "Would not a Vermont village furnish as American a background for a composition as the Great Plains? The self-conscious striving for nationalism gets in the way of the establishment of a strong school of composition and even of significant individual expression. If the composers will increasingly strive to perfect themselves in the art of music and will follow only those paths of expression which seem to take them the true way, the matter of a national school will take care of itself. And who can predict the time of its coming? Some say it is already here. Some say it has been here since the turn of the century. Others feel it will take time to show the true significance of the enormous development of these recent years. But the composer cannot afford the wild-goose chase of trying to be more American than he is."[17]

Ironically, this association between Piston and Boston, first imputed by the composer himself in this defensive rebuttal to the Americanists, became a commonplace after the Second World War. But it was often made in a derogatory sense, not to suggest internationalism and elegance, but rather parochialism and superficial charm. Elie Siegmeister says in 1978, "I think he was closer to the European neo-classicism of Stravinsky and Hindemith than to the native get-your-feet muddy spirit of Ives, Gershwin, Blitzstein, Thomson, et al. I guess the 'embrace-the-common' fellows ca. 1925–45 felt that way: a good, somewhat Boston-genteel composer of fine craftsmanship, a bit thin and academic."[18] But even though Piston had no interest in the descriptive titles and musical clichés of self-conscious nationalism, his early music sounds recognizably American. And as Piston's style grows less mannered, its national character becomes that much more perceptible.

# 5

## Piston, Patriot:
## From the *Violin Concerto* and the *Violin Sonata*
## (1939) to the *Violin Sonatina* (1945)

The national quality of Piston's music may vary from work to work, but it is inevitably to be found to some degree. Virgil Thomson, in a mood very different from his 1939 *State of Music*, writes in 1970:

> A European formation in music is seemingly ineradicable. And so indeed is the lack of one. The cases of Roger Sessions, Roy Harris, Walter Piston, Elliott Carter, Arthur Berger, and Ross Lee Finney, like Edward Burlingame Hill and John Alden Carpenter before them, are significant in this regard. No amount of European overlay, though it may have masked their essential Americanism, has deceived anyone into mistaking them for Europeans.[1]

Piston's Americanism is very evident and sincere in his 1939 *Violin Concerto*, dedicated to Ruth Posselt, an "able and indefatigable promoter of modern violin concertos"[2] for whom Hill, Duke, and Barber also wrote concertos. Posselt premiered the work on 18 March 1940, in Carnegie Hall with Leon Barzin conducting the National Orchestral Association. Of all Piston's works, the *Violin Concerto* is perhaps most pointed in its Americanism, and as Carter notes, "most of the materials suggest in a very discreet way various kinds of popular music."[3] But its style is not inconsistent with the composer at his most personal, and therefore provides a helpful focus for understanding the national attributes of his art.

Although Piston once wrote "that the basic facts of rhythm apply to music of all periods and nationalities, not just to some,"[4] in matters of rhythmic detail, Piston's music is undeniably influenced by the music of ragtime, the tango, and Tin Pan Alley. In the *Concerto*'s first movement, for instance, the violin's beautiful melody is supported by rhythms like $\frac{3}{4}$ ♩ ♫ ♩ ♫ and $\frac{3}{4}$ ♫ ♩ ♩ . Off-beat accents are also prevalent in the finale, whose main theme takes the following rhythmic shape:

Had Piston written the theme in mixed meter

it would have sounded more Stravinskian but less jazzy.

Piston's chords and textures, so lean and sparse, also sound American. As is well known, Piston prefers triads of fourths or fifths to simple triads, and the simple triads at the slow movement's climax are atypical. The second theme of the first movement (ex. 4) has the spaciousness of the American countryside, although it is only remotely reminiscent of Copland. And while Piston poked fun at Thomson's canon for tuba and piccolo in the *Symphony on a Hymn Tune*,[5] he often employs wide-open textures himself, a particularly beautiful example of which is the violin's entrance in the *Concerto*'s slow movement. In addition, the *Concerto*'s melodic language is colored by an American vernacular. The pentatonicism of the first movement, the important "blues" motive (m. 3) of the slow movement, and the "blues" notes of the finale all bespeak an American origin. Even the pristine and ethereal second theme of the first movement is transformed into a spicy tango in the finale. Aside from some snazzy passages for brass and percussion in the finale, however, Piston's orchestration, unlike Copland's, is not suggestive of the American scene, not at least in any obvious way.

The national elements of the *Violin Concerto*, undeniable though they may be, are subordinate both to a personal need for self-expression and a European canon of beauty. In the two years prior to the *Concerto*, Piston had made distinctive use of French, Spanish, and Italian styles in, respectively, the *Concertino*, *The Incredible Flutist*, and the *Carnival Song*. The use of American material is made not on principle but rather when it appears appropriate to a certain work, movement, or even theme. I am reminded of the appraisal of Glinka's nationalism that Stravinsky made before a Harvard audience the year in which Piston's *Violin Concerto* was written:

> It is in the opera *A Life for the Czar* that the "melos" of the people is quite naturally incorporated into art music. Glinka is not here obeying the dictates of custom. He does not think of laying the groundwork of a vast enterprise for export purposes: he takes the popular "motif" as raw material and treats it quite instinctively according to the usages of the Italian music then in vogue. Glinka does not hobnob with the common people, as certain of his successors did, to reinforce his vigor through contact with the plain truth. He is merely looking for elements of musical enjoyment.[6]

An even fairer analogy might be made with Tchaikowsky, for, as Stravinsky writes, "however attentive and sensitive he was to the world outside
of Russia, one can say that he generally showed himself to be, if not
nationalist and populist like The Five, at least profoundly national in the
character of his themes, the cut of his phrases, and the rhythmic phy-
siognomy of his work."[7] This analogy is especially relevant regarding
Piston's *Violin Concerto*, for it is, in fact, closely modelled after Tchaikowsky's *Violin Concerto*. From the standpoint of nationalism, their first

Ex. 4.   Piston, "Allegro energico," *Violin Concerto No. 1* (New
         York: Boosey and Hawkes, 1948), p. 5. Used by
         permission.

Ex. 4.   (continued)

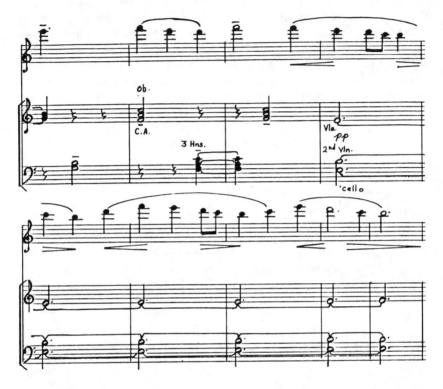

movements are the most personal, their slow movements are subtly tinged by popular song, and their finales are clearly evocative of national dance. The nationalism of the Piston *Concerto*, however, does not preclude a contrapuntal sophistication typical of its composer; and one finds a good deal of melodic inversion, contrapuntal inversion, and canon in the score. There are also two striking thematic transformations: the first movement's second theme becomes the last movement's second theme, and the slow movement theme becomes the finale's episodic E minor theme. Piston, ever crafty, has the solo violin simultaneously play both transformations in the cadenza to the last movement. It is as if Bach wrote the Tchaikowsky *Concerto*—in America.

These preoccupations with Bach and Tchaikowsky place the *Violin Concerto* in Stravinsky's orbit, and, in fact, the opening's violin double-stopping and the finale's bassoon ostinati are quite Stravinskian. Perhaps this is why Harold Shapero and Benjamin Britten liked the work so.[8] But even more Stravinskian is Piston's *Sinfonietta* of 1941, which is as conscious of Stravinsky's *Symphony in C* as the *Violin Concerto* is of the Tchaikowsky *Violin Concerto*. The *Sinfonietta* was dedicated to Boston Symphony harpist Bernard Zighera, who premiered the work with his Chamber Orchestra in Jordan Hall on 10 March 1941.

The *Sinfonietta*'s three movements, "Allegro grazioso," "Adagio," and "Allegro vivo," are modelled after the first three movements of Stravinsky's *Symphony in C*, "Moderato alla breve," "Larghetto concertante," and "Allegretto." Piston is obviously touched by Stravinsky's melodic material. He appropriates the main theme's motive, B-C-G-E, for his own main theme and subjects it to transformations that are all inspired by comparable Stravinsky transformations. Thus, the *Sinfonietta*'s first movement themes (p. 1, p. 5), second movement theme (p. 22), and third movement themes (p. 29, p. 37, p. 46) correspond, respectively, to the *Symphony*'s first movement themes (p. 1, p. 8), second movement theme (p. 41), and third movement themes (p. 52, p. 59, p. 60). In addition, Piston's *Sinfonietta* takes a more than characteristic delight in ostinati, jerky rhythms, tonal sequences, trumpet calls, and expressive horn lines, and this too must be ascribed to an intense involvement with the *Symphony in C*. The syncopations, cross rhythms, and contrametric patterns of the last movement are especially Stravinskian, but whereas Stravinsky's use of mixed meter is prodigious ("the most extreme," wrote the composer, "in the whole of my work"[9]), Piston works within a 6/8 meter, except for a 2/4 section towards the end.

Piston's finale is not particularly successful, however, and Stravinsky's brilliantly subtle "Allegretto" only reminds us how episodic and uninspired it is. When Piston composes a similar movement to conclude his *Fourth Symphony*, the design is much smoother and its relation to the whole more satisfying. Part of the problem stems from Piston's use of a scherzo to model a finale, a decision necessitated by the fact that he composed the *Sinfonietta* while Stravinsky was still at work on the finale. How indeed did Piston come to know the *Symphony* before its completion? When Stravinsky held the Charles Eliot Norton chair at Harvard during the academic year 1939–1940, he brought the first two movements with him, and he composed the third movement in Cambridge.[10] Presumably Piston had an opportunity to acquaint himself with the manuscript, or perhaps, like Sol Babitz,[11] he heard the composer discuss the work at the piano. Stravinsky composed the work's finale in Los Angeles, and the completed *Symphony in C* was first performed in Boston on 17 January 1941, less than two months prior to the *Sinfonietta*'s premiere.

More mysterious is how Piston's 1940 *Chromatic Study on the Name of Bach* for organ comes to resemble Schoenberg's 1941 *Variations on a*

*Recitative* for organ. This is Piston's first work to use the twelve-tone method. Furthermore, both works contain ten variations, though Schoenberg's variations are lengthier, and conclude with a fugue. It is doubtful that this is mere coincidence. As both works were commissioned by William Strickland and the H. W. Gray Company as part of the same contemporary organ series, Piston might have felt inspired to anticipate Schoenberg's contribution by writing in his style. Harold Shapero remembers that Piston made a year's investigation of Schoenberg in the late thirties, after which he remarked, "When you first look at that music it looks very strange, but when you get into it, it's not that strange anymore."[12] Another important influence may have been the publication in 1940 of Ernst Krenek's *Studies in Counterpoint Based on the Twelve-Tone Technique*. Piston, in fact, knew Krenek during these years, as the following anecdote, reported by Michael Steinberg, reveals:

> When I conducted the premiere of my First Symphony with the BSO, that was about 1938, Krenek was here, and I said to him, "Well, how do you like that old-fashioned music? Pretty different from yours." And he said, "Not so very," and next thing I heard he was analyzing it in his classes at Vassar. So I got out the score again and took another look, and of course I hadn't used any tone rows, but the ways in which I had developed material had a lot to do with 12-tone music, and so did the texture.[13]

Krenek also wrote a work, his *Sonata* for organ, for H. W. Gray.

The first four notes of the *Study*'s row spell out the name Bach, the second four notes transpose this motive, and the last four notes complete the chromatic spectrum within an octave compass (ex. 5).

Ex. 5.  Piston, *Chromatic Study on the Name of Bach* (New York: H. W. Gray, 1941), p. 1. Used by permission.

The *Study* itself combines elements of fugue, passacaglia, and variation within its small dimensions. After a four-voice fugal exposition, the twelve-tone melody is subjected to further variations including a statement in counterpoint with its retrograde-inversion in diminution (mm. 17–20), a retrograde statement in counterpoint with its inversion in diminution (mm. 21–24), an extended variation in three-part invertible counterpoint (mm. 25034), and a canon at the octave (mm. 35–39). Despite such twelve-tone orthodoxy, a vague feeling of key is nonetheless detected throughout. The theme itself suggests rising major thirds by whole-step, and towards the end of the piece Piston introduces triadic harmonizations and tonic pedals. Sometimes harmonic progressions arise from strict contrapuntal manipulations. At measure sixteen (ex. 6), for instance, the final notes of

Ex. 6.   Piston, *Chromatic Study,* p. 2.

$R^P$, $RI^9$, $I^9$, and $O^P$ combine to form a cadential progression in G. The *Study*'s harmonic language, unusually progressive for its composer, resembles Krenek, as well as Schoenberg at his more conservative, though Piston's textures and rhythms are more traditional.

Piston's involvement with both Schoenberg and Stravinsky finds expression in the 1939 *Sonata for Violin and Piano*. Jascha Brodsky, violin, and Frederic Pillotson, piano, premiered the work on 20 April 1939, and soon after it was recorded by Louis Krasner and the composer, who gives a fine rendition of the difficult piano part. The *Violin Sonata* does not integrate the influences of Schoenberg and Stravinsky as much as oppose them. In the first movement, for instance, the first theme (according to sketches) has a twelve-tone origin, while the second theme has a quirky diatonicism and a lively mixed meter reminiscent of Stravinsky. The last movement, also in sonata form, presents a similar contrast. In an article devoted to the *Violin Sonata*, Ross Lee Finney writes:

> Clarity and wit represent only one side of Piston's temperament. The other is more difficult to define, but whatever it is, it stands in almost exact opposition to the acid quality of the counterpoint so common to all of his works. It is, in effect, a sudden blurring or fogging of contrapuntal lines which results in a kind of impressionism that is never obvious and serves as relief from the drive of the rest of the composition. This duality of style is essential to his expression and represents no undigested eclecticism. . . . The new *Sonata for Violin and Piano* shows that the contrast of these two basic elements becomes more and more important in Piston's development.[14]

Although Finney sees this opposition as one of counterpoint versus harmony, this conflict between "clarity" and "a kind of impressionism" also points to the dual influence of Stravinsky and Schoenberg. At any rate, it is a sign of Piston's growing skill that Finney focuses on this conflict of material rather than on the conflict between form and content that concerned Citkowitz in 1935, although Finney's discussion still suggests some shortcomings of Piston's art.

Actually, the *Violin Sonata* is very like Piston's earlier chamber music, especially in its dreamy sensuousness. Finney cites a few measures from the slow movement that recall late Fauré. He also cites another example, the "tranquillo" and "dolce" return of the main theme in the coda of the first movement, that might have reminded him of Bloch. In addition, the "meno mosso" section of the first movement development is Scriabinesque, and the last movement's final harmonic progression ($D^b$-$G^b$-$F^b$-$B^{bb}$-f) is also quite rich. Even the tonal scheme of the three movements, F minor-B minor-F minor, is darkly romantic.

The *Violin Sonata*, written before the advent of the Second World War, brings Piston's early mannerist period to a close. The War evoked different responses from Piston, as evidenced by his greater adherence to Schoenberg in the 1940 *Chromatic Study*, and to Stravinsky in the 1941 *Sinfonietta*. Piston was deeply affected by the War, especially with America's entrance in 1942. During the War, he wrote to Arthur Berger:

> As a composer, I had a slump for the first year of the war, feeling that writing music was about the most futile occupation. What got me out of it chiefly was getting letters from men in the armed forces who said they hoped I was keeping on composing because that was one of the things they were out there for. I have now completely recovered a sense that it is important and that I am meant to do that job (along with other things like teaching and civilian defense). I am now on my second symphony, commissioned by the Ditson Fund in Columbia University.[15]

As part of civilian defense, Piston studied first aid and became, like Shostakovich, an air raid warden. He would drive about Belmont in his jeep during drills to insure that all lights were out. He also translated Italian material for the OSS.[16]

Piston wrote three short works directly related to the War. The 1942 *Fanfare for the Fighting French* for brass and percussion, commissioned by Eugene Goossens, was premiered by Goossens and members of the Cincinnati Symphony Orchestra on 23 October 1942. Goossens commissioned seventeen other American composers to also write fanfares. "It is my idea," he wrote to Piston on 30 August 1942, "to make these fanfares stirring and significant contributions to the war effort."[17] Only Copland's *Fanfare for the Common Man* survived the occasion. Goossens also commissioned Piston to write a "Variation" for a collaborative set of variations on a theme by the conductor. The other participants were Creston, Copland, Taylor, Hanson, Schuman, Harris, Fuleihan, Rogers, and Bloch, and the resulting 1944 *Variations on a Theme by Goossens*, with a finale by Goossens, was premiered by Goossens and the Cincinnati Orchestra on 23 March 1945. Since each collaborator was assigned a tempo and a tonality—Piston's variation is "allegro" and in F—the work is surprisingly cohesive, though its stylistic diversity is its raison d'être. The *Variations* celebrates not only the Cincinnati Orchestra's Golden Jubilee, but also the solidarity of American composers during the Second World War. Another work intended to commemorate the War was Piston's 1944 *Fugue on a Victory Tune*, one of eighteen works commissioned by the League of Composers with the assistance of the New York Philharmonic and the Columbia Broadcasting System. The League requested that each composer make use of a war-associated theme, and Piston accordingly based his *Fugue* on a Navy adjutant's call "which had impressed Piston greatly in 1918 with its spirited simplicity."[18] The *Fugue* was premiered by the New York Philharmonic under Artur Rodzinski on 22 October 1944, and Lou Harrison reviewed the performance, broadcasted by C.B.S., for *Modern Music*:

> Walter Piston's *Fugue on a Victory Tune* must be some newfangled kind of fugue because it starts right off with what seems like stretto stuff and furthermore with all voices at once being as busy as can be. The theme is, I presume, a bugle call of victory, and proceeds along to a chattery and confetti-throwing course for a brief moment to a gay ending. It is quite amusing and stunt-like, nothing more.[19]

The War, however, informs all of Piston's music of this period, though in different and less obvious ways. We have already noted Piston's growing closeness to the aesthetic of Stravinsky and Schoenberg as the composer moves further away from Hindemith and the late works of Ravel and Roussel. In addition, there is something better described in terms of mood rather than technique, namely lyric expressions of mourning and energetic expressions of resoluteness. While Piston's Stravinskian music tends to be diatonic, and his Schoenbergian music tends to be ultra-chromatic, both the mournful and the resolute music tends to be darkly modal. Furthermore, these mournful and resolute expressions are public and patriotic, which is not surprising if one remembers that the composer deeply felt the futility of his art during this national emergency, and that he became active in matters of civilian defense.

The 1942 *Quintet for Flute and Strings*, commissioned by and dedicated to the League of Composers, and first performed in New York on 9 December 1942, by the Budapest Quartet and Ruth Freeman, demonstrates these varied tendencies in the course of its four movements. The artful simplicity, graceful elegance, and exquisite scoring of the opening movement are inspired by Mozart, and thus suggest an affinity to Stravinsky. The 5/4 "Andantino" is in a dark, mournful C-sharp, a bridge, so to speak, between the nostalgic 5/4 "Andantino" of the *Violin Sonata* (1939) and the powerful 5/8 "Andantino" that is the *Passacaglia* (1943). The third movement's scherzo shows the influence of Schoenberg and Webern; and the fourth movement is an example of what this author has called "resolute" music, though such an association would seem somewhat far-fetched if the movement did not resemble the finale of the *Second Symphony* (1944).

Despite this rich variety, the *Flute Quintet* is not a particularly compelling work. The bland neoclassicism of the first movement is less memorable than Mozart or Stravinsky. The "Andantino" sags as much as it moves, and has an overlong, ponderous middle section. And the finale has a plodding third theme and an unsuccessful fusion of serious and lighthearted elements that results in an emotional ambiguity that also plagues the finale of the 1944 *Partita*. The third movement scherzo is, however, of importance—at least from the standpoint of Piston's development—for although its extreme chromaticism, its pointillistic "staccati" and "pizzicati," and its dense contrapuntalism were new for Piston in 1942, they become typical features of many later scherzos. These scherzos are, in fact, Piston's most obvious and characteristic response to the challenge of Schoenberg and Webern. Piston, however, does not forsake tonality in this movement; but, rather, tempers the flatness of his mosaic-like manipulations through such strategies as the tonic-dominant entrances in the five-voice exposition, the harmonic bass (at mm. 37ff and again at mm. 104ff), and the diatonic middle section which arches the movement. But although Arthur Berger[20] speaks highly of the *Quintet*, especially of its scoring, it is not one of Piston's better works.

It is regrettable, however, that so few violists know Piston's *Interlude* for viola and piano, also from 1942, and first performed on 4 September 1943, by Louise Rood, viola, and Irene Jacobi, piano. The work is a short, lovely "Adagio," with a beautifully idiomatic viola part and a gossamer piano accompaniment. Lyrical and elegiac, it resembles, in fact, Stravinsky's *Elégie* for solo viola of 1944 (though English critics have compared it to Edmund Rubbra). In addition, both works are in an ABA form, with a climactic B section, which, in the *Interlude*, reaches a dramatic statement in F-sharp through a minor cycle of fifths starting on C (m. 25). But while Stravinsky's *Elégie* is a memorial piece for Alphonse Onnou, Piston's intentions in the *Interlude* are much more private. The title at least offers a clue, as the interlude is, specifically, a short improvisatory organ work played between the verses of a hymn or psalm. The titles of the similarly mournful *Passacaglia* (1943) and *Improvisation* (1945), both short pieces for solo piano, are even more noncommittal. But all three works seem to be conditioned by sorrow for the War, not only because of what we know of Piston's feelings in this regard, but also because Piston never wrote anything like these works after 1945.

The *Passacaglia*, first performed on October 23, 1944, by Shura Cherkassy, is one of Piston's most powerful works despite its brevity (it is only four minutes long). It is the most angry of the mourning pieces, with a forceful climax at its end rather than at its center. The form in general is slightly fanciful for Piston. There are five statements of the passacaglia theme in B minor (mm. 1–20), and then two transitional statements (mm. 20–28) that lead to two cadential statements in C-sharp (mm. 29–38). Following this are five improvisatory statements (mm. 39–58) in different tonalities (C-sharp, G-sharp, D-sharp, A, D), two transitional statements (mm. 59–66), and finally three climactic statements in B (mm. 67–78). Thus, the work is in two parts, the first half moving from B to C-sharp, and the second half moving from C-sharp back to B. The *Improvisation* is also four minutes in length, but is a gentler work with no such tonal polarization. All of its cadences, with the exception of a half-cadence twelve measures from the end, are in a sober E minor.

The 1943 *Prelude and Allegro* for organ and strings is, like the *Improvisation*, in E minor. Much of Piston's music from this period is in E or A minor, and this is his repertory, in fact, for which the term "minor" can most safely be used. On a WGBH 79th birthday celebration for Piston,[21] E. Power Biggs, to whom the *Prelude and Allegro* is dedicated, explains the origin of the work as follows. In the early forties, Biggs decided to play a movement of a Soler concerto for two harpsichords on one of his C.B.S. broadcasts; but as he could not transcribe the work from a recording, and as the manuscripts were in Spain and unobtainable, he accepted Piston's offer to transcribe the movement, which only took the composer a day to do. Later, Piston similarly transcribed some of Haydn's "musical clocks," and finally he wrote a new work, *Prelude and Allegro*, for Biggs's radio program. The work was first performed on 8 August 1943, with Biggs at the organ and Fiedler conducting the Fiedler Sinfonietta. Daniel Pinkham remembers that an engineer approached Piston at the broadcast and said, "Mr. Piston, with this marvelous new microphone, I can make one viola sound like ten," to which Piston responded, "That's all very well, but can you make one viola sound like one?" Koussevitzky later took up the work, and he and Biggs played it in Symphony Hall and recorded it for Victor. This is the only piece by Piston that Koussevitzky ever recorded, perhaps because the work was so intended: the "Prelude" and "Allegro" are each four and a half minutes long, and thus perfectly fill out the two sides of a 78 RPM record.

The "Prelude" is Piston's only work that is entirely canonic, and yet, significantly, it is one of his most emotionally stirring works. The canon's three voices enter at the fifth and thus allow for characteristic quintal harmonies and strong progressions. While the organ sets forth the canon in the outer sections, the canon passes on to the strings in the middle section, which poignantly moves through the flat keys of C minor and E-flat major. Similarly, the vigorous and virtuosic "Allegro," after firmly establishing E minor, modulates to G minor, E-flat major, and G-flat major, before it returns, by way of B minor, to the original key. While the "Prelude" expresses the tragedy of the War, the "Allegro," which combines variation and ritornello forms, expresses the determination to win it. On the 1973 birthday program, Pinkham called the *Prelude and Allegro*, "a very marvelous piece, entirely accessible and warm, with a very joyous allegro," while Biggs agreed, saying "it is one of his most immediate works, it connects with people, Piston à la Handel to a certain extent. You know what Romain Rolland said about Handel: he was immediately understood by the people. I think you can say that about Piston in this work." The "à la Handel" may have been quite intentional. Leichtentritt[22] noticed a connection between the *Prelude and Allegro* and Handel's organ concertos, and the work's opening is indeed reminiscent of the canonic opening of Handel's *Tenth Organ Concerto*.

Biggs also premiered, along with Wolfe Wolfinsohn, violin, and Eugene Lehner, viola, the 1944 *Partita for Violin, Viola and Organ* on 29 October 1944. This premiere was part of an eightieth birthday celebration for Elizabeth Sprague Coolidge, to whom the score is dedicated, and through whose Foundation the work was commissioned. Piston, in fact, uses the initials E.S.C. to fashion the *Partitia*'s initial motive, $E^b$-C, an idea he seems to have borrowed from Harris's *Second Quartet*. It was actually

Harold Spivack and Archibald MacLeish, both at the Library of Congress, who suggested, says Piston,[23] that Coolidge approach him,

> to write for this outlandish combination something on words by Carl Sandburg from a poem called *The People, Yes*. I should have said no. Anyway, in those days, Mrs. Coolidge had done a lot for me, for all of us, and so I thought I would as a sporting thing, but I finally had to say that the words got in the way. It's one of those things you don't pull out of after you've said yes. So I think I gave the movements noncommittal titles.

Lengthy excerpts from *The People, Yes* were nonetheless printed in the program notes to the premiere, and according to Biggs, "there was very little connection." "There wasn't any connection," says Piston. "There was as little connection as there often is in an opera." How did such an unusual commission come about? Did MacLeish, who knew both Piston and Sandburg, see a basic affinity between the two men, or their work? Did the following lines from *The People, Yes* suggest Piston?

> Who shall speak for the people?
> who has the answers?
> where is the sure interpreter?
> who knows what to say?
> Who can write the music jazz-classical
> smokestacks—geraniums hyacinths—biscuits
> now whispering easy
> now boom doom crashing angular
> now tough monotonous tom tom
> Who has enough split-seconds and slow sea-tides?[24]

Did Spivack suggest the instrumentation in the wake of the success of the *Prelude and Allegro*? The *Partita*, as it happens, "ran off with the show," according to one reviewer.[25] And on the WGBH broadcast, Biggs says, despite Piston's protest, "It is a wonderful piece, I maintain that. It's a unique piece because I wouldn't think that bunch of instruments would go together."

According to sketches in the Library of Congress, Piston considered a number of "noncommittal" titles before he decided upon "Prelude," "Sarabande," "Variations," and "Burlesca" for the *Partita*. These included prelude, praeludium, fantasie, symphony, sinfonia, préambule, ouverture, and toccato for the first movement, sarabande and courante for the second movement, and burlesca, finale, gigue, fugue, rondeau, and caprice for the finale. The *Partita* sketchbook also indicates precompositional decisions about tonality, rhythm, form, and tempo; but more untypically, there are specific moods indicated as well: "tender" for the

"Sarabande," "serious, enigmatic" for the "Variations," and "rough, not humorous" for the "Burlesca." In addition, there is a short musical phrase, , with the description, "bird (mourning dove)," and the viola's last four notes in the "Sarabande" (ex. 7) are interesting in this regard. Furthermore, this phrase gives concrete evidence that Piston is quite intentionally writing elegiac slow movements during these years.

That Sandburg's words have little to do with the *Partita* is proved by the fact that the work so closely resembles the 1942 *Flute Quintet*. It too has a neoclassical first movement, a mournful slow movement, a Schoenbergian scherzo, and a "rough and ready" finale. The classical model for the first movement, with its E-flat major "Maestoso" introduction and its vigorously contrapuntal C minor "Allegro vivo," is not Mozart, but rather the Baroque overture. And the Schoenbergian scherzo actually makes use of the twelve-tone method. This is a variation movement, whose theme combines a row, A#-G#-D-C#-F#-B-G#-A-C-G-E-D#, with its retrograde inversion. The ten variations on this theme form a pyramid, so that variation six mirrors variation five, variation seven mirrors variation four, and so forth, while the coda completes the arch by restating the theme. Not all the material is strictly twelve-tone; when the organ is twelve-tone, the strings are freely chromatic, and vice versa. The music's large melodic leaps, muted sonorities, variation form, and waltz rhythms also bring it close to the music of the Viennese, though for Piston there is an important distinction, as the following anecdote reveals:

> You know Ernst Toch was there at the concert, and he came rushing up all excited to me after it, and he said, "How did you write a twelve-tone piece?" and I said, "You mean the second movement [sic]?" He said, "Yes," and I said, "That's not a twelve-tone piece, that's in F# major." Well as a matter of fact it goes through all the motions of twelve-tone music, but I wouldn't call it twelve-tone because it doesn't have the spirit of twelve-tone music.[26]

As a whole, the *Partita* is no more, though no less, successful than the *Flute Quintet*.

A better work, though far less ambitious, is the 1945 *Sonatina for Violin and Harpsichord*, dedicated to Alexander Schneider, violin, and Ralph Kirkpatrick, harpsichord, who premiered the work on 30 November 1945. The work was written after the War, and its graceful elegance, cheerful optimism, and neat proportions do indeed inaugurate Piston's post-War style. Even the elegiac slow movement in A minor, which clearly resembles the *Improvisation* of the same year, has a classical poise new to Piston, emphasized by the theme's return in a cool F minor. The opening

Ex. 7.   Piston, "Sarabande," *Partita for Violin, Viola and Organ*
(New York: Arrow Music Press, 1951; New York: AMP),
p. 15. Used by permission.

"Allegro leggiero" is one of Piston's wittiest creations, and the movement from the F-sharp minor second theme (m. 36) to the B-flat major recapitualation (m. 64) is especially masterful: the second theme, which exquisitely turns to the relative major (m. 41) and then back to tonic minor (m. 45), is used for the tiny development, which moves from F (m. 54) to F-sharp (m. 58) to G (m. 60), wavers between A-flat and A (mm. 62–63), and, with an abruptness that is comic, recapitulates the first theme in the home key, B-flat. This sort of restless, exhaustive energy typifies the whole movement, and the busy counterpoint can easily obscure such a classic maneuver as the "Stimmtausch" at mm. 10–18 and again at mm. 77–85. The coda delightfully welds elements from both themes and accelerates to a canon, "precipitoso."

The exuberant finale, also in sonata form, is like the first movement in many particulars, including the minor second theme's move to the relative major and its subsequent return. However, the main theme, subtly indebted to the chromaticism and athematicism of the Viennese, is experimental for Piston; and its humor, though more daring, is also more strained than that of the first movement. The second theme, on the contrary, is truly delightful, although its skillful invertible counterpoint is also taut. All in all, the finale is an appropriately modest and delicate conclusion to a small but intense chamber work, which, by the way, can sound as good with piano as with harpsichord.

The *Second Symphony* of 1943 towers above all the other wartime works, not only because it is the major symphonic work of the period, but also because it beautifully expresses the heroic struggle of American involvement in the Second World War. The work was commissioned by Columbia University's Alice M. Ditson Fund and was first performed on 5 March 1944, by the National Symphony Orchestra under the direction of Hans Kindler, who, on the following day, sent a note to Piston, saying, "[The *Symphony*] is without even the shadow of a doubt one of the half dozen great works written during the last ten years. It sings forever in my heart and in my consciousness, and does not want to leave me."[27] Similarly, Erich Leinsdorf wrote to Piston after a playing of the work with the Cleveland Orchestra in 1946, "The performance of your Symphony which took place last night was, to me personally, the most gratifying experience with any score that has seen daylight within the last ten or fifteen years."[28] All the critics[29] who reviewed the work for *Modern Music*, including Colin McPhee,[30] who criticized the *Passacaglia* and the *Prelude and Allegro*, and Donald Fuller,[31] who did not like the *Sonatina*, were unanimous in their praise of the *Symphony*, which won the New York Critics Circle Award of 1945.

While the *Second Symphony* reminded two critics[32] of French nineteenth-century music, no one placed the work in a patriotic context. The aforementioned letter to Arthur Berger might suggest such a connection, but so does the music itself. In the first movement, for instance, Piston contrasts a dark, desolate, and lyrical first theme with a jaunty and elegant bit of Americana for the second theme. Clearly the tragedy of the War and the spirit of the American people are the ingredients of this drama. The muted coda for brass choir is like a far-off battle or like taps, and is especially reflective of the War. The second movement, "Adagio," is justly famed for its beautiful opening clarinet melody, which, like the other elegiac melodies of this period, sounds almost improvised, though sketches reveal that Piston worked long and hard on this theme. This elegy is not morbid, but rather poignant and serene; and it was this movement that Leonard Bernstein chose to play in commemoration of the composer's death. Despite its general calm, there are, nonetheless, angry dissonances at the movement's two climactic points, and there is nothing sentimental about this movement. As for the finale, it is a call to arms, and its seriousness and urgency make it the most inspiring of all the resolute movements.

Although Piston's *Second Symphony* deserves to rank with Prokofiev's *Fifth Symphony* and Shostakovich's *Seventh Symphony* as one of the noblest expressions of the Allied cause, the work, unlike those Russian symphonies, was never taken up as a patriotic symbol. Even at his most patriotic and civic-minded, Piston is never, as Copland is in such moments, a stirring nationalist. And yet patriotism is at work in the *Second Symphony*, and this provides a clue for understanding Piston's other, even more private works, at least those written during the War.

**Plates**

Plate 1. Second grade class in Rockland, Maine, c. 1902. Piston is in the front row, second from right. (Piston Collection)

Plate 2.  Mechanic Arts High School Band, Boston, c. 1910. Piston is in the back row, far right. (Piston Collection)

Plate 3.  The Massachusetts School of Art, c. 1915. Piston is at middle-ground, center; Kathryn Nason stands to the right, Gertrude Nason, to the left. (Piston Collection)

Plate 4.  American students at the home of Nadia Boulanger, Paris, 1925. From the left: Herbert Elwell, Aaron Copland, Ada MacLeish, Walter Piston, Virgil Thomson. (Piston Collection)

Plate 5.    Irving Fine, Aaron Copland, Nadia Boulanger, Walter Piston, in Boston, October 1945. (Piston Collection)

Plate 6. Members of the Harvard music department, c. 1948. Seated left to right: Otto Kinkeldey, A. Tillman Merritt, Walter Piston; standing are Jules Wolffers (journalist) and Richard French. (Piston Collection)

Plate 7.  From the left: Walter Piston, John Alden Carpenter, Nadia Boulanger, Roy
Harris, Serge Koussevitzky, Zlatko Balokovic, Mabel Daniels, Jean Françaix,
Edward Burlingame Hill, in Boston, March, 1939. (Piston Collection)

Plate 8.   Hans Wiener (Jan Veen), Katrine Hooper, and the Wiener Troupe, *The Incredible Flutist*, in Boston, May 1938. (Piston Collection)

Plate 9.   Piston at work on the *Second Symphony*, in Belmont, c. 1943. (Piston Collection)

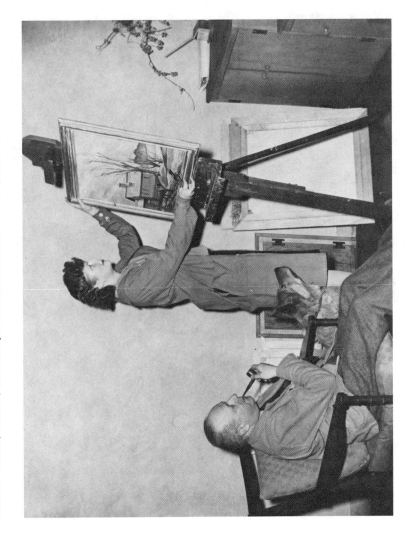

Plate 10. Piston, Bumble, and Kathryn Nason, in Belmont, c. 1943. (Piston Collection)

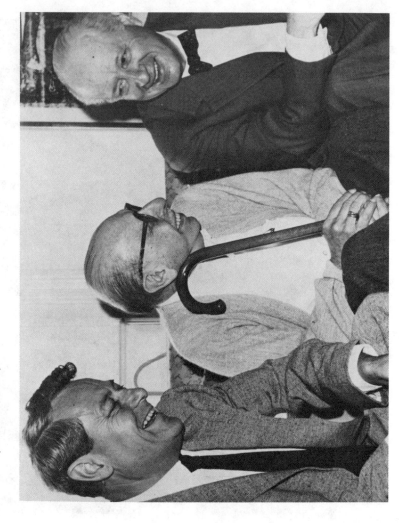

Plate 11. John Vincent, Igor Stravinsky, Walter Piston, in Beverly Hills, June, 1961. (Piston Collection)

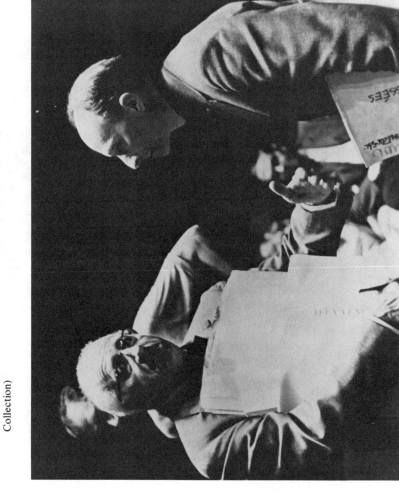

Plate 12.   Walter Piston and Witold Lutosławski, Dartmouth College, c. 1966. (Piston Collection)

Plate 13.   Leonard Bernstein, Virgil Thomson, Walter Piston, Aaron Copland, William Schuman, at Lincoln Center, New York, c. 1970. (Piston Collection)

# 6

## Nearer the Perfect Balance:
## From the *Divertimento* (1946) to the *Fourth Quartet* (1951)

The years 1946 to 1951 were peak ones in Piston's career. At the end of the War, Slonimsky wrote:

> In the constellation of modern American composers, Walter Piston has now reached the stardom of the first magnitude. He has not exploded into stellar prominence like the surprising nova, but took his place inconspicuously, without passing through the inevitable stage of musical exhibitionism or futuristic eccentricity.[1]

Looking backward, Virgil Thomson writes that the "slow-ripening" Piston, like Sessions, did not reach full maturity until the 1940s.[2] Piston's *Third Symphony* won the 1947 Pulitzer Prize and the 1948 Mark Horblit Award, while the even superior *Fourth Symphony* won the 1950 Naumburg Award. Piston's prestige was also bolstered by the growing prominence of younger composers who had studied with Piston at Harvard and who were deeply respectful of his music and his teaching. These included Carter, Bernstein, Fine, Berger, and Shapero. Elliott Carter's 1946 article, "Walter Piston," for *Musical Quarterly*, was the most substantial expression of such respect, and remains the most comprehensive piece of Piston criticism to date: Piston's work from 1925 to 1946 is summarized and evaluated. Carter's reservations are subordinate to a keen appreciation of the music, and his concluding remarks are almost panegyrical:

> In the whole field of contemporary music, Walter Piston occupies an important position. He has summed up the tendencies of the past twenty years both here and in Europe and given them broad and masterful expression. Although living in the time of the "lost Generation" he found himself in his devotion to music. His unique contribution is to have done this particular work with outstanding excellence in a country where few have ever made a name for themselves as thoroughly craftsman-like artists. In literature several names come to mind but in music there is hardly one to be found before our time.

> To have helped to establish a deep understanding of the value of craftsmanship and taste here and to have given such persuasiveness exemplification of these in his works is highly important for our future. For, not having as ingrained a respect and love for high artistic ideals as Europeans have had, we often slipped into the trivial, chaotic, and transitory. Piston's work helps us to keep our mind on the durable and most satisfying aspects of the art of music and by making them live gives us hope that the qualities of integrity and reason are still with us.[3]

These "tendencies" include "chromatic and diatonic elements, linear counterpoint, impressionist harmonies, twelve-tone techniques, and a-symetrical rhythms."[4] Carter admires their "broad and masterful expression," although he addresses the question of form and content all too briefly:

> One of his main concerns, of course, as of many other contemporary composers, has been the use of the contrapuntal style within the sonata principle. But this is done with a clear sense of harmonic structure and motion that distinguishes his tendency from that of many others with similar aims.

Carter communicates none of the tension between form and expression that in different ways struck Citkowitz, Finney, and Thomson; nor does he, like those other critics, note any growing improvement in Piston's formal skills or emotional expressiveness.

Carter does distinguish, however, Piston's prewar from his wartime works. He writes, "If in the first period he is occupied with integrating and assimilating modern techniques, in the second there is an urge towards directness and simplicity."[5] Now, in 1946, "the composer seems headed in a new direction, for the *Sonatina for Violin and Harpsichord* and the short *Divertimento for Nine Instruments* are written in a fresh vein that returns to the more pointed and terse style of his earlier works."[6] For Donald Fuller, the *Sonatina* "shows Piston reverting to his straitjacketed neoclassicism."[7] Peter Ustinov offers yet another perspective in a discussion of Piston's 1946 *Divertimento* and Carter's 1948 *Wind Quintet*. Says Ustinov, "I'd always heard of Piston . . . as being a classicist, but the Divertimento seems to me a romantic work. It seems to me extremely romantic, very ingratiating . . . I think Elliott Carter is much more classical, much more Hindemithian."[8] Since the tension between form and expression is less strained in the *Sonatina* and the *Divertimento* than in Piston's earlier works, the term "neoclassic," or "surreal," seems less applicable, because classic and romantic elements are blended in a way that might suggest Mendelssohn, another composer who might alternately be viewed as "pointed and terse," "neoclassical," and "romantic and ingratiating." The *Divertimento* is certainly closer to Mendelssohn's *Oc-*

*tet* than to any eighteenth-century serenade. Incidentally, both Mendelssohn and Piston, great craftsmen though they were, recognized the limitations of their art in similarly ironic ways: Mendelssohn referred to himself as a Philistine, while Piston placed his music in the orbit of Humperdinck.

The *Divertimento for Nine Instruments* was commissioned by the International Society for Contemporary Music, and first performed on 18 May 1946 at Columbia University by "nine of the best players in New York" under the direction of Dmitri Mitropoulous, "the most dynamic conductor you could think of," remembers Piston. "But he didn't turn on any dynamics; he just did a perfect job."[9] Ideally, the *Divertimento* does not require a conductor, although a lack of rehearsal time, as at the premiere, often necessitates one. Piston himself conducted the work on occasion. It is, after all, scored for a miniature orchestra: flute, oboe, clarinet, bassoon, two violins, viola, cello, and double bass. When asked if he chose the instrumentation to suit certain expressive aims, Piston answered:

> To tell the truth, I don't even know . . . I think I must have chosen the instrumentation first, because I don't remember any process of having an idea and saying, "This would be good for two basset horns and a piccolo." I've been tied down on a great many of my works with commissions. I think I am tempted to accept commissions because I am sure of a performance of the piece. But as soon as you do that you've got to find out what are going to be the resources to play it. For instance, if half-way through the piece you decide you want three harps, you're running the risk of losing a performance right then and there. So I think probably I've decided things on a practical basis quite a lot. Because what I want to do always is to hear the work and learn from it, and go on to the next work which I hope will be better. I still feel that way.[10]

Actually the *Divertimento* is one of Piston's few commissioned works that was written for an unspecified ensemble.

The *Divertimento*, as Carter notes, shows the composer "headed in a new direction," combining his prewar acidity and alertness with his "newly found Mozartean fluency." But the *Divertimento* is more profoundly different from its composer's earlier works than this observation suggests. Where prior to the *Divertimento* does one find the buoyant optimism of its outer movements? Here Piston's humor is neither cynical, as in the prewar works, nor anxious, as in the wartime works, but rather is relaxed and carefree. Similarly, the slow movement has a calm that is new for Piston and is, in fact, marked "tranquillo." In general, the *Divertimento* has a clearer and brighter tonal language than earlier Piston, although its melodic lines are still chromatic and its harmonic rhythm still subtle. There are other technical differences as well. The ritornello first movement has an adventurous metric scheme: while the episodes are in

3/4, the ritornello theme, stated, respectively, in D (m. 1), D$^b$ (m. 43), B$^b$ (m. 52), G (m. 83), and D (m. 132), mixes 7/8, 3/4, 5/8, 8/8, and 6/8. The soft and slow "Tranquillo" is a theme (mm. 1–7) and three variations (mm. 8–14, mm. 15–36, and mm. 37–45) with cadences in F minor concluding each section. Since the third variation is a reprise of the main theme, the movement combines variation and ABA forms, a procedure presaged by the passacaglia movements of the 1930s, but which first finds a classically characteristic expression with this movement. As for the last movement, it displays Piston's most personal assimilation of Schoenberg's music to date (ex. 8). This characteristic absorbtion of the Viennese school deserves comparison with another work of 1946, Session's *Second Symphony*, or, considering the medium, with the 1931 *Octet* of the Greek composer, Nikos Skalkottas.

Carter prophetically concludes his discussion of the *Divertimento* by writing. "There are a Third Symphony and a Third String Quartet in preparation that may apply this new found flexibility to the serious style."[11] This is very much the case, especially with the 1947 *Third Quartet*, commissioned by Harvard University, dedicated to Diran Alexanian, and first performed on 1 May 1947 by the Walden Quartet. Like the *Divertimento*, the *Quartet*'s first movement has a dynamic metric scheme, although here Piston opposes driving "staccato" lines with lyrical "legato" lines (ex. 9). Furthermore, the outer movements of the *Quartet* are not throughcomposed, as in the *Divertimento*, but are in sonata form. While the first movement has a spacious, whimsical, and bizarrely casual second theme

Ex. 8.   Piston, "Vivo," *Divertimento for Nine Instruments* (New
York: Broadcast Music, 1946), pp. 23–24. Used by
permission.

and a taut development, the finale, on the contrary, breathlessly moves through its second theme and finds some relaxation only with the melancholy viola solo in the development. These two sonata movements thereby quite strikingly complement one another. Like the *Divertimento*'s "Tranquillo," the *Quartet*'s "Lento" is a calm and beautiful variation movement. Although there are five variations (mm. 8–15, 16–21, 22–27, 28–35, 36–40) on the opening theme, the movement is not in the least episodic, but rather forms one smooth arch with subtle shifts of mood.

The *Quartet*'s dominant mood, in both the F minor outer movements and the C minor middle movement, is darkly solemn and utterly unlike the *Divertimento* in this respect. The work deserves comparison with Bartók's *Sixth Quartet*, which it resembles. However, its only critical review, written by William Bergsma,[12] compares it unfavorably to Piston's earlier works. Not insensitive to Piston's virtues, Bergsma nonetheless is critical of certain predictable features in Piston's style. While Bergsma's general observations are more or less accurate, his comments on the *Third Quartet* are distinctly not. He writes of the "lack of rhythmic interest" in the rhythmically adventurous first movement, and of "longish and exact" recapitulations in a work whose recapitualtions are all dramatically reworked. Bergsma's conclusion that Piston's earlier quartets are "likelier to attract quartet players and their audiences" is assumptive, for during the 1977 Troy Quartet Program, four student players found the work to be immensely pleasurable, and brought down the house with a skillful and suave rendition of it.

That the *Divertimento* ushers in a new stylistic period is also evidenced by a comparison with the 1947 *Third Symphony*. The *Symphony*'s second movement scherzo absorbs Schoenbergian chromatics and textures like the *Divertimento*'s finale; its slow movement has a theme, two variations, and a reprise very much like the smaller work's "Tranquillo;" and its last movement has the happy-go-lucky spirit of the *Divertimento*'s first movement. But Piston also has in mind Copland's 1946 *Third Symphony*, which was premiered by Koussevitzky and the Boston Symphony less than two years before the same musicians premiered Piston's *Symphony* on 9 January 1948. It could not have escaped Piston's attention that both works were commissioned by the Koussevitzky Music Foundation and dedicated to the memory of Natalie Koussevitzky. Nor could he overlook a work of such magnitude.

Like Copland's *Third Symphony*, Piston's *Third* has a slow opening movement that organically unravels three principal melodic ideas:[13] a scherzo and trio that suggest, respectively, city and country life; a contemplative variation movement; and a finale that celebrates the end of the Second World War. Furthermore, there are more minute reflections of

Ex. 9.   Piston, "Allegro," *String Quartet No. 3* (New York: Boosey and Hawkes, 1949), p. 1. Used by permission.

Copland in the Piston work, including falling fourths, ostinati, a xylophone solo, and, most important, overlapping phrases of rich contrapuntal interest. But there are significant differences as well. Piston's first movement is majestic, but it is also dense, chromatic, and middle-ranged, and more suggestive of the thickly forested Green Mountains than open prairies or empty city streets. The scherzo movements are perhaps most alike; and Copland did, in fact, once say of Piston, "Sometimes I think it's his scherzo movements that I enjoy the best: they literally crackle along,— snappy and alert, and so neatly put together (no seams)."[14] On the other hand, Piston's slow movement has a dark and tragic sensibility that is foreign to Copland; while his comic finale, whose first theme slyly quotes Copland's famous fanfare and whose second theme is a delicately festive march in three, is quite distinct from Copland's rhetorical and ecstatic finale.[15]

It is perhaps not as surprising that the introverted and conservative pedagogue Piston should write a different music from the extraverted and liberal critic Copland than it is that they should share a basic artistic affinity and a personal fondness for one another. For Stravinsky, they were the outstanding American composers of their generation. He told an American reporter in 1945:

> I think you have two here who have shown real talent. I mean Aaron Copland and Walter Piston. They have good musical ideas. They also have the requisite techniques. They are fine orchestrators, too.[16]

The 1948 *Second Suite for Orchestra*, commissioned by and dedicated to Antal Dorati and the Dallas Symphony Orchestra, and premiered by them on 28 February 1948, is a more delicate and, in this sense, a more characteristic work than the *Third Symphony*. The *Suite*'s four movements are entitled "Prelude," "Sarabande," "Intermezzo," and "Passacaglia and Fugue;" and while the passacagila theme is twelve-tone, the work has a calm and joy very much unlike the dissonant and ironic *First Suite* of 1929. It may be no coincidence that during this period, somewhat populist for Piston, he accepts commissions from Midwest ensembles like the Dallas Symphony, the Minnesota Symphony, and Michigan's Stanley Quartet. Furthermore, with his growing fame, he could doubtless expect some local performance of any new work.

The other works of this period can be grouped in pairs. Both the 1948 *Toccata for Orchestra* and the 1950 *Tunbridge Fair: Intermezzo for Symphonic Band* are colorful and lighthearted one-movement works which are similarly constructed: in each work, a short and catchy tune is repeated, often with charming twists, through a number of keys, and is contrasted by lyrical sections. The *Toccata* is dedicated to Charles Munch, who, with the Orchestre National de la Radiodiffusion Française, gave its first performance in Paris, and its first American performance in Bridgeport, Connecticut on 14 October 1948. Munch had introduced Piston's *Second Symphony* to France, and now requested one of the composer's shorter works for a planned American tour with the French Radio Orchestra. When Piston suggested that he write something especially for the tour, Munch responded, "Ce que vous dites me ravit."[17] It was fortunate for Piston that this ally succeeded Koussevitzky in 1949 as director of the Boston Symphony. During his eleven years with the Symphony, Munch programmed at least one work by Piston each season. Piston would often say, "Munch played my music because I spoke French;"[18] but, as the following remarks reveal, Munch held Piston in great esteem:

> To a degree Honegger, for instance, is to me a very great man, and Piston, too. Everything Piston does is perfectly organized; nothing is left to chance. It is all logical, as music should be. And, of course, there is Stravinsky. . . .[19]

*Tunbridge Fair* was commissioned by the League of Composers at the suggestion of Edwin Franko Goldman, and was premiered by the Goldman Band, Piston conducting, on 16 June 1950. The work depicts one of Vermont's oldest and most cherished events, the annual country fair at Tunbridge, and is markedly American, although it owes something to English band works like Holst's 1930 *Hammersmith*, which is also inspired by a rural fair. *Tunbridge Fair* is ABABA in form, and the A sections, which combine, in David Hall's words, "a kind of 'yokel' jazz with all manner of rhythmic and polyphonic intricacy,"[20] capture the rollicking merriment of Tunbridge Fair as described below:

> People from all walks of life are jostled together in the gay riotous turmoil that is Tunbridge Fair—the back-country folk of the soil mingle with people from the metropolitan districts; world travelers eat hot dogs at the same booth with native Vermonters; schoolteachers from Iowa, lumbermen, truck drivers, state officials, country storekeepers, college boys, school girls, bankers, and laborers are caught alike in the hilarious whirl.[21]

Contrastingly, the B sections are nostalgic, and as their theme suggests a sentimental song and their scoring suggests a reed organ, Piston may have been thinking of the parlor music performed in the Fair's Floral Hall, described by one writer as follows:

> Music is furnished throughout the day and for the dance by firelight and candlelight by Romeo's orchestra, composed of harp and violin, assisted at the melodeon by Mr.

Sawyer, while Mr. Wheelock plays the bass viol. The music seems most fitting in this atmosphere of the long ago. Old songs are sung several times daily by Miss Louise Farnham, soloist, in costume, with Paisley shawl.[22]

Although less picturesque than *Tunbridge Fair*, the *Toccata* is similarly populist in tone, despite Piston's assertion, "Many memories of student days in Paris returned during the composition of this piece and I continually sought to bring out in the music those qualities of clarity and brilliance which are so outstanding in the playing of French musicians."[23] The *Toccata* (was it possibly inspired by Fine's *Toccata Concertante* of the previous year, 1947?) is not as compelling as *Tunbridge Fair*; its fast parts are somewhat square and its slow section is lovely but pale. Fortunately, Piston varies the work's recapitulation in all sorts of ways, including a brief but moving interpolation on page 76. Hindemith liked the work well enough to program it on his German tour in 1950. And Mark DeVoto,[24] in a eulogy for Piston, cites the *Toccata*, along with the 1937 *Concertino* (also French-inspired and radio-premiered) as the quintessential Piston, although the conservative and populist *Toccata* and the exuberant and chic *Concertino* are different in their humor.

The *Quintet for Piano and Strings* and the *Duo for Viola and Violoncello*, both from 1949, are more serious works, but are nonetheless rather light for Piston chamber music. The *Quintet* was commissioned by the University of Michigan, and first performed by the Stanley Quartet (Gilbert Ross, Emil Raab, Paul Doktor, Oliver Edel) and Joseph Brinkman, to whom the work is dedicated. The *Quintet*, which one reviewer[25] compared to Brahms, is a full-bodied romantic work, especially the first movement, "Allegro comodo," which has a tender first theme in G minor and a sentimental second theme in D minor, not to mention rich textures, abrupt changes of mood, and distant key relations. The second movement, a theme-two variations-reprise form on the order of the *Divertimento* and the *Third Symphony*, sustains the first movement's melodramatic tone. For Virgil Thomson, this was Piston at his most memorable.[26] But the bright G major finale is the work's best movement, with two robust themes, respectively Latin and folksy in flavor, clever contrapuntal transitions, and a 6/8 scherzo section integrated as an episode. If the influence of Brahms, and even more, Dvořák, is in plentiful evidence, this is not surprising, as the piano quintet is a specifically nineteenth-century medium, and the traditional Piston would naturally give consideration to the masterpieces of the genre. The *Quintet* won an initially favorable press, and in 1968 Otto Deri looked back at the work as "one of his best chamber works,"[27] although in 1972 Piston refused a commission for another piano quintet, "saying that he had once written a piano quintet which he did not like."[28]

The elderly Piston, on the other hand, thought the 1949 *Duo*, "one of my best works."[29] Although there are similarities between the *Quintet* and the *Duo*, the latter's medium naturally suggested a smaller scale and a lighter touch. The *Duo*'s first movement, in fact, is a sonatina, with two extremely delicate 3/4 themes (one march-like in A minor, the other waltz-like in E-flat major), a brief fifteen-measure development, and a short and poignant "pianissimo" coda. Like the *Quintet*, the second movement, "Andante sereno," is in C and in 12/8, though its harmonies are less morbid and its rhythms are more gentle. The last movement, which retains the marchlike innocence of the first movement, is dazzlingly virtuosic.

The *Fourth Symphony* and the *Fourth Quartet* were written, respectively, in 1950 and 1951. The *Symphony* was commissioned for the Centennial Celebration by the University of Minnesota, and premiered on 30 March 1951, by the Minnesota Symphony Orchestra under Antal Dorati. The *Quartet* was commissioned by the Coolidge Foundation in celebration of another school centennial (namely, Mills College's), and the work, dedicated to Elizabeth Coolidge, was premiered on 18 May 1952, by the Hungarian Quartet. As the following outline suggests, the two works are closely related.

*Fourth Symphony*
I.   Piacevole (tonality: G, meter: C; form: binary sonata)
II.  Ballando (A; mixed; ABACABA)
III. Contemplativo (F; 12/8; ABA)
IV.  Energico (B$^b$; 6/8; sonata)

*Fourth Quartet*
I.   Soave (D; C; sonata)
II.  Adagio (F; 9/8; ABA)
III. Leggero Vivace (A; 2/4; ABA)
IV.  Con fuoco (B; 6/8; sonata)

The words "piacevole" (pleasant) and "soave" (gentle) are unusual tempo indications (they are more often used in association with wine than with music), and the music is indeed distinctively calm and peaceful. The movements' main themes are spaciously diatonic (the *Symphony*'s theme resembles, perhaps not coincidentally, the opening theme of David Diamond's *Fourth Symphony*, premiered in Boston in 1948). Their secondary themes, although more chromatic and cramped, are similarly sweet: Piston, in fact, writes "dolce" for the "Piacevole's" second theme, and "dolcissimo" for the "Soave's" second theme (ex. 10), one of his loveliest melodies. Piston attains a memorable peacefulness through means other than melodic construction, and these include extremely delicate contrapuntal textures, unhurried rhythms, slowly paced harmonic changes, and comforting, sometimes mesmerizing motivic repetitions. In addition, the formal structure of the "Piacevole" is particularly undramatic, a binary sonata whose recapitulation calmly interrupts the second theme. The coda is even more casual; it interrupts the second theme eight measures too soon, but the woodwinds at m. 230 remind us of the missing bassoon tag, and harmoniously resolve this pleasant argument.

The slow movements of the *Symphony* and the *Quartet* are also smooth and relaxed, not only because of their swaying melodies that languorously move through minor and major harmonies, but also because of their fluid structures. While their opening A sections subtly suggest an antecedent-consequent structure, the feeling is one of continuous, organic growth. In both cases, the B section is divided into two halves (mm. 20–25 and 26–30 in the *Symphony*; mm. 19–25 and 26–35 in the *Quartet*) that would be fairly well-defined variations in the other slow movements of this period, but not so here. Furthermore, the A section is thoroughly rewritten upon its return, especially in the *Symphony*. In program notes to the *Quartet*, Piston does not even draw attention to any ABA scheme, but states:

> In the second movement, *Adagio*, two thematic elements are simultaneously developed, melodically and harmonically, the formal design being created by the emotional consequences emerging from this development. The first element is presented by the two violins, as an introduction of the second element, which appears in the 'cello.[30]

On the face of it, the scherzi of the *Fourth Symphony* and the *Fourth Quartet* are worlds apart. The *Symphony*'s scherzo is in the festive, populist tradition of *Tunbridge Fair*; and its three contrasting ideas are indebted, respectively, to Spanish dance (perhaps the fandango), the waltz (especially of the carousel or melodeon variety), and the New England country reel. The *Quartet*'s fugal scherzo, on the other hand, has a fleetness as deft as Mendelssohn's and a chromaticism as dense as Schoenberg's (ex. 11). Nonetheless, this movement's scherzo and trio sections are also related, although far more subtly than in the symphonic scherzo, to, respectively, American and Latin idioms. As for the *Symphony*'s "Ballando," its chromaticism can get quite formidable, as in the passage beginning at m. 141. The finales of the *Symphony* and the *Quartet* are more similar: both are lively 6/8 sonatas, "energico" and "con fuoco," respectively. But while the symphonic finale's first theme is sharp and festive, the *Quartet*'s opening theme (ex. 12) is more expressionistic in tone, with crescendos from "forte," uncertain downbeats, abrupt rests, sharp dissonances, and dramatic formal and textural contrasts. And the

Ex. 10.    Piston, "Soave," *String Quartet No. 4* (New York: AMP, 1953), pp. 2–3. Used by permission.

Ex. 10.　(continued)

*Symphony*'s spacious second theme (a transformation, in minor, of the opening movement's first theme) is dissimilar to the grotesque marchlike second theme of the *Quartet*. Both movements, however, have an urgency comparable to the finales of the early 1940s; and they were, in fact, also written in wartime—this time during the Korean War.

In 1955, William Austin published a detailed and penetrating study of Piston's *Fourth Symphony*.[31] Austin prefaces his analysis by observing that the "chief beauties" of Piston's music "arc in the harmonious relation of diverse elements in long compositions, rather than in startling sonorities or obsessive bits of melody," and concludes his article, saying, "Melody and tonality are extended to allow for all sorts of new sounds and new rhythms, but melody and tonality organize the whole in essentially the same way they do in Mozart's world, as they rarely do in ours." A letter to Donald Ferguson in 1954 occasioned some words on the *Fourth Symphony* by the composer himself:

> I am at a total loss to know what to write about my symphony. It is not intended to convey other than musical thoughts, although I think you will agree that this leaves more freedom to the listener to bring to the music what he will. Needless to say, I could not write a symphony about Minnesota, since I have never set foot in that part of the country. I feel that this symphony is melodic and expressive and perhaps nearer than my other works to the problem of balance between expression and formal design. It should not prove complex to the listener in any way.[32]

Ex. 11.    Piston, "Leggero Vivace," *String Quartet No. 4,* p. 20.
Used by permission.

Years later, Piston told Klaus George Roy, "My music is becoming more
relaxed, I think, more flowing, less angular and nervous. I feel a greater
sense of ease in the Fourth Symphony than I have ever felt before."[33]
The *Fourth Symphony* may well be a turning point, but Piston's aspiration
to write a more relaxed and flowing music is pronounced throughout this
entire period, especially in his swaying 9/8 and 12/8 slow movements, his
agreeably spacious movements with titles like "Allegro comodo," "Piacevole," and "Soave," and in his vigorously populist works. The search
for the perfect balance between expression and form, however, already
takes new dimensions with the *Fourth Quartet* of 1951, and continues to
do so with the many works to follow.

Ex. 12.   Piston, "Con Fuoco," *String Quartet No. 4,* p. 28. Used
   by permission.

# 7

# Piston, Classicist:
## From the *English Horn Fantasy* (1952) to the
## *Seventh Symphony* (1960)

The works that Piston wrote between 1952 and 1960 have a good deal in common. With the exception of the *Wind Quintet*, they are all orchestral works. Again with one exception, the *English Horn Fantasy*, they are all multimovement in design. Complementing this grandeur of sound and size is an opulent tone—an emphasis on melody and color, and a more casual approach to counterpoint and form.

This impressionistic richness is a pronounced feature of the small and delicate *Fantasy for English Horn, Harp and Strings*, written in 1952 and first performed by the work's dedicatee, Louis Speyer, and the Boston Symphony under Munch on 1 January 1954. The chosen ensemble is, of course, a mellow one. Furthermore, the work's texture is relaxed: the harp and strings provide a fuzzy harmonic background to the long lines of the English horn, respectively "dolce e tranquillo" and "grazioso." The *Fantasy*'s homophony is in keeping with Piston's remark, "The work intends primarily to exhibit, and indeed may be said to have been inspired by, the poetic beauty of the English horn as played by Louis Speyer,"[1] but it is also symptomatic of a general trend towards homophony that characterizes Piston's music during this period. As Piston also writes, the work "is in a simple ternary form," but it is not as straightforward as that. The outer sections are separated from the middle section, "più mosso," by transitional but discrete sections: a variation (mm. 23–31) that precedes the B section and a cadenza (mm. 70–83) for English horn and harp that follows it. This blurring of the formal design is matched by the ambiguity of the tonal scheme, for D, E, G, and A fade in and out as possible tonal centers. Even the work's last four measures (ex. 13) move quickly from D to E to A, the tonality of the English horn's opening phrase.

These features—the mellow ensemble, the rich homophony, the

Ex. 13.   Piston, *Fantasy for English Horn, Harp and Strings*
(New York: AMP, 1955), p. 14. Used by permission.

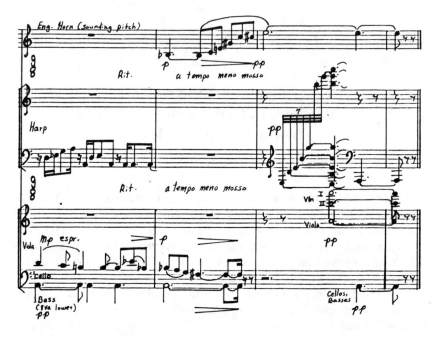

blurred form, and the ambiguous tonality—give the *Fantasy* a pastoral
quality. In this respect, the work is closer to Sibelius's *The Swan of
Tuonela* than it is to the works that Hill, Honegger, and Hindemith wrote
for Speyer. Like *Tuonela*, the *Fantasy* is ten minutes long, ternary in
form, with a tonal center of A and a meter of 9 (9/8, though, not 9/4).
Piston's landscape, however, is less bleak; it is a setting, perhaps, for a
New England mallard rather than for the black swan of death. Because
the *Fantasy*, like nearly all of Piston's ouevre, makes no explicit reference
to nature, any talk of landscape painting is purely hypothetical, but not
improbable. Each year Piston did most of his composing during the summer months on a hilltop with a magnificent view of the Green Mountains.
His artist-wife doubtless directed his attention to subtleties of light and
design, and he himself was a bird lover. At any rate, the works of this
period, beginning with the *Fantasy*, seem particularly responsive to nature; and the decade ends, in fact, with the *Three New England Sketches*
and the "Adagio Pastorale" from the *Seventh Symphony*.

Piston evokes a mood similar to that of the *Fantasy* in the "Lento" sections that frame the opening sonata allegro of the 1954 *Symphony No. 5*.

The first section opens with a "dolce" flute melody in the upper register against a misty chord (E-G, a tenth higher-A#-D#-A#-D-F#) in the strings, "tremolo" and "pianissimo." When the "Lento" returns, an additional harp part makes the effect even more atmospheric. The movement's internal "Allegro con spirito" sonata has a secondary theme that is also sweet, although most of it is heavy-handed and uninspired. Further, the "Lento" arch smothers, rather than highlights, whatever significance the "Allegro" may be said to possess, and the whole movement is daringly poetic in a somewhat contrived fashion. The "Adagio" variation movement is also experimental. The theme's twelve-tone introduction, for instance, is subjected to discrete variations. And Piston ends the movement not with a reprise but with the second, climactic variation. There are also some fashionable twelve-tone textures, although the twelve-tone bass lines support clearly tonal melodies. Like the first movement, the "Adagio" is strained in its modishness. The *Symphony* was commissioned by the Juilliard School of Music in honor of its fiftieth anniversary, and first performed on 24 February 1956, by the Juilliard Orchestra under Jean Morel. Perhaps Piston was too conscious that his *Fifth Symphony* was to be first played among new works by Mennin, Foss, Babbitt, Fine, Finney, and Schuman.

The finale, "Allegro lieto," pays tribute to New York in a more carefree way. This movement has melodies that are clearly indebted to the up-tempo cabaret songs of Broadway, and Piston's classy treatment of such material is witty, but also dated and somewhat trivial. Like the preceding movements, this finale also makes use of the rhythm of the "fate" motive from Beethoven's *Fifth Symphony*, although Piston attains little organic unity by this means. The movements are curiously independent; and while not without moments of beauty, they do not form a symphonic whole as satisfactory as that of the *Fourth Symphony*.

In the following year, however, Piston wrote one of his most outstanding works, the beautifully luminous and finely crafted *Sixth Symphony* (1955). Commissioned by the Boston Symphony in celebration of its seventy-fifth season, and dedicated to the memory of Serge and Natalie Koussevitzky, the work was first performed by Munch and the Boston Symphony on 25 November 1955. In program notes for the premiere, Piston discussed the powerful inspiration the Boston Symphony exerted upon the composition of the work:

> While writing my Sixth Symphony, I came to realize that this was a rather special situation in that I was writing for one designated orchestra, one that I had grown up with, and that I knew intimately. Each note set down sounded in my mind with extraordinary clarity, as though played immediately by those who were to perform the work. On several occasions it seemed as though the melodies were being written by

the instruments themselves as I followed along. I refrained from playing even a single note of this symphony on the piano.[2]

And indeed the music is very smooth and compelling. Unlike the disjointed first movement of the *Fifth Symphony*, the first movement of the *Sixth Symphony* (aptly titled "Fluendo espressivo") is one flowing gesture. The two themes of this sonata movement are in a fluid 3/4; but whereas the violins uninterruptedly spin out the first theme, the woodwinds pass about phrases of the second theme in an overlapping fashion, like birds in the woods. The movement's entire design is extremely smooth. The development reworks the opening of the exposition, and recapitulates at an internal but memorable spot in the first theme group. The restatement of the theme comes only at the movement's end. In some ways this movement resembles the binary "Piacevole" from the *Fourth Symphony*, although here the structure is more dramatic and poignant.

The second movement scherzo is also incredibly smooth, although the link to the coda at m. 191 is a bit weak. This coda, by the way, is unusual for Piston in that it gradually disintegrates over forty-two measures. The scherzo itself wittily features folk elements, chromatic intricacies, fugal techniques, and brilliant instrumental writing, including effective use of the percussion battery, "pianissimo." But the real gem of the *Sixth Symphony* is the magnificent "Adagio sereno." As in the *Piano Concertino*, a solo cello inspires Piston to write one of his most moving melodies (ex. 14). Piston's own satisfaction with the melody is evident from the fact that he does not subject it to variation treatment, but rather uses it as the basis for an ABABA rondo movement. The second A sweetly embellishes the theme, while the last statement is a powerful reprise for full orchestra. These statements are perfectly complemented by the beautiful but more delicate contrasting theme.

The vigorous "Allegro energico" finale is like Piston's more populist works of the late forties, although the second theme is utterly suave. One might question, however, whether this movement truly achieves a classic balance or whether form imposes itself upon the material in too prim and careful a manner. The four movements of the *Sixth Symphony* are not only lovely in themselves, but combine to form a beautiful and poised whole. The work's key scheme is particularly classical: i (A minor)—IV (D major)—vi (F-sharp minor)—I (A major). Furthermore, Piston uses mode, motive, form, color, and mood to pair the first and third movements and the second and fourth movements. This establishes the sort of balance missing in the *Fifth Symphony*.

In his book on American music, *Music in a New Found Land*, Wilfred Mellers discusses the *Sixth Symphony* as the basis for his appraisal of the composer. Some of Mellers's statements are inaccurate. The first movement, as discussed above, is not "a normal classical sonata structure;" nor is its first theme built "around a tonic C," but rather it is in A (Mellers compounds this error by stating that the second theme is "in the mediant (not dominant)" whereas it is, in fact, in the dominant).[3] Further, Mellers's aesthetic generalizations, based as they are on a very incomplete

Ex. 14.   Piston, "Adagio sereno," *Symphony No. 6* (New York: AMP, 1957), p. 74. Used by permission.

Ex. 14.   (continued)

knowledge of Piston's music, seem untenable. But even his remarks on the *Sixth Symphony* are provocative. Mellers claims that Piston's "Boston gentility," like Moore's "American Past" and Hanson's "Puritanic nature-mysticism," has its "own partial truth. But more was asked of an American composer if he was to face up to the central American themes: to something comparable with Whitman's 'multiplicity in unity,' with Melville's transcendental terror, with Hawthorne's conscience, Thoreau's and Dickinson's search for the music in the pool at noon, Twain's vision of the boy-child's integrity."[4] Mellers finds that the four movements of the *Sixth Symphony* are touched by, respectively, American "spring and open-air resilience," "American bounce," "American hymnody," and "American zest." But he concludes:

> Indeed, the total effect of the symphony, which was written for the Boston Symphony, is in every sense Bostonian; and while both the polish and reticence are admirable, they are somewhat negative values. As a Bostonian, Piston takes something from both worlds, the old and the new, while getting the best of neither; something valuable is lost, along with primitive crudity, and even in the lovely Adagio the strength of the melodies is less remarkable than the radiant gravity of the sonority. Piston is a composer to be grateful for, since his beautifully written music is always delightful to play and agreeable to listen to, and his professionalism marks the beginning of a truly American—as opposed to the old-fashioned Teutonicized—academic tradition. When

one has said that, however, one has to admit that his somewhat clinical music is "civilized" only because it is in part ignorant of what America is and might be.

This final assessment is compelling, but it is plagued by too many vague qualifications. Furthermore, important questions arise, such as: how different in fact are the old and new worlds? There seems to be vague mythology at play in Mellers's criticism. Why conjure up Melville and Dickinson rather than, say, Henry James and Edith Wharton? Some other critics not bothered by such aesthetical considerations found that Piston's later symphonies consolidated his stature. In a 1956 review for *Pravda*, Kabalevsky says of the *Sixth Symphony*:

> This composition confirmed our impression that he was an excellent composer and a good orchestrator who is completely at ease with the symphonic form, and if his music somehow lacks melodic interest, it develops naturally and convincingly. There is artistic temperament and fantasy.[5]

Vernon Duke calls Piston "America's best symphonist"[6] in his 1963 publication, *Listen Here!*, and in a 1967 survey of the American symphony, Peter Jona Korn writes:

> Piston is without question America's most mature composer. This maturity is reflected in the consistently high level of his output—there is virtually no such thing as "bad Piston". . . . Walter Piston has never been the subject of a heated controversy, and never will be. He has established a reputation as a good, solid craftsman who turns out one splendid work after another. He has not passionate detractors nor adulating disciples. There is, in other words, nothing extraordinary about him—except, perhaps, the strong possibility that his symphonies may well turn out to be the most durable written in America today.[7]

The 1956 *Serenata*, commissioned by the Louisville Philharmonic Society, dedicated to Robert Whitney, and first performed on 25 October 1956, by Whitney and the Louisville Philharmonic, is a little symphony. Its three movements take only twelve minutes to perform, and its instrumentation (2 flutes, 2 oboes, 2 clarinets, 2 bassoons, 4 horns, 2 trumpets, timpani, harp, and strings) is only slightly larger than that employed for the *Sinfonietta* for chamber orchestra.[8] The *Serenata* combines a pre-fifties crispness with a post-fifties lushness, and the result is a style that comes closer to Mozart than any of Piston's so-called neoclassical works from the 1930s. There are some Mozartean details as well—the title, the D major key for the outer movements, an occasional melodic gesture— but the work still remains more distant from eighteenth-century classicism than comparable pieces by Poulenc, Prokofiev, and Stravinsky. The work's first movement, "con allegrezza," is Piston's only orchestral piece from this period to employ mixed meter, and it possesses something of the verve of the *Divertimento*. The tender and moody slow movement, "con sentimento," presents a spacious theme against an impressionistic background, followed by two variations and a reprise. The final "con spirito" is elegant and carefree, although tonal emphasis on the tonic minor, the subdominant, and the dominant minor gives the tonic major conclusion an ambiguity peculiar to Piston. The entire work is a bit thin and routine, and its classicism, while charming, is not a great achievement.

Piston's major work of 1956, however, is the *Quintet for Wind Instruments*, for which he wrote the following record liner notes.

> The Quintet for Wind Instruments was commissioned by the Elizabeth Sprague Coolidge Foundation in the Library of Congress and was first performed at the Library on Jan. 24, 1957, by the Boston Woodwind Quintet (five members of the Boston Symphony Orchestra: Doriot Anthony Dwyer, Ralph Gomberg, Gino Cioffi, Sherman Walt, and James Stagliano). The Quintet is in four movements: I. Animato; II. Con tenerezza; III. Scherzando; IV. Allegro comodo. Beyond these general characterizations the listener needs no further preparation, as the music is straightforward and without formal complexity.
>
> The makeup of the traditional woodwind quintet may be said, in a sense, to be ideal as chamber music, in which the individual voices' blend complement one another without giving up any of their distinction and independence. These five instruments differ strikingly in tone color, tone weight, intensity, dynamic range, expressive power and technical capability. Furthermore, each instrument by itself presents similar differences between the parts of its range. Difficult and fascinating problems arise from these physical facts, not only for the composer but for the performer as well.[9]

It was perhaps these "difficult and fascinating problems" that discouraged Piston from completing a wind quintet he had begun in 1930, but with thirty years experience and a text on *Orchestration* behind him, this second attempt is so expert and inspired that, as William Flanagan writes, "one is inclined to forget that this is the same instrumental combination that, in other hands, produces so cool, brusque, and unsentimental a coloration."[10] In the *Wind Quintet*, more than in the orchestral works of this period, harmony and counterpoint are conceived for their coloristic properties. The first movement is especially gorgeous, with an imaginative handling of the medium that results in an evocative array of instrumental sonorities. And yet the movement's form is a fastidiously neat sonata, as the following outline suggests (arrows indicate cadential points).

| *introduction* | *theme 1* | *transition* | *theme 2* | *development* |
|---|---|---|---|---|
| | ↓ ↓ ↓ | ↓ ↓ ↓ | | |
| E♭————N | E♭–B♭–(C)–B♭ | E♭– – –F | E– – –A | – – – – – |

| *theme 1* | *transition* | *theme 2* | *coda* | |
|---|---|---|---|---|
| ↓ ↓ ↓ | ↓ | ↓ ↓ | ↓ ↓ | |
| E♭–B♭–(F)–B♭ | A– – –C♭ | B♭–E♭ | E♭–B♭–E♭–#IV–E♭ | |

The ensuing tension between romantic expression and classical form is reminiscent of Piston's music from the 1930s, except that here the conflict is between form and color as opposed to form and counterpoint. The conflict is accordingly less traumatic and surreal, yet similarly disturbing and intriguing.

Form and color are better integrated in the *Wind Quintet*'s three other, less dramatic, movements. Each section of the slow movement, for instance, highlights a particular instrument: the theme—the oboe; variation 1—the flute; variation 2—the horn (though this variation features mutable doublings); variation 3—the clarinet; variation 4—the flute; and variation 5—the oboe. Throughout the third movement scherzo, by contrast, all five instruments are more or less equally prominent; and if the players do not attend to Piston's "marcato" markings, the movement's intricate fugal design can be easily obscured. Similarly, sensitivity to the movement's sequential melodic patterns can give spring to its waltz rhythms and shape to its chromatic lines. The delicate rondo finale is similar to the last movement of Arthur Berger's *Woodwind Quartet*. It has a nimble but pastoral first theme, a more spirited second theme, and a contrapuntal episode which is "meno mosso" and distinctive in mood, but which perfectly fits the rest of the movement. This contrapuntal excursion is yet another sonic adventure, and it concludes with one of Piston's most luminous moments, an exquisite cadence in the key of the Neapolitan (ex. 15).

The concerto is a suitable vehicle for the exploration of both melody and color, and towards the end of the 1950s, Piston concentrates on this genre, writing three great concertos: the *Concerto for Viola and Orchestra* (1957), the *Concerto for Two Pianos and Orchestra* (1959), and the *Violin Concerto No. 2* (1960). The *Viola Concerto* was commissioned by and dedicated to Joseph de Pasquale, "and many of its musical thoughts," writes Piston, "may be said to have been inspired and motivated by his superb viola playing."[11] The work was premiered by Pasquale and the Boston Symphony on 7 March 1958, and critical reaction was tentative. Irving Kolodin felt that Pasquale's performance could not answer the question of whether "Piston's melodic seeds can blossom, like the primrose, or merely bud,"[12] and the New York Critics Circle gave the *Concerto* its 1958 Award only after numerous balloting and much debate. Many violists, however, have since recognized the *Concerto*'s importance to the repertory, including Paul Doktor, who recorded the work with the Louisville Orchestra, and the Czech violist Jaroslav Karlovsky. Karlovsky wrote

Ex. 15.    Piston, "Allegro comodo," *Quintet for Wind Instruments*
(New York: AMP, 1957), p. 30. Used by permission.

to Piston in 1965, "I love this Concerto and I am sure that it enriches the literature of viola music."[13]

In notes similar to the aforementioned ones for the *Wind Quintet*, Piston discusses composition for viola and orchestra:

> The viola has greater tone weight [than the violin], but it cannot penetrate or soar, unless permitted to do so by carefully adjusted accompanying parts. . . . The two most important problems in this combination of viola solo with orchestra proved to be balance of sound and association of tone colors. These problems are not exactly peculiar to this combination, but they seemed here more pronounced and ever present. I was more than ever impressed with the necessity for the most intimate knowledge of every instrument. Likewise indispensible is the faculty of hearing mentally what one writes, and writing accurately what one hears mentally. The scoring had to be of a transparency to allow the solo voice to be heard in all registers at all times.[14]

Piston continues by listing some sounds, including "viola between oboe and horns, harp" and "high viola with mirror in bass clarinet," that he found particularly appealing. But the *Concerto*'s principal concern is with melody, and even form accomodates the viola's untrammeled lyricism. In the first movement sonata, for instance, Piston minimizes transitions and developments and concentrates on the viola's two highly idiomatic themes: the first supple and waltzlike, and the second, rigidly Hindemithian. The simple ABABA rondo finale similarly features two contrasting themes for the soloist, topped off by a long and impressive cadenza. The relationship between melody and form is even closer in the beautiful and soothing slow movement, for each of its two halves is further subdivided into an improvisatory section, like a recitative, and a "cantabile" section, like an aria. This preoccupation with melody makes the *Viola Concerto* one of the more refreshing and successful examples of Piston's art.

The *Concerto for Two Pianos and Orchestra* was commissioned by and dedicated to Melvin Stecher and Norman Horowitz. "I was pleased by the invitation," writes Piston, "not only because of their brilliant playing, but also I found it intriguing and romantic that their tours took them far and wide with two Steinway concert grands in a truck which they drove themselves."[15] Stecher and Horowitz were originally scheduled to premiere the work in 1959 with Leinsdorf and the Boston Symphony, but a tiff between the piano-duo and the conductor led to a cancellation, and the work was not performed until 4 July 1964, when Stecher and Horowitz premiered it with the Dartmouth Symphony Orchestra under the direction of Mario di Bonaventura. In 1968, the piano-duo played the Piston *Concerto* in London, Munich, Amsterdam, Copenhagen, Brussels, Salzburg, Stockholm, and Berlin, and they wrote the composer from abroad, "Absolute phenomenal success in Europe. Reviews almost unbelievable. They love you."[16] When Horowitz asked the composer whether he would be interested in a poster from Berlin that advertised the *Concerto*, Piston replied, "No, I already have one in Russian announcing a performance of my symphony."[17]

In the *Two Piano Concerto*, Piston understandably enough emphasizes texture and counterpoint rather than melody and color. From this standpoint, the work resembles his 1958 choral work, *Psalm and Prayer of David*. In fact, the opening movement has a mixolydian and quasi-Oriental main theme similar to the melody, "O sing unto the Lord a new song" (ex. 16 and 17), whereas its second theme, in contrast, is sparkling and virtuosic. Like the first movement of the *Sixth Symphony*, this "Allegro non troppo" recapitulates the first theme at an internal, climactic point, and returns to the opening only at the coda. The second movement "Adagio" is more special, ten variations on a theme that is unusually

Ex. 16.    Piston, "Allegro non troppo," *Concerto for Two Pianos and Orchestra* (New York: AMP, 1966), p. 1. Used by permission.

succinct for Piston. These short eleven sections allow for a variety of textures, including impressionistic tone clusters and romantic arpeggios, but they group to form a smooth ABA structure related to the opening movement.

*A*
Theme (mm. 1–7)
Var. I (8–14): extension
Var. II (15–22): transition

*B*
Var. III (23–29)
Var. IV (30–33)
Var. V (34–35)
Var. VI (36–39)

*A*
Var. VII (40–48): climactic return
Var. VIII (49–54): extension
Var. IX (55–62): extension
Var. X (63–71): reprise

After the $B^b$ major first movement and the F minor middle movement, the sprightly C major finale sounds particularly bright. This movement, writes Michael Steinberg, "is full of bounce in the French cafe-concert tradition of the twenties,"[18] much like the 1937 *Concertino*. However, it is also characteristic of Piston's fifties style in that it is less satirical in its wit, but rather closer to Mozart's humor. It is a joyous conclusion to a work that, like the *Viola Concerto*, is an important addition to an under-sized repertory.

At about this time, the violinist Joseph Fuchs, who had given the New York premiere of the *Violin Sonata* and who had recorded that work as well, took advantage of a grant from the Ford Foundation to commission Piston to write the *Second Violin Concerto*, which is dedicated to him.[19] Fuchs premiered the work on 28 October 1960 with the Boston Symphony under the direction of William Steinberg. He subsequently performed it with Paul Paray and the Detroit Symphony, and with the composer and the Los Angeles Symphony. According to Fuchs, Piston was not a great executant, and his finest performance of the work, he claims, was given with Leonard Bernstein and the New York Philharmonic at that orchestra's farewell concert in Carnegie Hall on 18 May 1962. This concert, stated Bernstein in an opening speech, both commemorated Stravinsky's eightieth birthday and paid homage "to my beloved teacher, Walter Piston."[20]

Ex. 17.    Piston, "Psalm," *Psalm and Prayer of David* (New York: AMP, 1959), pp. 2–3. Used by permission.

The *Second Violin Concerto* is less compelling and more subtle than the two preceding concertos, and marks a transition to Piston's intimate and romantic style of the 1960s. The first movement, with its dissonant harmonies, lush textures, changing tempos, and static sonata form, is especially adventurous; and in a review of the work, Paul Henry Lang writes, "I am still puzzled why I could not penetrate into the first movement."[21] The second movement, "Adagio," and the third movement, "Allegro," are more conventional. The "Adagio" has a theme which, in striking contrast to the short, melodramatic, and dark theme of the "Adagio" from the *Two Piano Concerto*, is lengthy (ABA in design), pastoral, and light, though its cadences are unexpectedly in minor. The three variations that follow are as lovely and as delicate as the theme. The first two variations are highly florid, with the violin first in sixteenth-note triplets, then in thirty-second notes. The last variation opens not with a reprise, as one might expect, but more romantically with an anguished version of the theme freely inverted in minor, although Piston does eventually return to the serenity of the opening statement. The finale, like the *Carnival Song*, is in Piston's Italian idiom: the first theme is a waggish tarantella, while the second theme is the sort of simple melody Piston so often favors for the violin.

Although all three concertos have moments like those found in the 1958 choral work, *Psalm and Prayer of David*, it is impossible to know whether these or any of Piston's other instrumental works were religiously inspired. Piston seems to have inherited the austere and private religiosity of his parents, who cherished Biblical wisdom but who did not attend church. Piston also avoided any church affiliation, although he occasionally contributed to Woodstock's North Universalist Chapel Association.[22] He and Kathryn, in fact, were married in a Unitarian church, but their funerals were private and civil affairs. Further, he would not have Kathryn decorate their home during Christmas.[23] *Psalm and Prayer* is Piston's only work on a religious theme. It was commissioned by Brandeis University, where it was premiered on 9 May 1959, by the Chorus Pro Musica and Alfred Nash Patterson. From these circumstances it is difficult to ascertain the nature of Piston's religious convictions, although one cannot doubt the heartfelt sincerity of *Psalm and Prayer*.

Whereas Piston decided upon Lorenzo's sensuous celebration for his *Carnival Song* for the Harvard Glee Club, he chose two psalms, Psalm 96 and Psalm 86, for this choral work for Jewish-sponsored Brandeis. The two psalms, as they appear in Piston's score, are as follows (Piston sets all but one line of Psalm 96, and most of Psalm 86).

### Psalm 96

O sing unto the Lord a new song:
sing unto the Lord, all the earth.
Sing unto the Lord, bless his name;
shew forth his salvation from day to day.
Declare his glory among the heathen,
his wonder among all people.
For the Lord is great, and greatly to be praised:
he is to be feared above all gods.
For all the gods of the nations are idols:
but the Lord made the heavens.
Honor and majesty are before him:
strength and beauty are in his sanctuary.

Give unto the Lord, O ye kindreds of the people,
give unto the Lord, glory and strength.
Give unto the Lord the glory due unto his name:
bring an offering, and come into his courts.
O worship the Lord in the beauty of holiness:
fear before him, all the earth.

Say among the heathen that the Lord reigneth:
he shall judge the people righteously.

Let the heavens rejoice, and let the earth be glad;
let the sea roar, and the fulness thereof.
Let the field be joyful, and all that is therein:
then shall all the trees of the wood rejoice
before the Lord: for he cometh,
for he cometh to judge the earth:
he shall judge the world with righteousness,
and the people with his truth.

Psalm 86

Bow down thine ear, O Lord,
hear me: for I am poor and needy.
Preserve my soul; for I am holy:
O thou my God, save thy servant that trusteth in thee.
Be merciful unto me, O Lord:
for I cry unto thee daily.
Rejoice the soul of thy servant:
for unto thee, O Lord, do I lift up my soul.
For thou, Lord, art good, and ready to forgive;
and plenteous in mercy unto all them that call upon thee.
Give ear, O Lord, unto my prayer;
and attend to the voice of my supplications.

Teach me the way, O Lord;
I will walk in thy truth:
unite my heart to fear thy name.
I will praise thee, O lord my God, with all my heart:
and I will glorify thy name for evermore.
For great is thy mercy toward me:
and thou hast delivered my soul from the lowest hell.

O turn unto me, and have mercy upon me;
give thy strength unto thy servant,
and save the son of thine handmaid.
Shew me a token for good;
that they which hate me may see it, and be ashamed:
because thou, Lord, has holpen me,
and comforted me.

It is indicative of Piston's development that while Lorenzo's poem is taut and formal, the psalms are soft and rhapsodic, although Piston imposes a rondo musical structure on both poems as outlined below.

*"Psalm" (Psalm 96)*

A.  lines 1–6: "Con moto," ♪ = 168, and in mixed meter (5/8, 6/8, 3/8, 3/4)
B.  7–12: "meno mosso," ♪ = 144, and in 6/8
C.  13–16: ♪ = 168, and in 5/8
A.  17–22: ♪ = 168, and in mixed meter
B.  23–26: ♪ = 144, and in 6/8

A.   27–28: $\flat$ = 168, and in mixed meter.

*"Prayer" (Psalm 86)*
A.   1–4: "Molto Adagio," $\quad \boldsymbol{\downarrow}$ = 40
B.   5–10: "poco più mosso," $\quad \boldsymbol{\downarrow}$ = 60 (lines 9 and 10 are in the original tempo)
A.   11–12: $\boldsymbol{\downarrow}$ = 40
C.   13–19: $\boldsymbol{\downarrow}$ = 60 (line 19 is in the original tempo)
A.   20–26: $\boldsymbol{\downarrow}$ = 40.

The feeling in both settings, however, is one of fluidity, especially in the "Prayer," where lines 9 and 10, and line 19 function as transitions.

The opening "Psalm" is surprisingly like the *Carnival Song*, although instead of the festive merriment and tender romance of an Italian processional, we have the exuberant worship and quiet reverence of a Hebraic celebration. There is even one moment, at the words, "for he cometh," of hushed Messianic wonderment. In this movement (ex. 17), Piston combines modal chant, chromatic melody, jazz harmony, mixed meter, Baroque counterpoint, and delicate orchestration to convey a mood, somewhat related to contemporary American psalm settings by Bernstein and Foss, of ancient and sacred revelry. The "Prayer," on the other hand, is extremely dark, with some climaxes that struggle towards the light. Its opening chromatic incantation for cello suggests the East, although its brooding canonic choral writing is clearly in the Protestant tradition of Bach and Brahms. The "Psalm" and "Prayer" are, in fact, markedly distinct, although the "Prayer's" C tonality resolves the "Psalm's" ambiguous G mixolydian modality. In addition, both movements share a restrained intensity that is not merely decorous, but that illuminates these profound texts in beautiful ways.

Another novelty of the period is Piston's *Three New England Sketches* (1959), commissioned by the Worcester County Musical Association for its 100th Annual Music Festival, and premiered by Paul Paray, the work's dedicatee, and the Detroit Symphony Orchestra on 23 October 1959.[24] The work's three movements are entitled, "Seaside," "Summer Evening," and "Mountains," and while it is not Piston's first programmatic work—that distinction belongs to *Tunbridge Fair* of 1950—it is uniquely impressionistic and descriptive. The first two movements are especially picturesque. In "Seaside," a somewhat chilly shoreline is vividly depicted by a softly undulating bass, tremolo strings, and swashes of harp, percussion, and woodwind. The movement's principal theme, first put forth by the oboe, "come da lontano," is nostalgic, a remembrance of Rockland's coast, perhaps, and we learn at the movement's end that this melody is indeed derived from a sailor's chanty. There is nothing nostalgic, however, about the huge, almost terrifying climax that caps this movement. In "Summmer Evening," the melodic thread, faintly pastoral, aimlessly drifts towards its sleepy final cadence against suggestions of bird and insect sounds from the other instruments. The chirps and buzzes are amazingly life-like, although Piston writes that the *Sketches* "are not intended as descriptive or representational tone painting, and any chance impressions of realism or specific reference come as incidents in the art of composition."[25] And to the man who smelled clams during a performance of "Seaside," Piston remarked, "That is quite all right. They are *your* clams."[26] While "Seaside" and "Summer Evening" are loosely binary in structure, "Mountains" is in an aptly arched ABCBA form. Each section has a distinct tempo and mood: A, "Maestoso," is monumental; B, "Risoluto," is energetic and lively; C, "Meno mosso," is misty and atmospheric. The music bears special resemblance to "Marching Mountains" from Carl Ruggles's *Men and Mountains*, another work composed in the Green Mountains of Vermont. But as its title suggests, *Three New England Sketches* is possibly a response to more contemporary American works such as William Schuman's *New England Triptych* (1956) and Quincy Porter's *New England Episodes* (1958), although perhaps to Ives and MacDowell as well. Piston's effort is ambitious, but not representative of the composer at his best.

The masterful *Seventh Symphony* (1960) was commissioned by the Philadelphia Orchestra Association and is dedicated to Eugene Ormandy, who premiered the work with the Philadelphia Orchestra on 10 February 1961.

Ex. 18.    Piston, "Con moto," *Symphony No. 7* (New York:
AMP, 1961), p. 3. Used by permission.

The *Seventh Symphony* is much like the *New England Sketches* of the preceding year, and can be said to be Piston's 'Pastoral' Symphony. Its opening movement, "Con moto," bears close affinity to the "Maestoso" from "Mountains" (exs. 18 and 19), although here the mountainous landscape is more stormy than calm. The slow movement, significantly entitled "Adagio pastorale," has not only a pastoral main theme, but a first variation that recalls the bird imitations in "Summer Evening," and a second and third variation that are reminiscent of the burblings from "Seaside." And like Beethoven's *"Pastoral,"* Piston's *Seventh Symphony* concludes with a festive celebration, "Allegro festevole," a movement that also finds parallels in the *New England Sketches*: its two main

Ex. 19.   Piston, "Mountains," *Three New England Sketches*
(New York: AMP, 1964), p. 38. Used by permission.

themes are related, respectively, to the "Risoluto" from "Mountains," and the principal melody from "Summer Evening." But the *Seventh Symphony* is a far greater work than the *New England Sketches* because its forms are brilliantly concise and logical. Its three movements never slacken for a moment. The "Con moto" is a taut sonata, the "Adagio pastorale" is a beautifully clear variation movement, and the "Allegro festevole" is most terse of all, for each section of this ABACABA rondo is comprised of only two phrases. The work richly deserved the 1961 Pulitzer Prize.

While the *Seventh Symphony* is a particularly fine work, Piston's music from this period in general has a beauty and a clarity that brings him yet closer to classical perfection, and that led him to contemplate God and nature in musical terms. This classicism betokens not only Piston's growing skill and maturity, but also a harmonious relationship to the times. Piston welcomed Eisenhower's presidency, which he actively supported in 1956, and although neither smug nor uncritical,[27] he seems to have been heartened by the peace, prosperity, and conservatism of these years. The music of this period, in contrast to the earlier music reflective of the ordeals of the Great Depression, World War II, and the Cold War, is refreshingly buoyant and optimistic. The memories of a painful past and the expectations for a hopeful future combine to give this music a classical equilibrium that is always steadying, and, at its best, that is very impressive.

# 8

# Under the Stimulus of New Musical Meaning: From the *Symphonic Prelude* (1961) to the *Ricercare* (1967)

Piston was less in tune with the 1960s. He did not care for Kennedy-Johnson liberalism,[1] and he was troubled and perplexed by the decade's social unrest, especially by campus disturbances.[2] Interviews from this period find Piston conservative, sceptical, and wise. "Now only the new is good and the old is bad," he tells one interviewer, "and that's what I call the bulldozer approach, like urban renewal."[3] He often reminds us that his generation had also disinherited the past in their youth ("we wouldn't have gone to a Beethoven symphony if you had paid us"[4]), but had come, in time, to cherish the past. On occasion he jibes at such contemporary trends as aleatoric composition, computer music, and the composer-in-residence, but only in an off-hand way. And when he is asked why he doesn't write "modern" music, his answers ("I'm not dead, you know;" "I'm deficient in herd instinct;" "I work very hard to make it new, but when I get through and look at it, it's the same old Piston") explode with irony. Actually, listeners and musicians would have found Piston's music from the 1960s surprisingly modern had they paid it any serious attention. But despite the many high honors[5] and birthday salutes accorded to Piston during these years, performances of this new music were rare, and criticism of this music was negligible. Significantly, only two of Piston's numerous works written between 1961 and 1976 were recorded during the composer's lifetime.

This situation kept Piston as reliant as ever on commissions, and, in fact, the only noncommissioned work of the period—*Souvenirs*—has gone, to date, unpublished and unperformed. Some of these commissions were carefully prescribed, such as the request by the Association of Women's Committees for Symphony Orchestras for a work to prelude a Cleveland Orchestra performance of Beethoven's *Ninth Symphony*. "The assignment to compose a piece suitable to precede Beethoven's Ninth," writes

Piston, "was further complicated by the realization that the other nine orchestras scheduled to play the work would very likely not contemplate a similar program."[6] The work, entitled *Symphonic Prelude*, was completed in 1961 and premiered by George Szell and the Cleveland Orchestra on 20 April 1961. It is described by Piston as "a kind of discourse about a melody given out by the violas and clarinets" which explores a dozen or so aspects of this theme based on the variation principle. The *Prelude*'s tonal center, F, seems cognizant of the *Ninth*'s D minor opening; but an investigation of the work's relationship to Beethoven's *Symphony* is hampered, for now, by the score's relative inaccessibility.[7]

Eugene Ormandy similarly commissioned Piston to write a work to open the Philadelphia Orchestra's debut concert in the newly created Lincoln Center on 25 September 1962. Piston's *Lincoln Center Festival Overture* (1962) is a one-movement work divided into sections with different time signatures and tempos as follows.

A.   3/4, "Sostenuto" ( ♩ = 44)
B.   2/4, "Allegro" ( ♩ = 126)
C.   5/8 and 3/4, "Andantino" ( ♪= 88)
B.   2/4, "Allegro" ( ♩ = 132)
A.   3/4, "Sostenuto" ( ♩ = 44)
B (coda).   2/4, "Allegro" ( ♩ = 132)

This *Overture* works better than the similarly arched "Mountains" movement from the 1959 *Sketches*, and points ahead to the remarkable one-movement works of the late 1960s. Its "Sostenuto" music has a stately grandeur like that of "Mountains," but is less awesome and more ceremonial. The faster music is festive in an extremely urbane and contemporary way, suggesting patrons in tuxedos and gowns arriving in limousines and sedans. The *Overture* might be unusually slick for Piston, but it is neither pretentious nor corny, but rather the perfect music for a gala event.

Most of Piston's other commissions from this period called for more substantial works than either the *Symphonic Prelude* or the *Lincoln Center Festival Overture*, but for nothing as weighty as an opera. Nonetheless, a letter from Betty Thorndike to Piston, dated 23 May 1962, indicates that during this time Piston gave at least passing thought to writing an opera with a Maine coastal setting.[8] Perhaps Piston had in mind an American *Peter Grimes*, but the project never materialized. It was sometimes thought that Piston's Italian background might predispose him to the genre, and the composer once admitted, with characteristic understatement, that he had "nothing against opera," but that without the assurance of a performance, the three years of work an opera would demand held little incentive for him.[9] In another interview, Piston discusses his reasons for not setting texts in general:

> Well, one is that I'm not very good at it. Somehow or other the words tie you down. But I won't say that I really dislike it because it just turns out that I've been more interested in other things.[10]

Ned Rorem writes:

> Walter Piston once exclaimed to a pupil who brought in a word setting, "Anything but that!" Songs, he felt, were beyond his ken; he could neither write nor judge them. Still, there *are* principles by which one can assess, if not necessarily feel, a song. More subjectively, the arch and flow of much of Piston's own instrumental output could be described as "vocal". . . . Roger Sessions' vocal output conversely could be described as instrumental.[11]

Another outstanding song composer, Samuel Barber, holds a differing opinion:

> There are composers who avoid the voice completely and they are probably quite right to do so. Among Americans I think of Walter Piston, who was not a very lyric composer anyway. Men like Piston, Roger Sessions, and Aaron Copland (although Sessions and Copland have written songs and operas) are essentially instrumental composers.[12]

I suppose, though, that if a reputable opera company or a fine singer had commissioned a work from Piston, he may well have tried his hand at opera or song. In fact, towards the end of his life, he seriously considered writing an opera for New York's Tri-Cities Opera Company.[13] As it was, his abilities as a composer for voice, as distinct from chorus, went untested.

Two works from this period—the *String Quartet No. 5* (1962) and the *Capriccio for Harp and String Orchestra* (1963)—were commissioned for European premieres. Is this the reason that both works are in Piston's bright and breezy international style of the 1930s, or could it be that the Kennedy years provoked a similar response to that of the Roosevelt era? At any rate, the *Capriccio*, ABABA in form, has a thirties waggishness in its "Animato" and 4/4 A sections, and a thirties sensuousness in its "Calmo" and 6/4 B sections. This eight-minute work is, in fact, very much like the 1937 *Concertino for Piano and Chamber Orchestra*, not least in the jazzy syncopations that open the work, or in the misty atmosphere of the second "Calmo." In addition, Piston's writing for harp is similar to his writing for piano in the *Concertino*: he emphasizes scales and arpeggios rather than chords and glissandi; and, in his own words, he has sought "to utilize various melodic and rhythmic capabilities of the harp, rather than to exploit its commonly employed decorative and coloristic effects."[14] Commissioned by Broadcast Music, Inc., on the occasion of its twentieth anniversary, the *Capriccio* is dedicated to Spanish harpist Nicanor Zabaleta, who premiered the work on 19 October 1964, at an Inter-American Festival in Madrid that featured works by such American composers as Chávez, Ginastera, Villa-Lobos, Copland, and Somers.

The *String Quartet No. 5* was commissioned for the 1962 Berlin Festival by the Kroll Quartet, who premiered it on 8 October 1962. This work, with its brisk sonata "Allegro," its dreamy "Adagio," and its witty rondo finale, is reminiscent of Piston's two quartets from the 1930s, especially the 1933 *String Quartet No. 1*, which it matches in vitality and lightness. This later quartet, however, is more personal and subtle. In the first movement, for instance, the statement of the B-flat opening theme in G-flat at m. 74 seems to be the start of a development, and the statement of this theme in D at m. 101 seems to be a recapitualation. However, the entire section from m. 74 to m. 120 is more accurately described as a recapitulation of the exposition's first theme group (mm. 1–37). Piston had written a number of similarly binary sonata movements throughout the 1950s, but in this movement, texture, tonality, and dynamics give this conception some new twists. There are formal ambiguities in the "Adagio" as well, including an opening section (mm. 1–18) that sets forth the violin theme upon which this variation movement is based, but that also resembles a four-voice fugal exposition. And while the finale is essentially an ABACABA rondo movement, a good deal of formal play obscures its design: the second A section (mm. 70–107) is invertibly counterpointed by the B theme; the third A section (mm. 129–150) reduces the A theme to a barely recognizable skeleton of its former self; the second B section (mm. 151–174) is invertibly counterpointed by the C theme; and the final A section (mm. 175–224) is invertibly counterpointed by both the B and C themes. This obscure rondo scheme led one observer to believe the movement, "a fugue on three subjects."[15] In addition to its formal ingenuities, the *Fifth String Quartet* has a complex and distinctive tonal language. Each of its movements is based on a twelve-tone idea, and the music is indeed very chromatic, although Piston's harmonic sense is, as ever, cool and refined. He shows less interest in confining himself to Schoenbergian manipulations of the basic set than he did in the early forties with works like the *Chromatic Study* and the *Partita*. The *Fifth Quartet* won the composer his last major prize, the 1964 New York Music Critics Circle Award.

Piston's 1964 *Sextet* for stringed instruments is, surprisingly enough, a much different work from the *Fifth Quartet*. Far from the style of the 1930s, the *Sextet*, commissioned by the Elizabeth Sprague Coolidge

Foundation and first performed on 31 October 1964, at the Library of Congress, has a somber grandeur very likely inspired by the two Brahms sextets. The romantic opening, "Adagio espressivo," is a massive variation movement (theme: mm. 1–28; Var. I: 29–41; Var. II; 42–62; Var. III: 63–77; Var. IV and coda: 78–99) that is seamlessly put together, but not as through-composed as may appear. Its huge dimensions, not to mention its jagged lines (based on the ten-note melody played by the first cello in ex. 20), rich textures, and intense counterpoint, suggest a certain monumentality that one rarely encounters in Piston's music, especially the chamber music. This morbid and brooding opening is followed by a brisk, cheerful scherzo: an ABABA movement with a witty, "staccato" first theme, and a slinky, tango-like second theme that reappears in the second B section in six-voice canon. Here we find, in utter contrast to the murky textures of the first movement, some of Piston's most brilliant writing for strings. The last movement attempts to reconcile these opposite moods within its spacious sonata form, which has a lengthy development section balanced by a truncated recapitulation. It is a strenuous conclusion, however, to a somewhat strained work.

Commissioned by the Harvard Musical Association and first performed on 27 April 1964, by Robert Brink, violin, George Humphrey, viola, Karl Zeise, cello, and Bruce Simonds, piano, the 1964 *Piano Quartet* is more agreeably lyrical and less severely chromatic than the *Sextet* of the same year. Its first movement, which opens with a beautiful theme for unison strings, is pretty much melodious throughout, even in its dramatic development section. The modest "Adagio sostenuto" that follows is a straightforward variation movement whose tender and touching lyricism is not obscured by some subtle counterpoint. Its ambiguous tonic center of D nicely prepares the G major tonality of the finale, a tuneful ABABA rondo whose second B section is drastically reworked. The *Quartet*'s lyricism, however, has little of the relaxed spontaneity found in the music of the 1950s, but rather exhibits the meticulous and intricate care that characterizes Piston's melodic language of the 1960s. In the *Quartet*, these melodies are not so much shaped by rows or motives as by specific intervals, and, to take two contrasting examples, one might compare the role of the minor second in the somewhat erotic theme of the slow movement (ex. 21) with that of the perfect fourth in the whimsical second subject of the finale (ex. 22).

The circumstances surrounding Piston's major orchestral work of the 1960s, the *Eighth Symphony* (1965), are told by the composer as follows:

When my Fourth Symphony was performed recently by the Boston Symphony under Erich Leinsdorf, a lady stopped me in the corridor and said, "Please excuse my asking

Ex. 20.    Piston, "Adagio espressivo," *Sextet* (New York: AMP, 1965), p. 2. Used by permission.

Ex. 21.  Piston, "Adagio sostenuto," *Piano Quartet* (New York:
AMP, 1974), p. 12. Used by permission.

a personal question, but I want so much to know what you and Mr. Leinsdorf were
talking about while taking a bow." I had thought all the questions one could ask a
composer had been put to me, but this was new. Furthermore, and oddly enough, it
happened that I did have something to tell. Mr. Leinsdorf was saying, "Now you must
write something for us," the Fourth Symphony having been composed for the Minneapolis Symphony, the Third and Sixth for the Boston Symphony but under Serge
Koussevitzky and Charles Munch, respectively. It is well known that the Orchestra
has shown different qualities of sound and style under the regular leadership of these
three distinguished conductors, so the proposal was for me timely, logical, and intriguing. We continued our conversation in the Green Room. Replying to my query as
to the kind of piece he would like, the maestro put forth several attractive suggestions,
all of which I hope one day to carry out. When I voiced a preference for the Eighth
Symphony he heartily agreed.[16]

The score is dedicated to Leinsdorf, who premiered the work with the
Boston Symphony on 31 March 1965, in Philharmonic Hall, New York.
Not since the premiere of the *First Symphony* was the reception to a new
Piston symphony so largely negative. Such sympathetic listeners as Michael Steinberg and Harold Shapero found the work disappointing[17] and
dreary,[18] although Louis Biancolli thought it "Piston's finest symphony
to date,"[19] an appraisal echoed ten years later by David Hall in a review
of the work's first recording by the Louisville Symphony Orchestra.[20]

The *First* and *Eighth Symphony* were similarly received because they
have a good deal in common, including murky and surreal details that
overwhelm the formal design. In a discussion of the *Eighth Symphony*,
Harris Lindenfeld is reminded of an early work like the *First String Quartet* in the way "canon, motivic transformation, simultaneous inversion
and strict imitation pervade the entire work," although, he adds, Piston
also makes use of a twelve-tone series in the later work.[21] Actually, Piston's music from the 1930s, as already noted, also makes use of tone-
rows, and by the composer's, and Krenek's, admission, the *First Symphony* has a lot to do with twelve-tone music. Furthermore, it is only the
*Eighth Symphony*'s first movement, "Moderato mosso" ( ♪ = 80), that
is based on a twelve-note idea. In this, the work's finest movement, the

Ex. 22.    Piston, "Allegro vivo," *Piano Quartet,* p. 20. Used by
permission.

initial twelve-tone melody for cellos and basses twists and winds through a number of colorful textures, creating a loosely arched design. Like "Seaside," it is dreamy and austere, and both pieces, in fact, conclude open-endedly, with a sustained note that does not seem to be the movement's tonic.

After this slow, preludial movement, one might expect, as in the *Third Symphony*, the *Sketches*, and the *Sextet*, a scherzo movement, or at least some fast movement. But in what is decidedly a risky venture, Piston offers us a slow variation movement, "Lento assai." The opening theme for bassoon and then flute (mm. 1–27) and the first variation for, primarily, strings (mm. 28–44) are warm and introspective, and they nicely complement the suspenseful "Moderato mosso;" but the next three variations (mm. 45–57, 58–78, and 79–93) and the reprise (mm. 94–105) dissolve into impressionistic musings too similar to the opening movement for sufficient contrast.[22] The finale, "Allegro marcato," is happily brisk and lively, with a forceful first theme and a marchlike second theme. This movement resembles the finales of other wartime works—the *Second* and *Fourth Symphony* and the *Fourth Quartet*—although the war in question, it seems, is neither World War II nor the Korean War, but rather the undeclared War in Vietnam. Here, in what Louis Biancolli calls a "smart American salute," we find loyalty and courage expressed in a more contemporary language. The possibility that Piston grew disillusioned with this War, however, is suggested not only by the lack of such patriotism in the music of the late 1960s and early 1970s, but by this later music's intimate romanticism.

Piston's other work from 1965, the *Pine Tree Fantasy* for orchestra, is one of three works from this period that clearly evokes a world of the past. The first, the 1963 *Variations on a Theme by Edward Burlingame Hill* for orchestra, is based on a 1942 *Prelude* for unaccompanied flute that E. B. Hill wrote for his friend, Herbert Kibrick, an amateur flutist and Laurent disciple who had studied with Hill and Piston at Harvard, class of 1938.[23] After Kibrick's death in 1960, his father, Isaac, asked Piston to write a work in Herbert's memory for the Boston Civic Symphony (of which Isaac was then President) and suggested that the composer use the tiny Hill *Prelude*. Piston, who was somewhat acquainted with Isaac and Herbert's widow, felt obliged to honor their request. Since Hill had died in 1962, Piston wrote to the composer's son George for permission to use the *Prelude*, and in a letter of assent, George writes, "I do know how much Father admired you and your music and since Mr. Kibrick was a student of both of you, the combination should be a very beautiful memorial."[24] The *Hill Variations*, which was first performed on

30 April 1963, by Kalman Novak and the Civic Symphony, opens with the entire *Prelude* played by the flute supported by an orchestral accompaniment that well suits Hill's sinuous and exotic melody. It is the only time Piston ever made use of another composer's music in one of his own compositions; and even here Piston touches up the original, changing a few notes, but mostly shaping the whole into a smoother and more varied rhythmic design (ex. 23). The three variations and reprise that follow are particularly literal, and retain the "art nouveau" quality of Hill's aesthetic. It is not a very interesting work, but the scoring throughout is appealingly delicate and piquant.

The *Pine Tree Fantasy* is a better work, more nostalgic but less sentimental. It was commissioned by Mary Castleman Lipkin, and dedicated to Arthur Bennett Lipkin, who led the Portland Maine Symphony in the work's premiere on 16 November 1965, as part of a program that was a "Voice of America" musical salute to Kyoto, and that was broadcast throughout Japan. Piston writes:

> As this work was composed especially for the Portland Maine Symphony it seems natural that the expressive content of its musical ideas may have been influenced by contemplation of the Pine Tree State, and perhaps more specifically by recollection of early boyhood days in Rockland. I have not wished to evoke a picture of those dim memories that came to mind, allowing them to make their impression upon my musical thinking. No doubt some of the melodic turns and patterns heard can be found among the songs of seafaring men and woodsmen, but no such tunes have been quoted, unless unintentionally. All is imperfect remembrance of things past and having been long forgotten.[25]

The three themes that form the *Pine Tree Fantasy*'s ABCBA design are all related to folk song. The first theme, introduced by the clarinet in m. 5, is "Largo," dreamy, and supple, and is supported by a winding, chromatic accompaniment, much as in "Seaside" Piston's slow-moving chanty is set against a wavelike ostinato. The other two themes, "Allegro deciso," are more realistic: the B sections suggest the bustle of turn-of-the-century New England, while the C section has a tuneful, seafaring quality. Sketches reveal that Piston studied traditional Yankee songs for this work, and that its three themes owe something to "Shenandoah," "Sally Brown," and "Blow the Man Down," respectively. Indeed, the *Pine Tree Fantasy* comes surprisingly close to Ives, especially to a work like *Washington's Birthday*, and might reflect that composer's growing popularity during these years.

Another work that may be grouped with the *Hill Variations* and the *Pine Tree Fantasy* by virtue of its title is the 1967 *Souvenirs* for flute,

Ex. 23.  Hill, Prelude for Flute (unpublished); Piston, *Variations on a Theme by E. B. Hill* (New York: AMP, 1964), pp. 1–3. Used by permission.

viola, and harp, a short rounded "Tranquillo" movement only 57 measures long. The work is dedicated to Nadia Boulanger, ostensibly in honor of her eightieth birthday, whose celebration (given by Prince Rainier and Princess Grace of Monaco) Piston could not attend. A few years earlier, Boulanger had similarly declined an invitation to a seventieth birthday party for Piston, and had written him the following note:[26]

> Not to be amongst your friends Friday is saddening! But, as I feel always near, I will imagine I am there, happy . . . and silent. For what I have to say is too serious for a joyful gathering. Indeed I join in expressing wishes, affection and gratefulness. But your contribution to the musical life in Harvard, to the musical life universally speaking, your influence . . . to place higher and higher the great values which open on the past, the future and give all its strength to the present, are of such weight that . . . well, out of my reach, and out of place, maybe!
> I admire you and I do love you, Dear Walter, and this implies all the unsaid.
>
> Most faithfully,
>
> Nadia Boulanger

Is *Souvenirs* a comparable birthday salutation to Boulanger? When the work is published and performed, we might better know.

A year earlier, in 1966, Piston had written another trio, his *Trio No. 2* for violin, cello and piano. The work was commisioned in memory of Robert Wurlitzer by his family, and is dedicated to the Balsam-Kroll-Heifitz Trio (Arthur Balsam, piano, William Kroll, violin, and Benar Heifitz, cello), who premiered the work on 10 October 1966, in Pittsburg. Although Piston's post-1965 orchestral works, as we shall soon see, are in complex one-movement forms, this *Second Trio* has three movements: "Molto leggiero e capriccioso," "Adagio," and "Vigoroso." These movements, however, are particularly interdependent. Their melodies, for instance, are derived from the work's opening phrase (ex. 24), which contains the tone-row, B-A#-C#-D-E♭-A-G#-E-F-F#-G-C. As a result, the minor second colors the entire score, and gives this severely contrapuntal work a monochromatic consistency. Furthermore, the three movements have similarly arched structures. The opening movement combines sonata and arch form by reversing the order of the first and second theme groups in the recapitulation, while the "Adagio" combines variation and arch form in the following way:

Theme (mm. 1–8)
Variation I (9–19; the violin and cello lines of the theme are subjected to melodic and
    contrapuntal inversion)
Variation II (20–27; an embellished version of the theme)
Variation III (28–36; rhapsodic in style, this central variation is itself arched)

Ex. 24.   Piston, "Molto leggiero e capriccioso," *Piano Trio No. 2*
(New York: AMP, 1974), p. 1. Used by permission.

Variation IV (37–46; see Variation II and the last two measures of Variation I)
Variation V (47–56; a reprise of the Theme)

The finale is an ABA movement whose outer sections are in 3/4, and whose middle section is in 9/8. This scherzo-like 9/8 middle section is itself in three parts; the first two of these subsections (mm. 33–42, 43–53) are full of intricate mirror, melodic, and contrapuntal inversions, while the third subsection (mm. 54–78) is a fugato in three-voice invertible counterpoint. Another, less strict fugato, whose four statements (beginning, respectively, at mm. 92, 98, 102, and 106) ascend by perfect fourth, is interpolated into the second A section to intensify the movement's dramatic close. Throughout this movement, the minor second is as important harmonically as it is melodically (ex. 25) and this imparts an angry tone to the vigorous A sections, and a macabre quality to the witty B section.

Ex. 25.    Piston, "Vigoroso," *Piano Trio No. 2*, p. 18. Used by
           permission.

The *Variations for Cello and Orchestra*, another work from 1966, is dedicated to Mstislav Rostropovich, who premiered the work with Gennadi Rozhdestvensky and the London Symphony Orchestra at the Carnegie Hall concert of 2 March 1967. In an interview with Peter Westergaard, Piston says:

Let me tell you of my experience with the cellist Mstislav Rostropovitch. I met him for the first time when he appeared with the Boston Symphony in 1966. Through an interpreter, he asked me to write a cello concerto for his Carnegie Hall series in February 1967. But for one very short letter thanking me for accepting, not one word of communication took place between us until the rehearsal the day before the concert. He played the rehearsal, and of course the concert, with no music before him, and it sounded just as I had dreamed it would. Also he knew all the orchestra parts, and at the rehearsal he was constantly prompting the members of the London Symphony. As for the contribution, over and above a performance that was a true and faithful statement of my communication, in the process of relaying this to the listeners he gave his own reaction to the communication without in any way altering its musical meaning. A great artist rather intensifies that meaning.[27]

Piston says in another interview, "I put everything I had into that piece . . . it takes a lifetime of knowledge to write for a man like that," and Rostropovich could not believe that the composer of the *Cello Variations* did not himself play the cello.[28] Piston tells Westergaard:

When he asked me to write it he said, "Please don't write for the player—write for the instrument." I think that's a most unusual request from a virtuoso. He wants to increase the literature for all cellists. Now, I know it is a difficult piece. But it wasn't written to exhibit things that Rostropovitch can do that others can't.[29]

And yet Piston admits "it was impossible to put down a single note without hearing him."[30] Boston Symphony cellists anxious to study the work in the wake of Rostropovich's performance doubted whether or not they could "hack" it, although Luis Leguia did, in fact, perform the work a few years later.

The 1966 *Cello Variations*, even more than the 1959 *New England Sketches* or the 1962 *Fifth String Quartet*, may be cited as the beginning of Piston's late period. Certain formal and stylistic innovations set this work apart from previous efforts, and bring it close to the music of the following ten years. Its formal innovation entails a synthesis of variation form, as in the *Sextet*'s slow movement, and sectional form, as in the *Lincoln Center Overture*. The result is a one-movement work whose sections, distinct in tempo and time signature, form a set of variations.

Variation I (mm. 1–41): 3/4, "Adagio" ( ♩ = 58)[31]
Variation II (mm. 42–85): 3/4, "Poco più mosso" ( ♩ = 72)
Variation III (mm. 86–130): 3/4, "Allegro moderato" ( ♩ = 76)
Variations IV and V (mm. 131–187; 188–259): 5/8 and 3/8, "Allegro vivo" ( ♪ = 160);
    one might prefer to think of this section as a single variation
Variation VI (mm. 260–298): 4/4, "Lento assai" ( ♩ = 40)
Variation VII (mm. 290–382): 4/4, "Allegro giusto" ( ♩ = 126)
Coda (Variation VIII? mm. 383–412): 3/4, "Allegro con Spirito" ( ♩ = 132–138)

In this way Piston uses variation form to suggest the introduction (Var. I and II) and "Allegro" (Var. III), scherzo (Var. IV and V), slow movement (Var. VI), and finale (Var. VII and coda) of a traditional four-movement structure, and the additional variations for the "introduction" and the "scherzo" help further this impression. Piston discusses the work's unusual formal scheme with Westergaard.

WP: When Rostropovitch asked for a cello concerto I thought, "I've done so many concertos, all in three movements." The plan "fast-slow-fast" is not bad. But I have on occasion heard entire programs of my works, and heard that way I have found it a bit dreary. The idea of movements is a little hackneyed, and I thought, "Wouldn't this be an interesting project: to make one continuous work—variations, but not theme and variations, rather six or seven ways to regard a musical idea, different aspects or facets, each growing out of another."

PW: Six or seven variations of an underlying theme that is never stated, or each variation a variation of the preceding one?

WP: Well, both. I think they are all variations of one another. But I can't sell the idea.

PW: It doesn't sound that different from Schoenberg's notion of perpetual variation.

WP: I suppose you could say that. Probably one could apply it to more music than one might suspect.[32]

And indeed the *Variations* is closer to a work like Tchaikowsky's *Variations on a Rococo Theme for Cello and Orchestra* than to the music of Schoenberg.

The *Cello Variations'* other innovative feature is its melodic language, based, as Piston tells us, on a musical idea—probably the cello's opening three notes, G#-E-D#. The cello part, while neither erratic nor particularly rhapsodic, has a rhythmic and tonal fluidity that is as novel as the work's formal design, or, for that matter, the work's colorful orchestral effects. Without losing its cool or reserve, the *Cello Variations* has an improvisatory quality—sometimes tentative, sometimes impulsive—that is very personal and direct. The work, however, is not as "episodic" as one reviewer may have thought.[33] The variations, for one thing, are recognizable as such, most obviously at their "meno mosso" climaxes, or rather anticlimaxes. Furthermore, the work moves smoothly from its fuzzy tonal beginnings to its bright conclusion in D. Shortly after its premiere, the *Cello Variations* was deemed by Piston to be his best work.[34]

The similar *Concerto for Clarinet and Orchestra* of 1967 gives further evidence that Piston was pleased with the new directions the *Cello Variations* had taken him. This is another variation cum four-movement work, though here the scheme is simpler:

Variation I (mm. 1–141): 3/4, "Con moto" ($\downarrow$ = 132)
Variation II (mm. 142–298): 2/4, "poco più mosso" ($\downarrow$ = 138)
Variation III (mm. 299–342): 4/4, "Assai lento" ($\downarrow$ = 63)
Variation IV (mm. 343–417): 7/8, 5/8, 3/4, 2/4, "Vivo" ($\downarrow$ = 126)

In addition, each variation has a clear-cut ABA design, except for the binary, and more complex, "Assai lento." The work's finely etched form is matched by clear textures, sparse harmonies, and straightforward rhythms reminiscent of an earlier Piston. In fact, the *Clarinet Concerto*'s gentleness and humor, so becoming to its medium, is untypical for its time, even for Piston. On the other hand, the clarinet writing, with its wide leaps and jagged runs, is decidedly "au courant." The work was first played by Donald Wendlant, clarinet, and the Dartmouth Symphony Orchestra, conducted by Mario di Bonaventura, on 6 August 1967. The work was commissioned for Dartmouth's Hopkins Center "Congregation of the Arts" by Bonaventura, who became Piston's close friend and active supporter during these years. In fact, between 1963 and 1969, the "Congregation of the Arts," under Bonaventura's leadership, performed twenty-three works by Piston, including four world premieres. Piston occasionally attended these summer festivals, where he coached his own music, heard concerts, and met such distinguished colleagues as Dallapiccola, Henze and Lutosławski, all of whose music he admired.

The 1967 *Ricercare* for orchestra was one of eighteen works commissioned by the New York Philharmonic in celebration of its 125th anniversary[35] and is dedicated to Leonard Bernstein, who conducted its premiere on 7 March 1968. The *Ricercare* is Piston's last major work of the 1960s, and it culminates the decade. The work, Piston tells us, is an "investigation" of three notes "whose identity is of no importance to the listener," but which would seem to be the motive, C-D$^b$-E. This "investigation" forms a complex and improvisatory arch divided by changes of tempo and time signature as follows: "Adagio," 3/4; "Vigoroso," 2/4; "Lento," 5/4; and "Adagio," 3/4. The *Ricercare* thus combines the through-composed arch of the *Eighth Symphony*'s first movement, and the sectional variations of the *Cello Variations* and the *Clarinet Concerto*. Further, in its eleven minutes, Piston encapsulates the nostalgia, the uneasiness, and the introspection that characterizes much of his music from the 1960s. These and other moods fluctuate with more rapidity and uncertainty than ever before, and sometimes with a theatricality that might be reflective of Bernstein's dynamic personality. Gunther Schuller spoke of the work as "one of my special favorites, the beautiful Ricercare."[36]

Piston's *Ricercare* more closely resembles the ricercari of the late Renaissance than the ricercari of the high Baroque, and it might therefore be grouped with such kindred works as Hindemith's 1958 *Madrigals* and Stravinsky's 1960 *Monumentum pro Gesualdo*. As we have already noted resemblances between mannerist art of the late 16th century and Piston's surrealist art of the 1930s, and have further drawn parallels between his music of the 1930s and the 1960s, this connection is neither inconsistent nor surprising. The unity between Piston's early and late works is intriguing, and may be related, as noted before, to similarities in political and social climate. Might another factor be that in both periods Piston frequently composes music for close friends and acquaintances? In some ways, then, Piston comes full circle.

And yet Piston's compositions from the 1960s show the composer departing from his established style in ways reminiscent of contemporary works by Copland and Stravinsky. Indeed, Piston believed that any artist "worth his salt" sought both to perfect his craft and explore new ways. During these years, Piston leaves behind modal chromaticism and classical forms, and takes up the challenge of creating a more thoroughly chromatic syntax and a more personal and complex architecture. Gone, for the most part, are any overt references to Bach and Mozart, marches and tangos, or fairs and forests. This music—and the music to come—is without question the most abstruse and difficult music of Piston's career. Despite widespread clichés about Piston's academicism, the music often surprised and baffled the few who took notice of it. There are no texted works to help us appreciate this ouevre, although three titles (*Variations on a Theme by E. B. Hill*, *Pine Tree Fantasy*, and *Souvenirs*) and the projected Maine opera suggest that remembrance is an important source of inspiration. The music, however, is more often anguished, sensual, and jovial than nostalgic. These and other moods are easily accessible to the listener, but an understanding of whole melodies requires patience and study.

# 9

# Piston, Romanticist:
# From the *Ceremonial Fanfare* (1969) to the *String Quartet Concerto* (1976)

Piston continued to compose, amid physical and emotional hardships,[1] until his death, at age eighty-two, in 1976. He was less prolific than usual, however, and it was not until three years after the 1967 *Ricercare* that Piston finished another major composition, the 1970 *Violin Fantasia*. In between there is only the small *Ceremonial Fanfare* (1969), commissioned by the New York Metropolitan Museum of Art for one of the five centenary exhibitions held there in 1969 and 1970 (the other four opened with fanfares by Bernstein, Copland, Schuman, and Thomson). Piston's *Fanfare* for six horns, four trumpets, three trombones, tuba, and percussion, makes use of such typical fanfare gestures as triplet rhythms and open intervals, especially the perfect fourth, which often determines melodic shape, chordal structure, harmonic motion, and contrapuntal design. Like the last movement of the 1967 *Second Piano Trio*, the *Ceremonial Fanfare*'s outer sections are in 3/4 and its middle section is in 9/8. These two movements offer other similarities as well and suggest that fanfare, whose influence was so strongly felt in an early work like the scherzo to the *First Piano Trio*, is still an important component of Piston's musical imagination even in his late, intimate style. Some years later, in 1975, Piston wrote another fanfare, the *Bicentennial Fanfare* for orchestra, commissioned by the Cincinnati Symphony, Thomas Schippers, music director, on the occasion of the 200th anniversary of American independence, and first performed by Schippers and the Cincinnati Symphony on 14 November 1975. Piston provided the following notes for the work's premiere:

> The idea of marking our bicentennial year by opening programs with fanfares written by different composers I found most intriguing and singularly appropriate. I was pleased and honored when invited to participate in this project by Thomas Schippers,

whom I have long admired. It seemed to me fitting to compose a fanfare in festive character for the full symphony, so as to hear the whole sound of this great orchestra.

The Fanfare is an ABA form, the A section slow and dignified. In contrast, the middle section is lively, exploiting various instrumental combinations and developing material from the first part. The final section is a return of A, played softly with new color, and building to a sonorous climax.[2]

Here is the culminating fanfare of a musician whose composing career began with the writing of fanfares.

Another occasional piece that may be grouped with these two fanfares is the 1970 "Variation of Happy Birthday" for piano. It is one of a set of *Variations on Happy Birthday* written for Eugene Ormandy on the occasion of the conductor's seventieth birthday, and first played on 24 January 1970, in Philadelphia's Academy of Music. Also contributing variations to this work were Barber, Berger, Bernstein, Copland, Creston, Dello Joio, Diamond, Einem, Finney, Nabakov, Orff, Persichetti, Rochberg, Rózsa, Schuman, Sessions, Thomson, and Zador. Piston's "Variation" (ex. 26) is an exquisite joke full of "double entendre." It puns, in succession, the "Menuetto" from Beethoven's *Piano Sonata Op. 31, No. 3* (mm. 1–4), "Columbia, the Gem of the Ocean" (mm. 5–6), and "Home on the Range" (mm. 7–9). which provides a funny, asymmetrical cadence. The coda, an almost exact quote from Strauss's "Presentation of the Rose" from *Der Rosenkavalier*, is, in this setting, evocative of birthday candles. This quodlibet thus alludes to staples of the Ormandy repertoire: Beethoven, American folk song, and Strauss.

The 1970 *Fantasia for Violin and Orchestra* was commissioned for Salvatore Accardo and the "Congregation of the Arts" at Dartmouth College by Mario di Bonaventura, and was first performed on 11 March 1973, by Accardo and the Dartmouth Symphony Orchestra, conducted by Bonaventura. Piston was familiar with Accardo's playing through a private exhibition, arranged by Bonaventura, at his Belmont home, and was much impressed with the Italian violinist's renditions of Paganini and Bach.[3] The *Fantasia*'s solo part accordingly has the violinist play fast, tricky passages of Paganinian virtuosity, as well as slow, supple melodies of Bachian intensity, such as one finds in the work's opening phrase (ex. 27). This melody, which sets forth the work's basic set, opens with a falling tritone (perhaps related to Accardo's initials) that colors the entire score and that gives a dark and misty edge to the music. Even at the final cadence, in which the soloist and the lower strings play a widely spaced open fifth, the harp plays a nontriadic, midranged chord that includes the tonic's tritone.

The *Fantasia* is divided into five sections as follows:

"Lento sereno" ♪ = 48, 5/8
"Allegro" ♩ = 120, 3/4
"Adagio" ♩ = 50, 6/4
"Allegro energico" ♩ = 84, 5/8, 6/8 and 3/4
"Lento" ♪ = 48, 5/8

The beautiful "Lento" sections that bear the weight of this arched work are at once painfully aware and transcendentally serene, and provide a dreamy refuge from the turbulent emotions of the middle sections. In the first of these, "Allegro," the violin's frantic perpetual motion and the orchestra's strident and busy commentary join to suggest a sense of disorientation in an overwhelmingly hectic world. The need to unwind, it seems, prompts Piston to write a cadenza at this point. This cadenza leads into an "Adagio" in which the violinist's quiet and tragic aria is supported by the orchestra's rich, dark chords, often proceeding by par-

Ex. 26.  Piston, "Variation on Happy Birthday" (unpublished).
Used by permission.

allel motion, and with major-minor clashes reminiscent of Schuman. The dancelike "Allegro energico" is the most joyous section, although there is a desperate quality about it, not least because it is over so quickly. These five sections not only form a slow-fast-slow-fast-slow arch, but are themselves arched, and may be thought of as a set of variations. Of all such similarly arched designs—including the *English Horn Fantasy*, the first movement of the *Fifth Symphony*, and the *Ricercare*—the *Fantasia* is the most perfect and the most profound of them all.

Piston had wanted to write a flute concerto for Doriot Anthony Dwyer at least as early as 1964, when he suggested as much to Leinsdorf, who preferred, instead, an *Eighth Symphony*.[4] Michael Tilson Thomas, more responsive to the idea, conducted the premiere of the 1971 *Concerto for Flute and Orchestra* on 22 September 1971, with Dwyer and the Boston Symphony. The score is dedicated to Dwyer, who had recorded Piston's

Ex. 27.   Piston, *Fantasia for Violin and Orchestra* (New York: AMP, 1975), pp. 3–4. Used by permission.

Ex. 27. (continued)

*Flute Sonata* even before her appointment as first flute with the Boston Symphony, with whom she played many of Piston's orchestra scores. A member of the Boston Woodwind Quintet, Dwyer also premiered Piston's *Woodwind Quintet*, about which she tells the following anecdote:

[At Tanglewood] one of my pleasures is to coach the students on the Piston Woodwind Quintet. So, the class read through it. They were all very good players, but they read through it rather coldly, I thought, and very literally and staid. And I said to them, "Do you know something about Walter Piston? Do you know that his name is really Pistone?" And they looked at me in such amazement. And I said, "Now that you know that, look at your music; don't play it. You see those long melodic lines? It means something." And they all relaxed and they all smiled and they played it very differently.[5]

In 1973, Dwyer, soon to hold the Boston Symphony's Walter Piston Chair, considered the *Flute Concerto* a "major activity" of her life.[6] For his part, Piston once stated, "Mrs. Dwyer is one of the best flutists around. She's amazing."[7]

The *Concerto*'s flute part is likewise amazing, especially in its opening section, "Alquanto largo," which is, melodically, Piston's most remarkable and adventurous accomplishment. Here the florid flute line, ornamented by trills, grace notes, flourishes, and flutter-tonguing, comes close to the music of the post-War avant-garde, especially Messiaen, who, like Piston, loved birds. This dramatic and declamatory "Alquanto largo" is in a broad 4/4, although there is a change of tempo and meter in the B section of its ABA design. The next two sections, "Lento espressivo" and "Allegro," are also in ABA form, and they too have changes of meter, though not tempo, in their middle sections. The delicate "Lento" is nostalgic at times, while the rousing "Allegro" is like those merry orchestral finales from the 1950s, except that here the sonorities are chamberlike and exquisite. The *Concerto*'s three sections might be likened to a recitative, aria, and cabaletta, although certain elements romantically interweave throughout the whole. Most romantic of all is the "Allegro's" cadenza (ex. 28), which includes a haunting "Lento" passage that looks back to the "Lento espressivo."

A final version of the *Flute Concerto*, with a revised finale, was premiered by Dwyer, Thomas, and the Boston Symphony in Providence, Rhode Island, on 6 December 1973. The work's cadenza had originally been followed by a short, up-tempo coda as in the *Viola Concerto*, not, as remembered by Leighton Kramer in the *Village Voice*, "a quiet, wispy, but interestingly unorthodox trailing-off."[8] Michael Steinberg wrote in the *Boston Globe* that this ending was "perfunctory and therefore disappointing,"[9] and Dwyer used Steinberg's review:

. . . to strengthen my own impression and resolve to speak to Walter about it. . . . I asked him to revise the work. He said, "I know how hard it was for you to say this." It was! "But I never would have forgiven you if you didn't—since you feel this way about it. I'll think about it." Later he called and said he agreed, that actually he had "been rushed" into finishing this work and he wasn't happy with it either. He sent

Ex. 28.  Piston, *Concerto for Flute and Orchestra* (New York:
         AMP, 1977), p. 19. Used by permission.

the one version which was changed before he wrote it permanently, and I changed a
few things once again, of which he approved. He also said I could make my own
cadenza or add to his.[10]

Piston expanded not only the *Concerto*'s coda, but, in the interest of
balance and symmetry, the "Allegro's" opening as well. In addition, there
are numerous refinements of a more minor sort throughout the entire
"Allegro," including added orchestral parts that could not be the work
of Dwyer. The *Flute Concerto* is Piston's only work to undergo such
drastic revision, and thus affords a rare opportunity to study Piston's

creative process. Otherwise Piston refrained from altering works upon their completion unless, as Dwyer's account testifies, he was asked to do so by an executant of his music. He did, in fact, lengthen the coda of the *Viola Concerto* for Pasquale, and edit the harp part of the *Capriccio* for Zabaleta.[11] "No note is sacred,"[12] he told Rostropovich during a rehearsal of the *Cello Variations*, but the cellist loved the work just as it stood.

Piston wrote his last two chamber works, the 1972 *Duo for Cello and Piano* and the 1973 *Three Counterpoints for violin, viola and cello*, for friends in the Boston Symphony. The *Duo* was written for Luis Leguia, cellist with the Boston Symphony, and Robert Freeman, pianist and present director of the Eastman School of Music, and was premiered at the Library of Congress on 13 December 1974. In the following passage, Leguia recounts the work's origins and offers other observations:

> Bob and I played cello-piano recitals, and several times had played some of our recital music for Walter Piston, generous friend that he was, for the benefit of his keen and sharp ear and mind. Of course, he listened to his Duo.
>
> I felt that 20th century cello and cello-piano compositions were rather limited, and thought it a good thing to ask Mr. Piston if he would be interested in writing for cello-piano. He stated he would do it, much to my happiness. But at that time he was working on another composition. The resulting Duo for cello-piano is a first-class composition, a joy for cellists and pianists, and it displays the cello mood and characteristics beautifully. Piston knew well the instruments he wrote for.[13]

The *Three Counterpoints* was commissioned by and dedicated to a violist with the Boston Symphony, George Humphrey, who, a decade earlier, had prompted the Harvard Musical Association to commission the Piston *Piano Quartet*, at whose premiere he played viola. Now Humphrey requested a piano quintet, but Piston suggested a string trio " since he felt that his catalogue needed one."[14] A close companion to Piston in the composer's last years, Humphrey copied out parts for the work's premiere, which he gave with Robert Brink, violin, and Karl Zeise, cello, in the rooms of the Harvard Musical Association on 8 March 1974.

While the *Flute Concerto* is a particularly accessible late work, the *Duo for Cello and Piano* is Piston's most impenetrable score from the 1970s. Little mention has been made of the melodic and rhythmic advances that mark Piston's late style; but ever since the 1962 *String Quartet*, Piston's music, often based on twelve-tone ideas but rarely serially conceived, constantly, and almost imperceptibly, grows more intricate and obscure. This obscurity becomes quite formidable, almost hermetic, with the *Duo*, which has a tonal complexity comparable to Carter's 1948 *Cello Sonata*. This complexity is due, in part, to the stringent independence of the cello and the piano that makes this piece a real duo. In addition, the work's textures are often thick, and Piston's typical fluidity is here a bit viscid. These features—tonal and rhythmic ambiguity, disjointed contrapuntalism, and textural richness—are epitomized by the *Duo*'s surprisingly inconclusive final cadence. Here is a turgidity greater than any that Citkowitz complained about in the 1930s.

The form of the *Duo*'s three movements, however, are clear enough. They all, in fact, have a similar five-section design that arches at the center. The "Calmo e ritenuto" first movement, ABCBA, is full of contrast, not only of tempo and meter, but of mood as well: the A sections are grave and serene, the B sections are gentle and romantic, and the C section is tense and explosive. The second movement scherzo, on the other hand, disguises its ABABA scheme in an essentially through-composed movement that is consistently ironic and grotesque throughout (ex. 29). The last movement is an ABABA rondo with a yearning and somewhat sad main theme, and a playful "delicato" secondary theme. Such stark contrast makes this movement particularly disturbing and personal, as does the music's limp, unsteady lyricism.

Ex. 29.  Piston, "Animato," *Duo for Cello and Piano* (unpublished). Used by permission.

The first movement of the *Three Counterpoints for violin, viola and cello* is similar to this rondo finale, for it too alternates a weary, yearning theme with an energetic, playful one. It is also like the *Duo*'s finale in its use of inversion and retrograde, although here, as outlined below, such artifice is even more extensive and thorough:

A   1.   mm. 1–10: antecedent
    2.   mm. 11–18: consequent
B   1.   mm. 19–37: antecedent
    2.   mm. 38–59: consequent, with some material from B1 in inverted counterpoint
A   3.   mm. 60–67: mm. 11–18 in retrograde
    4.   mm. 68–77: mm. 1–10 in inverted counterpoint
B   3.   mm. 78–96: mm. 38–59 in retrograde
    4.   mm. 97–116: mm. 19–37 in retrograde
A   5.   mm. 117–28: mm. 1–10, with some material in inverted counterpoint

Both emotionally and intellectually complex, this sort of thing is more digestible a first movement than, as in the *Duo*, a finale. The other two *Counterpoints* also have analogues in the *Duo* of the preceding year. The second movement, "Adagio sereno," is like the *Duo*'s opening, slow movement, though it is simpler and less gloomy, a theme with three variations in which the violin is preeminent throughout, although the viola and cello grow more assertive with each new section. The finale, "allegro spiccato," is like the *Duo*'s second movement scherzo, although it is neither as subtle nor as grotesque as that movement. The *Three Counterpoints* is less ambitious than the *Duo*—Piston himself referred to it as a bit of "Hausmusik"[15]—but it is an appealingly translucent and impressively skillful work.

The history of Piston's last work, the *Concerto for String Quartet, Wind Instruments and Percussion*, goes back to 1968, when the Portland Symphony Orchestra (which had commissioned the 1965 *Pine Tree Fantasy*) asked Piston to write something for the Maine sesquicentennial in 1970. Piston proposed an "Overture to the State of Maine," but on 1 January 1970, he wrote Paul Vermel, director of the Portland Symphony, "The recent months have brought a steady procession of frustrating and upsetting events making life almost unbearable and the creating of music well nigh impossible."[16] Vermel subsequently requested a work for the 1974–75 season in celebration of the Symphony's 50th anniversary, and suggested either a regular orchestral work, or a concerto for organ or for the Portland Symphony String Quartet. Piston preferred this last suggestion, for, as he told Harold Brown, "I admire that wonderful Portland Quartet, for they gave me the finest performance of my Fourth Quartet that I ever heard. When your director, Vermel, asked me if I would be interested in writing a work for them, I responded quickly."[17] Once again, however, Piston could not meet the Symphony's deadline. "I am determined to write the concerto," he writes, "but I am also determined to do a good job." Vermel, in the meantime, left Portland, so the 1976 *Concerto for String Quartet, Wind Instruments and Percussion* was premiered on 26 October 1976, by the Portland Quartet and the Portland Symphony under the direction of its new conductor, Bruce Hangen. The *Concerto* is dedicated to the members of the Portland Quartet: Stephen Kecskemethy, Ronald Lanz, Julia Moseley, and Paul Ross.

The *String Quartet Concerto* is the last of a series of concertos—the *Cello Variations* (1966), the *Clarinet Concerto* (1967), the *Violin Fantasia* (1970), and the *Flute Concerto* (1972)—that are in one movement and that combine sectional and variation form. But this work is the deepest and most fascinating of them all. Certainly the circumstances surrounding its composition were unique: Piston wrote most of the work in the hospital,[18] and completed it during the months following his wife Kathryn's death. The work's five variations, which form a fast-slow-fast-slow-fast design, cover a broad range of feeling: the first is madcap; the second is melancholy and nostalgic; the third is witty; the fourth is contemplative; and the fifth is marchlike and festive. These moods are familiar enough, but they unfold with a spontaneity and an impulsiveness that is novel. Piston himself acknowledged a change at this time in his compositional method: "I hear a sound and I write it."[19] To a degree, the *String Quartet Concerto* is like a nineteenth-century tone poem, a genre that had long been fundamentally antithetical to Piston's aesthetic. The slow cadenza for viola that concludes the work is especially poetic: a powerful and moving final soliloquy that is simple, poignant, and bittersweet. There are other particularly romantic features of this work, such as its dense harmonies and brilliant colors. Piston chose this fanciful medium because he was wary lest the soloists be "swamped" as they are in most concertos for string quartet,[20] or "absorbed" as they are in Tippett's *Symphony No. 3*.[21] The result is a feast of gorgeous sounds, including such exotic moments as, in the first "lento" section, passages for quartet, gong, and cymbals, and quartet, flutes, timpani, and tambourine. Neither "orchestral" nor "chamber" music, the *String Quartet Concerto* fulfills Piston's own prediction, made in 1967, that the future of the symphony orchestra might lie in its flexibility.[22]

The premiere of the *String Quartet Concerto* was a great success, and the soloists played, as an encore, the last movement of Piston's *String Quartet No. 4*. First violinist Stephen Kecskemethy told the audience, "I think you will admit and share with us the remarkable feeling this piece leaves,"[23] and critic John Thornton wrote in the *Portland Express*, "About 17 minutes long, it is magnificently fashioned, inventive without being avant garde, logically explorative, full of melody, laced with subtle changes in dynamics and rhythms."[24] Piston was too weak to attend the premiere, but he heard a tape of the performance a few weeks before he died. The *String Quartet Concerto* has since been recorded by the Emerson Quartet and the Juilliard Orchestra; but it is hoped that the Portland Quartet, who play the piece with greater sensitivity and understanding, might too have an opportunity to record it. In a letter to this author dated 28 December 1978, Julia Moseley, violist of the Portland Quartet, writes that the Quartet, in fact, hopes to record Piston's five string quartets as well as the *Concerto*. She also offers the following thoughts on these works:

> We in the Portland String Quartet believe that his chamber music is unexcelled in quality and sheer musicality, and we are grateful to have known Mr. Piston. We like to perform his quartets when we tour overseas for the State Department. In July 1977 we performed what was probably a premier of his *Fourth String Quartet* in Italy. The Italian public and the Ravenna press were thrilled with this exciting and beautiful work, which, by the way, was Piston's favorite string quartet. The next one he recommended to us, with a wink in his eye, was No. 5—a very compelling, intricate piece with a final movement of surprising jazz-like vitality.
>
> The *String Quartet Concerto* seems to me to have been almost intentionally a final statement. As the violist of the Portland String Quartet, I was curious about the viola solo at the conclusion of the work and the dissonant resolution which seems filled with philosophical implications. I asked the composer if there was particular meaning in this statement and, in typical fashion, he would not comment with any further clarification. It was almost as if he wanted my thought (or anyone's) to stand on their own merit. He always wanted his music to speak for itself, and he had great respect for musicians and their interpretative integrity.

The *String Quartet Concerto* is the most romantic work of Piston's career, but all of his music from the 1970s has a passion and a spontaneity that is extraordinary for an octogenarian. Further, this lush repertory emphasizes color and sound in ways that bring it close to the vanguard music of Piston's most youthful contemporaries. And yet these works are among the most mature and profound music of the decade, and their romantic freedom is the fruit of a lifetime of discipline and experience.

# 10

# Piston, Pragmatist:
# The Pedagogical and Critical Writings

Like Rameau and Fux, Piston is as well-known for his writings on harmony and counterpoint as for his musical compositions. His three major texts—*Harmony, Counterpoint,* and *Orchestration*—have been long admired by students and musicians around the world. Piston was especially amused to learn that a pirated Chinese translation of *Harmony* was in circulation in mainland China, even though this, of course, denied him some royalties. But Piston differs from Rameau and Fux, and, for that matter, from contemporary theorist-composers like Hindemith and Schoenberg, in that he does not offer theoretical rules for composing music, but rather deduces principles which have hitherto provided composers with a common practice. Piston had nothing against the first approach. He gladly submitted to the rigorous, scholastic training of Nadia Boulanger, and often encouraged his students to do the same. Further, he found much merit in the training manuals of Tchaikowsky,[1] Hindemith,[2] Edlund,[3] and Sessions.[4] He also respected Schoenberg's "highly developed theories,"[5] and, as stated before,[6] his reading of Krenek's *Studies in Counterpoint based on the Twelve-Tone Technique* was probably the stimulus for his first twelve-tone work in 1940. But such abstract methodology did not suit his own teaching purposes; and his textbooks, after all, were primarily intended for his classes at Harvard. Piston must have been pleased and surprised to find such a large international audience for his pragmatic approach to music theory.

This approach is given preliminary expression in Piston's first book, *Principles of Harmonic Analysis* (Boston, 1933). Dedicated to Nadia Boulanger, this text classifies and labels chords and nonharmonic tones,[7] and observes their function in musical examples from Couperin to Strauss. Such observation leads to a number of generalizations: vii is best considered as V; iii and $I_4^6$ are often contrapuntal elaborations of V; secondary dominants do not disturb the tonality; the Neapolitan chord is almost always found in the first inversion; pivot chords are discernable in all modulations, from those without chromatic alteration to those that are extremely sudden; the simpler the analysis, the better; and so on. Piston argues that the study of music literature also allows the student to observe the relation of chords and nonharmonic tones to melody, rhythm, texture, and dynamics. He therefore not only provides numerous musical examples himself, but encourages the student to consult whole compositions "so that the chord may be seen and heard in its entire context."[8] The author provides a start in this direction by concluding the book with harmonic analyses of ten complete pieces and extended fragments. These analyses reveal the skillful interaction of musical elements that one finds in good music. Naturally ambiguities arise: is the final cadence of Bach's choral, "Christus ist erstanden," an authentic cadence in the tonic or a half cadence in the subdominant? is the best harmonic explanation for m. 21 of the Haydn "Minuetto" V, bVI, iv, or ii°? The principles of harmony and counterpoint are clearly not rules that composers slavishly follow, but rather the background of musical meaning against which each composer finds his individual expression.

These concepts are familiar enough today, but in 1933 they were quite original. Ross Lee Finney writes of *Principles of Harmonic Analysis*, "It stimulated a great deal of new musical thought and gave the student a new technic for analyzing musical scores of the past two centuries."[9] How did Piston come by these ideas? In essence, it would seem, they derived from the pragmatism of C. S. Pierce and William James. Whether Piston actually read Pierce or James is not of decisive importance, for their writings had an enormous impact on the intellectual life of New England and Harvard in particular during the first quarter of the twentieth century. Piston's contention that a chord acquires meaning by means of a rational relationship to its surrounding context bears close resemblance to Pierce's theory that a sign is meaningful in virtue of its relation to a pattern of conduct. Similarly, Piston's empirical search for harmonic principles is methodologically akin to James's work in ethical behavior. Piston, however, is not as radically empirical as either Pierce or James. He acknowledges the indefinable, subjective part of artistic experience—the "content" of a work of art—and in this respect he is closer to latter day pragmatists like John Dewey and C. I. Lewis, who was a contemporary at Harvard. But a broad perspective allows us to rank Piston's contribution to music theory with Pierce's linguistics and James's ethics as well as Dewey's aesthetics and Lewis's logic.

The originality of Piston's achievement is not belittled by analogous developments in contemporary French theory much as James is not minimized by Bergson. Further, Piston's debt to Walter Spalding and Arthur Foote's *Modern Harmony in its Theory and Practice* (New York, 1905, revised 1924) offers additional proof for speaking of a distinctly New England approach to music theory. This debt is especially evident in Piston's *Harmony* (New York, 1941) which owes much to the Spalding-

Foote text in its format, its terminology, and its approach. Piston even adopts some of Spalding's musical illustrations: Mendelssohn's *Midsummer Night's Dream Overture* for a plagal cadence with a minor subdominant; Beethoven's *Piano Concerto*, Op. 37, for a dominant ninth; and Brahms's *Intermezzo*, Op. 119, No. 1, for a complete thirteenth chord. Piston began his teaching career as an assistant to Spalding's harmony classes, and was thereby thoroughly familiar with *Modern Harmony*. Spalding's appreciation text, *Music: an Art and a Language* (New York, 1920) also seems to have left its mark on Piston. For instance, Piston's ambition to find the perfect balance between expression and form, and his claim that "the two fundamental values in music are melody and form,"[10] echo concepts voiced by Spalding in his appreciation text.[11] Spalding, a contemporary of John Dewey, seems to have helped point the way towards Piston's pragmatic sensibility.

Whereas *Principles* is intended for the advanced student of harmony, *Harmony* is for the beginner. It is a longer, more basic text with exercises at the end of each chapter. Its principles and approach are those of the earlier text, but it covers some new ground, especially in the chapters entitled "The Harmonic Structure of the Phrase" and "Harmonic Rhythm." In these chapters and in his article on "Harmonic Rhythm" for the *Harvard Dictionary of Music*, Piston emphasizes the point that harmonic rhythm—the rhythmic movement of roots—is an important and often overlooked element of tonal music. It gives life to harmonic movement, provides a foil for melodic rhythm, articulates form, and "reveals important and distinctive features of style and texture."[12] This recognition has significant repercussions on Piston's view of twentieth-century music and on his own musical style as well.

Many of Piston's convictions as a harmony teacher are discernable in a 1953 review of Sessions's *Harmonic Practice*.[13] Sessions, claims Piston, is too abstract; he composes pedantic examples to illustrate observations that do not always agree with the actual practice of composers. His treatment of the leading-tone chord is likewise theoretical and ignores the fact that the chord sounds like an incomplete dominant—an empirical deduction on Piston's part. Further, Sessions treats harmonic rhythm lightly, and confuses (at times) suspensions with appoggiaturas and strong beats with upbeats (Piston also levels this last criticism at Virgil Thomson in another review[14]). Finally, Piston notes some instances of convoluted language and fussy terminology in *Harmonic Practice* (his own writing style, like his musical style, is a model of clarity and precision). Notwithstanding these many criticisms, the review ultimately affirms the value of Sessions's text. Piston is even more positive about Sessions's Norton lectures of 1968–69, *Questions about Music*, although here too he objects to Sessions's assertion that roots have been superseded in twentieth-century music.[15]

Piston's treatment of counterpoint and orchestration is even more empirical than his treatment of harmony for the reason that composers have shown less conformity in their contrapuntal and orchestral practices. *Counterpoint* (New York, 1947) is essentially the study of principles of eighteenth-century counterpoint, and especially of Bach. "This harmonic, rhythmic, instrumental attitude toward the contrapuntal texture is not only typical of Bach's immediate predecessors, but one may safely assert that most composers after Bach, including those of the present century, have looked up to his manner as the ideal of contrapuntal technique."[16] Medieval counterpoint, on the other hand, "has ceased to exert an active influence on our music." As for the Franco-Flemish school, Piston refers students to the studies of such scholars as Jeppesen, Morris, and A. Tillman Merritt, to whom this text is dedicated. *Counterpoint* is a particularly concise and lively text, and is neither pedantic nor old-fashioned. Three of its eleven chapters, for instance, discuss aspects of the single melodic line.

*Orchestration* (New York, 1955) benefits from Piston's fastidious ear, his easy familiarity with orchestral scores, and his thorough knowledge of instruments, as exemplified by his drawing of the French horn and his remarks about triple-tonguing the trumpet. Again, the method is empirical and the text's observations are based on a critical appreciation of the orchestral uses of other composers. Piston urges composers to investigate a work like Carlos Salzedo's *Modern Study of the Harp*, but such an approach is obviously antithetical to his own. Since *Orchestration* is a practical guide for the composer, however, Piston does set some of the capabilities and limitations of the instruments in a theoretical context. Moreover, he also expresses some value judgments, as when he steers the composer away from the up-beat harp glissando, the triangle trill, and the saxophone (as played today). In this sense *Orchestration* is different from the other textbooks. It is also distinctive in its use of examples from the work of twentieth-century composers, including Bartók, Schoenberg, Berg, Shostakovich, and Britten. To judge by the musical examples from his textbooks, Piston thought that the heights of counterpoint, harmony, and orchestration were attained, respectively, in the eighteenth-century (Bach, Handel, Haydn, Mozart), the nineteenth-century (Beethoven, Chopin, Brahms), and the early twentieth century (Strauss, Debussy, Ravel, Stravinsky). His own music would seem to reflect this belief.

Piston's textbooks point the way towards "a comprehensive, philosophical, deductive exposition of musical practice as seen in the works of composers right up to the middle of the present century,"[17] something that Piston saw as one of the pressing needs of his time. He himself hoped to write a book on contemporary harmonic and contrapuntal practices, but this ambition went unfulfilled. Privately, he made harmonic reductions of twentieth-century music by Debussy, Griffes, Bartók, Webern, Prokofiev, Sondoval, and others.[18] He also gave seminars on modern music at Harvard. But his most comprehensive survey of contemporary musical practices is only the four-page chapter entitled "The Twentieth Century" that concludes the 1933 *Principles*. Here Piston specifies the evolutionary nature of twentieth-century music by noting harmonic deviations found in the music of Puccini, Chabrier, Debussy, Strauss, and other transitional figures. He also shows how their use of unresolved dissonances becomes an important contrapuntal principle with contemporary composers. When describing such contemporary trends as artificial scales, polytonality, and atonality, his empirical mind makes refreshing distinctions between theoretical intent and actual experience. In general, Piston finds that twentieth-century music tends to emphasize one or another of the musical elements: counterpoint (Hindemith, Toch, Schoenberg, Berg), harmony (Schoenberg's Op. 16, No. 3), rhythm (Stravinsky, Bartók), and sound (Webern, Varèse, Mossolov's *Iron Foundry*, Honegger's *Pacific 231*). For Piston this has led to an increase of technical resources but also limitations of one sort or another. Still, good music can survive such limitations, as Piston makes explicit in a 1961 newspaper article: "Values such as beauty of sound, melody, design, expert workmanship, and rhythmic vitality are to be found in good music but a given piece will not necessarily contain them all."[19] The one indispensable attribute of good music, Piston continues, is that it communicate.

Piston's major harmony text, *Harmony*, makes even fewer references to contemporary practice than *Principles*. Encouraged by Norton Press to update the book, Piston wrote a chapter entitled "Extension of Tonality" for the third edition in 1962, but ironically this chapter deals mostly with the extension of the secondary dominant principle as seen in the work of common practice composers. Piston finally agreed to treat modern harmonic principles more extensively for the fourth edition in collaboration with a former student, Mark DeVoto, but he died shortly thereafter. There is conflicting evidence as to how enthused Piston was about the project in the first place.[20] In any case, the section entitled *After Common Practice* with which the fourth edition concludes is essentially the work of DeVoto, and is best considered as such. In fact, although DeVoto makes use of Piston's teaching and conversation for this section, he feels certain that Piston "would have hated many of the things I did to his book, taken in isolation; I think that had he considered them all as a whole, he would have accepted the motivations behind them."[21]

The few articles that Piston wrote often take twentieth-century music as their subject. They are extremely thoughtful and illuminating, and it is regrettable that they are not as well-known as the theory books. Most important are three articles that Piston wrote in the late 1950s concerning Schoenberg's twelve-tone method: "Thoughts on the Chordal Concept,"[22] "Problems of Intonation in the Performance of Contemporary Music,"[23] and "More Views on Serialism."[24] Although written during a time when Schoenberg's methods were hotly contested, Piston's attitude is coolly sympathetic. It should be remembered that Piston made use of the twelve-tone method himself, and even recommended it to other composers.[25] In the third edition of *Harmony*, he calls the twelve-tone system "probably the most important musical event of the first half of the century."[26] Even so, Piston recognized, as these articles show, that Schoenberg's method poses tricky problems.

"Thoughts on the Chordal Concept" mentions Schoenberg only at the end. It first raises a basic, philosophical question: how do we come to know the meaning of a chord? Piston takes for this inquiry an unusual four-note chord and then explores different ways to interpret it: as an arrangement of particular intervals, as a combination of two familiar chords, as a chord with nonharmonic tones, and as a chord derived from an artificial scale. Each explanation is persuasive but inconclusive, for the meaning of the chord must ultimately be determined by its context— which in this case happens to be a Bach fugue. As Piston writes in the much earlier *Principles*, "The most important observation about a given chord does not concern its make-up as regards intervals between the notes, etc., but rather what its relation is to the rest of the music."[27] The identical chord can mean one thing in Bach and quite another in Schoenberg, a point Piston humorously illustrates by placing the aforementioned chord in a twelve-tone texture scored for Eb clarinet, 2 basset horns, and heckelphone. Its meaning here is elusive and obscure, bringing Piston to the following observation:

> We have the right to judge unfamiliar music against the background of conventional usage, and to find in it musical meaning in so far as it appears to have a relationship to what we feel to be musical sense. But we must realize that usage is a powerful force against the introduction of new sounds in music, and that intelligent appraisal or analysis cannot be made without consideration of the composer's intent.[28]

The other two articles reach conclusions similarly evasive and tolerant. In "Problems in Intonation," Piston ponders the discrepancy between the tradition of wind and string playing that teaches the modification of leading-tones, thirds, and accidentals, and the twelve-tone theory that asserts the equal importance of each note. If an instrumentalist brings tonal nuance to a twelve-tone phrase, is he disclosing the music's meaning or is he obscuring the composer's message? This question is further complicated by the fact that composers of twelve-tone music seem to have very different expectations in this regard. Again Piston counsels a balanced understanding of common usage and individual intention tantamount, incidentally, to his own aspirations as a composer.

"More Views on Serialism" was written in response to an article by Peter Stadlen, a friend and associate of Webern's. Stadlen's article, "Serialism Reconsidered,"[29] argues that Schoenberg's method is harmonically inadequate and inconsistent, and that chordal meaning in twelve-tone music is incomprehensible. This assault on Schoenberg prompted responses from Piston, Sessions,[30] and Roberto Gerhard.[31] All three defend harmonic procedure in twelve-tone music both theoretically—by analogies to conventional tonal music—and empirically—by references to the varied and significant achievements of Schoenberg, Berg, and Webern. Unlike Sessions and Gerhard, however, Piston shares some common ground with Stadlen. First, Piston sympathizes with Stadlen's desire to hear the harmonic logic of twelve-tone music. "It is not necessary that the means serving the composer in writing his music be detected and followed in detail by the listener," Piston writes, but "a knowledge of the composer's method adds to one's aesthetic appreciation of the music, it is true."[32] Second, Piston himself observes a limitation of the twelve-tone method: the absence of harmonic rhythm.

> The sensation of root change is a tonal one and so perhaps it is not wanted. But its loss is an impoverishment in rhythmic resources, not to be compensated for by intricate counterpoints of melodic rhythmic patterns. The constant presence of all twelve tones creates a motionless harmonic texture just as it previously did in styles of overdone chromaticism.[33]

The greatest problem posed by the twelve-tone method, then, is not a chordal one as Stadlen would have it, but rather a rhythmic one. Significantly, Piston does not deprive himself this resource in his own twelve-tone music, a subject that awaits further study.

Piston's ambivalent attitude towards the twelve-tone method is expressed in yet another article, "Can Music be Nationalistic?"[34] Here Piston writes, "We are waiting for a genius to come along and tell us how, for example, twelve-tone technique and electronic music are related to a great mass of musical meaning."[35] Since this "great mass of musical meaning" includes tonality, a serious conflict arises, one that Piston, like Copland and Stravinsky, confronts in some of his own music. It is interesting to see Piston speak approvingly of electronic music. In the same year, 1961, he tells Russell Kerr, "Even in electronic music one at times hears something that has musical meaning. . . . Sometimes combining these tapes with other instruments such as a solo violin, or using them with the dance, is quite successful."[36] On the other hand, he humorously suggests to Kerr that music written by a computer would be best appreciated by another Univac. Piston also disapproved of aleatoric music. "What can be more aleatoric than the risk a composer takes by having one performer play it, then another performer play it? . . . The only objection I have to self-conscious aleatoric music is that I think it's awfully sad for a composer to abdicate his responsibilities."[37]

Only once does Piston refer to specific composers or works in the previous discussions of the twelve-tone method. In "More Views on Serialism," he writes:

> In the light of this freedom [of harmonic procedures in serial technique] it is at least permissible to view the tonal aspects of Berg's *Violin Concerto* as something more than a hangover from an outmoded style or nullification of serial principles. And it makes a vast difference that the unprecedented strictness and rarification of Webern's personal style is self-imposed and not produced by rigidity in the twelve-tone system.[38]

Berg's *Violin Concerto* is prominently featured in Piston's *Orchestration*, where it is used to illustrate not only violin but viola, clarinet, bass clarinet, bassoon, trombone, and harp techniques. Piston makes no secret of his admiration for these passages, for example, "The evocative color of the chalumeau tones, combined with harp and solo violin, create a fascinating atmosphere in the opening measures of Alban Berg's *Violin Concerto*."[39] In contrast, *Orchestration* cites Schoenberg only for instances of unusual and rarely used practices, and makes no mention of Webern whatsoever. As mentioned earlier,[40] Piston concluded after intensive study in the 1930s that Schoenberg is less strange than he at first appears. But it seems certain that Berg came closer to Piston's ideal balance of expression and form than either Schoenberg or Webern.

*Orchestration* cites Stravinsky more often than Schoenberg, Berg, or any other composer except Strauss. Piston's occasional writings about Stravinsky stress his brilliance as an orchestrator. In a review of the *Symphony of Psalms*, he writes, "This stimulating instrumentation is handled with his customary skill and artistry. One forgets that the orchestra which he has abandoned is the normal one and feels relief rather than regret at the complete lack of violins and violas," and later, "These persistent rhythmic figures in their peculiar gaunt orchestral settings lend the work some of the earthy and elemental character found in the music which will always represent the real Stravinsky, notably *Le Sacre du Printemps, Les Noces, Mavra,* and *Oedipus.*"[41] Similarly, in an article entitled "Stravinsky's Rediscoveries," Piston ponders Stravinsky's joy at discovering a D major triad at a critical moment in *Oedipus*:

> The particular and marvelous combination of tones in question owed its unique character to the exact distribution of the tones in relation to the spaces between them, to the exact placing of the instrumental voices in reference to the special sound of a given note on a given instrument, to the dynamic level indicated, and to the precise moment of sounding of the chord. . . . When we realize that such precision marks Stravinsky's approach to every technical and esthetic problem connected with musical composition, we begin to see why his music has been so great a stimulation to other composers.[42]

Eric White, Stravinsky's biographer, found these observations particularly insightful,[43] and Piston himself was fond of repeating this story.[44]

Although Piston actively supported a number of societies and leagues for American composers, he wrote very little about their music. The most notable exception is his 1934 article on Roy Harris.[45] Piston may have hoped to present a more balanced appraisal of Harris than those in general circulation in the early 1930s. In this he succeeds. While he commends Harris's classical approach to form, and notes music of real power and beauty, he criticizes Harris's strict avoidance of sequence and regular rhythmic pulse, as well as some of his contrapuntal efforts. Piston is especially satiric about Harris as the supposedly one-hundred-per-cent American composer, noting the influence of Strauss, Mahler, and Franck on his music, and even finding the German love ditty, "Ach, wie ist's möglich," in the slow movement of the *Sextet*. "Of course, your one-hundred-percenters say it is a gospel hymn—they might just as well say a West Point football song. The Teutonic flavor of this movement is heightened by the composer's harmonization. Harris would probably be surprised to hear of any foreign or German implications in his work, but more than one listener has found suggestions of a wooden-shoe dance toward the end."[46]

His sentimentality notwithstanding, Harris may well be the American composer of his generation whose achievement comes closest to Piston. It seems, however, that Piston had greater respect for Copland. *Orchestration*, for instance, cites Copland as often as it does Berg, Milhaud, and Shostakovich(the only other American music in *Orchestration* are single examples by Creston and Riegger). When on sabbatical from Harvard, it was Copland that Piston invited to teach his classes. But as Piston tells one interviewer, they were not in total agreement on artistic matters:

Copland and I had a friendly war about American music. Aaron and I were very thick.
We practically grew up together. He had hopes of producing an American music that
was just as recognizable as French and German music. I told him that America had
so many different nationalities that it would be nearly impossible. I felt the only
definition of American music was that written by an American. He had to agree, but
he felt there ought to be a vernacular.[47]

Since Piston believed that the use of folk song was based "on a naively
mistaken conception of the nature of musical expression,"[48] this may
have alienated him from such works as *El Salón México, Billy the Kid,* and
a *Lincoln Portrait.* In fact, the Copland examples in *Orchestration* bear
out assertions[49] that Piston admired above all Copland's earliest works:
*Music for the Theatre,* the *Piano Concerto,* and the *Symphonic Ode.*

Similarly, Piston probably had little use for the folkloric styles of
Ives and Thomson.[50] It is worth remembering, however, that Thomson
and Piston were almost exact contemporaries, and that they had the same
teachers: Davison, Spalding, Hill, Dukas, and Boulanger. This shared
background prompted an interest in each other's work, about which they
had mixed feelings. Piston disliked Thomson's simplicity and buffoo-
nery,[51] but admired his flair for opera.[52] For his part, Thomson thought
Piston's music "an easy way out, a way to show-off everything he knew,
a way to be modern and respectable, and another way of concealing the
Italian," and yet he found some slow movements from the 1940s direct
in their emotional appeal.[53] Their mutual respect survived Thomson's
ridicule of neoclassicism and composer-professors in *The State of Music*
(a book Piston actually rather liked) and Piston's attack on journalistic
music criticism in a review of a collection of Thomson's newspaper articles, *The Musical Scene.* Although it was Thomson himself who recommended that Piston review *The Musical Scene* for *Modern Music,* its
editor, Minna Lederman, rejected a first draft on grounds of supposed
harshness and hostility. She wrote Piston, "I don't expect a libel suit
exactly, but I can easily forsee consequences."[54] Piston revised the article, but first wrote back to Lederman, "No, there is no issue between
me and Virgil, and I am not trying to start a feud, public or private.
. . . My article is not half so edgy as many of Virgil's."[55] Actually, Piston's satiric tone in this instance is much like Thomson's:

The newspaper employs the music critic for his entertainment value, to attract
readers and sell papers, the way the comic strips do. His articles must therefore be
interesting and zestful. That means get out the axe and criticize, because there is
nothing the general reader loves more than to see someone lambasted in print, especially someone with a high reputation. This necessity doesn't impair the product's
usefulness for quoting, however, since even the most violently adverse write-up will
lend itself to quotations out of context which sound perfectly fine. Moreover, there is

no field better than this one to prove the old saying that every knock is a boost. It is a matter of history that careers of performers and composers are rarely affected by professional criticism, complimentary or otherwise.[56]

As for Thomson's articles, Piston finds the operatic reviews "by far the best."
In this same article, Piston writes:

> Criticism of one composer's work by another is most valuable as self-revelation on the part of the composer-critic. As a composer he spends his life working out as definite a pattern as he can for the approach to composition. Unless he is a weak spirit he will in the nature of things come to feel that his way is right and that other ways are partly or wholly wrong.[57]

This perspective helps explain a general reluctance on Piston's part to discuss other composers. We can nonetheless supplement the preceding discussions of Harris and others with a brief survey of Piston's likes and dislikes based on some first-hand as well as second-hand sources. In a review of Paul Henry Lang's *Music in Western Civilization*, for instance, Piston cites Roussel and Holst as two outstanding composers of the twentieth century.[58] Of his own generation, he had special respect, according to Harold Shapero, for Hindemith;[59] and in a letter to a young admirer, Piston expresses a favorable opinion of Orff:

> As for Carl Orff, I do not know him personally, so I cannot say what I think of him as a man. However, I admire his music, especially as it stands out as individual in times of conformity to stylistic trends.[60]

Other sources report that Piston thought Sessions too convoluted[61] and Chanler too thin.[62] Upon receiving a copy of the Carter *Piano Sonata*, he wrote, "It is indeed a fine work, an excellent piece of creative writing for the piano, music of beauty and nobility."[63] Years later, he also expressed fascination with the Carter *Piano Concerto*,[64] enigmatically adding, "I had some pretty funny pupils."[65] Takemitsu's *November Steps* fascinated him too, while the extensive program notes, musical quotations, and so-called blues elements of Tippett's *Third Symphony* put him off.[66] One friend remembers that Piston appreciated the music of Dallapiccola, Henze, and Lutosławski.[67] As for Boulez, Piston tells an interviewer:

> I'm beginning to see relations between these sounds and the sounds we're accustomed to hear in music. Of course, there's no sign that these relations are what he wanted. There are always two parties to communication, and the hearer contributes as much as the composer.[68]

Piston once told Shapero that "he thought Boulez was a real musician but Stockhausen was a fake."[69] Shapero guesses that Piston rejected such composers as Steve Reich and Philip Glass, but there is evidence to suggest that he might have tolerantly viewed their achievements in the tradition of nineteenth-century exoticism.[70]

Finally, in one article, "Teaching as a Composer's Craft,"[71] Piston defends college teaching as a congenial life style for some composers. Although teaching can be mentally exhausting, it can also replenish the composer. And in two short articles, "What a Young Composer Should Know"[72] and "The Composer Must Stay Individual,"[73] as well as in various interviews, Piston counsels young composers to both explore new musical trends and preserve and develop their individuality. In other words, the young composer is advised to find his own balance between form and expression, a balance which Piston found in all great musical works through pragmatic observation.

# Conclusion:
# Piston, Humanist

Piston kept a humble and respectful distance from the question of the creative process. Only once, in fact, did he publicly discuss this subject in any depth, and that was with Margaret Fairbanks in 1967. He gets a general concept, he tells her, and then begins to write. "The initial stages are the most mysterious, but one shouldn't wait too long for this." One note will eventually lead to another.

> You always keep an open mind on this all through the piece. I used to tell my students, as soon as you put down one note you've changed the conditions, and then you have to consider the others in relation to this, whereas before you put it down, you're free. On the other hand, you've got to be ready to throw that away, and that takes courage if you've done quite a lot of good looking pages. . . . I write about ten times as much music as I keep.

There are, however, not too many discarded pages among the Piston sketchbooks in the Library of Congress and the Boston Public Library. Piston mostly worked, in pencil, on a single draft, erasing as he went along. He would often joke that it would take him one hour to decide upon a note, and another hour to decide to erase it. This is, of course, a comic exaggeration. The entire ballet score to the *Incredible Flutist*, for instance, was written within a few months. And how often was Piston carried away by a melodic flow as he was, at times, in writing the *Sixth Symphony*? But Piston did indeed work cautiously. His distinctive penmanship was immaculately refined, and his holographs often served publishers as their final copies (this, in fact, was a written agreement with AMP). He never needed to revise, except when a performer requested it, as with the *Flute Concerto*. And finally, each composition by Piston shows the same careful attention to detail, whether this be precise dynamic and expressive markings, or thoughtfully cogent tonal and formal schemes.

Piston was, at any rate, a steady worker, and he averaged about three major works every two years. In the half century that marked his creative life, from 1925 to 1976, he composed seventy-six works of impressive diversity: many orchestral works, including eight symphonies and a ballet; a band work; two choral works; concertos, and the like, for violin, viola, cello, string quartet, flute, clarinet, English horn, harp, piano, two pianos, and organ; a string duo, trio, and sextet; five string quartets; a piano quartet and quintet, and two piano trios; a wind quintet; and assorted chamber pieces, including works for piano and flute, oboe, violin, viola, and cello. The traditional nature of this oeuvre is partly due to Piston's conservative tastes, but also due to the fact that nearly all of these works were commissioned. Piston welcomed commissions not only for their financial rewards, which were usually slight or nonexistent (although sometimes significant) but, more importantly, because they promised a performance. Although his fabulous inner ear allowed him to compose away from any instrument, Piston found nothing as edifying as a live performance of his own music; and he early gave up playing and conducting his compositions so as to be able to hear what others would do with them. Throughout his career, he was fortunate to have great musicians—from Koussevitzky and Laurent to Rostropovich and Accardo—play his music, and he rarely wrote works for second-rate artists. And yet Piston was responsive to all performances of his music, including those by amateurs; and his music—with such obvious exceptions as the concertos—has the virtue of suiting a wide spectrum of players. Similarly, his music can appeal, I think, to listeners of varying degrees of sophistication.

It is sometimes charged that "Piston never changed," but this indictment unfairly confuses style with stasis. In this author's investigation into Piston's sizeable output, the thought, "it's the same old Piston," (to quote the composer in a typical moment of self-deprecation) occurred only rarely. One reason for the diversity is that every instrument, and therefore every medium, draws a distinctive and special response from Piston. Furthermore, Piston's work constantly evolves, and may even be said to comprise four periods. The music of his first period, 1926 to 1938, is neoclassical in a mannered and surreal way, and is international in style, although distinguished by its Yankee verve and Boston chic. This early music is often referred to as Gallic or Parisian, although this writer considers it at least as close to Germans like Hindemith and Toch, and Italians like Casella, Petrassi, Rieti, and especially Malipiero, as it is to Frenchmen like Roussel, Milhaud, and Honegger. In the next period, 1939 to 1945, Piston's deeply felt response to the War brings him closer to Stravinsky and Schoenberg (he writes his first "twelve-tone" composition in

1940), as well as to patriotic feelings. The smooth and relaxed works from 1946 to 1960 have a truly classical poise, and glow with a folksy humor and a serene melancholy. In his final period, 1961 to 1976, Piston returns to a more mannered and surreal style, although this music becomes, especially after 1965, more and more romantic, personal, and complex. But even two works of the same genre and period—the *First* and *Second String Quartet*, for instance, or the *Fifth* and *Sixth Symphony*—can be significantly different from each other.

There are, however, some constant features that undeniably go to characterize Piston's style. It is difficult to generalize in the matter of technique, for Piston used all manner of melody, rhythm, harmony, and texture in the course of his long career, and did so in no strikingly original way. But one steady and important aspect of Piston's music is his ability to give an advanced twentieth-century idiom the sort of motion and direction one finds in eighteenth and nineteenth-century classics, and this he does by asserting such principles as pulse, melodic curve, harmonic rhythm, tonal design,and symmetrical form. In fact, all the musical elements, including dynamics and color, are responsive to form and movement. Another feature of Piston's art is its cosmopolitanism, for it is nourished not only by an encyclopedic knowledge of Western classical music, but by a love for the folk and popular musics of Europe, the East, and the Americas—most notably marches, tangos, ragtime, jazz, and New England country music. This eclecticism shows through a bit in Piston's early years, but is soon thoroughly assimilated into a markedly individual style. Finally, one might mention the sense of struggle that pervades all of Piston's work: the conflict between clarity and confusion, restraint and sensuality, wit and gloom, humanity and loneliness. And yet the music is full of a calm and a confidence rarely found in twentieth-century music, and that is in harmony with Piston's own quiet and settled life in which reading, chess playing, and gardening—and an occasional evening out—were the principal diversions from study and work.

Piston might have preferred the term humanist to surrealist, nationalist, classicist, romanticist, pragmatist, or any other label. His humanism attracted him to the writings, among contemporaries, of Lamont, Huxley, Gide, Camus, Sartre, Moravia, and Lin Yu-tang. However, it found expression neither in leftist politics nor in religious orthodoxy, but in an open-minded, but critically astute, interest in the great art and philosophy of all times and places. It was a Harvard humanism, indebted to the writings of Irving Babbitt, but more accurately expressed, as mentioned before, in the novels of Aiken, Marquand, and Cozzens. (Piston's ability to combine Aiken's sensuousness, Marquand's wit, and Cozzens's elegance makes him, perhaps, a greater artist than any of these.) One also finds comparable, though distinct, sensibilities in the poetry of a number of Harvard graduates including Aiken and Wheelwright (both of whom were friends of Piston's) as well as Eliot, Fitts, MacLeish, and cummings. But the refined atmosphere of Harvard and Belmont was countered, for Piston, by a childhood in Rockland, Maine, and a summer home in South Woodstock, Vermont; and this gave his music, and his person, an austere and rustic temperament reminiscent of such older American poets as Robinson, Sandburg, and Frost. In the light of both backgrounds, Piston's admiration for Greta Garbo and Humphrey Bogart is significant, for these film actors embody, much as Piston's music does, a blend of exquisite sophistication and earthy humanity.

As for modern art, Piston doubtless knew that Louise Nevelson, like the poet Edna St. Vincent Millay, grew up in his native Rockland; and that Homer and Wyeth did much of their work in that region. But American painters more comparable to Piston would be Stuart Davis, or, even more so, Milton Avery. Some magazine reproductions in the Piston Collection indicate that he preferred the paintings of Modigliani to those of any American artist. Indeed, Piston's attraction to such Italian humanists as Modigliani, Moravia, and Malipiero warrants special study. Piston never spoke of modern architecture, and if he took a special interest in Gropius's arrival at Harvard, this had gone unrecorded. The Harvard tradition of philosophical pragmatism, however, seems to have profoundly influenced his pedagogical and critical writings.

These writings help us to better understand what Piston meant by the perfect balance between expression and form. This is tantamount first to a balance between melody and design, the two elements Piston held to be fundamental values to music. A discordant relationship between melody and design can lead, on the one hand, to unshaped emotion, and on the other, to rigid contrivance. He thought Harris rare among American composers in his desire to avoid either of these pitfalls. But Piston's "perfect balance" may also be said to be a balance between individuality and common usage. Here again, it behooves a composer to avoid the extremes of either obscurantism or banality. Piston felt he approached "the perfect balance" with three works written about 1950: the *Duo* for viola and cello, the *Fourth Symphony*, and the *Fourth Quartet*. This suggests different theories concerning the balance of expression and form as it relates to Piston's entire opus. First, Piston's career may be viewed as a slow evolution from the 1926 *Three Pieces*, with its emphasis on design and common usage, to the 1976 *String Quartet Concerto*, with its emphasis on melody and individuality. According to this scheme, the works from 1946 to 1960, and especially those from around 1950, would provide a harmonious middle ground between the formalism of Piston's early works and the hermeticism of his later ones. A second interpretation, equally valid it seems to me, would find a series of individual accomplishments that conform to no chronological pattern. Such a theory might argue, for instance, that the 1937 *Piano Concertino* comes nearer the perfect balance than either the more difficult *First Symphony* of 1937 or the more popular *Incredible Flutist* of 1938. Yet another theory might view the *Fourth Symphony* as yet another step towards the balance one finds in a work like the 1966 *Cello Variations*.

Piston once stated, with characteristic humility, that he did not write for posterity, and that he did not expect to be remembered after his death. If this is true, it is to his credit that he could write such noble music with his eye to the present. But Piston is indeed a memorable figure in American music history. Copland often implied as much, as when he wrote, in a letter to this author dated 5 August 1977, "In my opinion, his music represents a thoroughly professional contribution, thereby supplying a model to the younger generation." This professionalism is distinguished not only by Piston's technical brilliance—perhaps the most formidable of any composer born in America—but by his cosmopolitanism and his individuality, his knowledge of the past and his sense of adventure, his broad culture and his unflagging labor. In his book on American music, Wilfred Mellers intends to slight Piston by pairing his photograph with one of Edward MacDowell. But this is a fair comparison, and one that the composer would probably not have objected to; he doubtless appreciated MacDowell's achievements as much as his own limitations. Piston's accomplishment might one day be rated even higher than MacDowell's: time has already revealed how enduringly fresh and beautiful the early works are. But in the meantime, one might say of Piston's music, to use one of the composer's expressions, "It'll be around."

# Appendix A

## Awards and Honors

This is a list of the awards and honors that Piston received from his graduation from Harvard in 1924 to his death in 1976. Most of these certificates and medals are now in the Piston Collection of the Boston Public Library. Piston may have received other awards as well, including some medals that were stolen when his home was ransacked in the early 1970s.

As much as Piston may have prized these honors, he was anything but sanctimonious about them. Upon learning that his stolen medals were probably melted down and irretrievable, he told the police, "Now I can't park anywhere I want to in Boston." And when he would be asked to make a speech on receiving some honorary award, he would often simply tell a New England joke in his wry, deliberate, twangy Maine accent. At one such dinner, given by the French Embassy in honor of his election to "Officier dans l'ordre des Arts et des Lettres," he told the following story.

I was driving up to Maine from Vermont, and came to White River Junction, and there was a branch in the road, and both of them said, "to White River Junction." There was a farmer leaning up against the fence there, and I said to him, "Does it make any difference which of the roads I take to get to White River Junction?" And he said, "Not to me it don't."

So I took one and got through to White River Junction, and then I got across New Hampshire, which of course is a wasteland in the opinion of Maine and Vermont, and I got up around Skowhegan and I saw three branches in the road, and I didn't know which to take to get to Millinocket. So I looked around, and sure enough there was another farmer leaning up against the fence. And I said, "Can you tell me how to get to Millinocket?" And he says, "Don't move a goddamned inch."

In the same 1973 radio interview in which Piston retold this story, he also spoke about his medal from the Vermont Council on the Arts.

Well, that was the surprise of my life, you see. We'd been living summers in Vermont since 1933 or 4, and nobody ever said anything about my writing music. Last year, a year ago, the telephone rang, and a fellow introduced himself, "This is the Vermont Council on the Arts, and we'd like to give you a medal." I dropped dead, but I survived. He said, "Yes, we're going to have a governor's dinner, and it will be at the Woodstock Inn, the 29th of September." And I said, "That's very nice. I'll be there." Well, I had a communication a little bit later, in which they said, "We discovered that you live in the little town of South Woodstock" (which has only one street, but it has a country school with a large room) "so we want to have the dinner there, so you won't have to go to Woodstock'' (which is five miles away). We struggled down there, and there were 150 people from all over the state of Vermont, and here was the Governor and various other officials.

So I made a few remarks, which they urged me to do. And I told this about Vermonters, how they didn't let on, but they knew it all the time, see. And I said, "I'm going to tell you a Vermont story that I bet you haven't heard: I read it in the Maine Farmer's Almanac. It's about Mark Twain. It seems that Mark Twain came to give a lecture in Vermont, and he told all his stories, and there wasn't so much as a smile; they all sat there, poker-faced. And he was worried. He said to his wife, he says, "I don't know what's the matter," he said, "I told my funniest stories and nobody laughed. I'm going to go out in the crowd when they're going out to see if I can overhear anything." So he went out, and sure enough there was a couple getting into a buggy, and the man was saying, 'You know, Mabel, that speaker was real good. It was all I could do to keep from laughing.' " And you know, those Vermonters had not heard that story.

Piston's awards and honors follow:

A.B. in music, summa cum laude, Phi Beta Kappa, Harvard University—1924
John Knowles Paine Travelling Fellowship, Harvard University—1924
Guggenheim Fellowship—1935
Coolidge Medal—1935
Certificate of membership, National Institute of Arts and Letters—1938
Certificate of fellowship, Academy of Arts and Sciences—1941
New York Music Critics Circle Award (for *Symphony No. 2*)—1945
Honorary Doctor of Music, Philadelphia Academy of Arts and Sciences—1946
Honorary Doctor of Music, Bowdoin College—1948
Pulitzer Prize (for *Symphony No. 3*)—1948
Boston Symphony Mark M. Horblit Prize (for *Symphony No. 3*)—1948
Honorary Doctor of Music, Harvard University—1952
Naumburg Award (for *Symphony No. 4*)—1953
Honorary Doctor of Music, New York College of Music—1953
Award for Musical Composition, Huntington Hartford Foundation—1954
Certificate of membership, American Institute of Arts and Letters—1955
Certificate for 25 years of service to the University, Harvard University—1957
New York Music Critics Circle Award (for *Concerto for Viola and Orchestra*)—1959
Award of Merit, National Association of American Composers and Conductors—1959
Gold Medal Award, Italian-American Charitable Society—1960
Pulitzer Prize (for *Symphony No. 7*)—1961
Honorary Doctor of Music, Colby College—1962
Medal of Achievement, Brandeis University—1963
Pierian Sodality of 1808 Award—1963
New York Music Critics Circle Award (for *String Quartet No. 5*)—1964
Honorary Doctor of Fine Arts, Massachusetts College of Art—1964
Arts Award, St. Botolph Club—1965
Certificate of Award, Metropolitan Washington Board of Trade—1965
Proclamation of Walter Piston Day in the State of Maine—9 March 1965
Arts Award, Dickinson College—1966
Composer's Award, Lancaster Symphony Orchestra—1966

Distinguished Service Award, Civic Symphony Orchestra of Boston—1966
Honorary Doctor of Fine Arts, University of Maine—1967
Honorary Doctor of Music, New England Conservatory of Music—1969
Decoration, "Officier dans l'ordre des Arts et des Lettres"—1969
Governor's Award for Excellence in the Arts, Vermont Council on the Arts—1971
Honorary Doctor of Music, Boston University—1975
Acknowledgement of Outstanding Contribution, Funk & Wagnalls, Inc.—1976

# Appendix B

# Catalogue of Works by Walter Piston

There are already two fairly comprehensive catalogues of Piston's music. The first, published in 1964 by BMI, is organized alphabetically by genre, and includes the date of composition (sometimes erroneous), publisher, scoring, and duration of each work. It also features, along with 70th birthday greetings from some eminent friends, the best photographs of Piston yet to be published. A more complete list, organized chronologically by genre, was assembled by AMP shortly before the composer's death. In addition to dates, publishers, scorings, and durations, it notes movement titles, commissions, dedications, premieres, and prizes. The following catalogue, chronological throughout, lists only dates, movement titles, and publishers, but is more complete than either of these other catalogues.

| Date of Composition | Work | Publisher |
|---|---|---|
| 1925 | *Orchestra Piece* | Ms. (Library of Congress) |
| 1925 | *Three Pieces for Flute, Clarinet and Bassoon*<br>I. Allegro moderato e grazioso<br>II. Adagio<br>III. Allegro vivace | AMP |
| 1926 | *Piano Sonata*<br>I. Allegro con fuoco<br>II. Lento e sostenuto<br>III. Allegro energico | Ms. (lost?) |
| 1927 | *Minuetto in Stile Vecchio for String Quartet* | Ms. (lost?) |
| 1927 | *Symphonic Piece* | Ms. (Library of Congress) |
| 1929 | *First Suite for Orchestra*<br>I. Allegro<br>II. Andante<br>III. Allegro | AMP |

1930    *Sonata for Flute and Piano*                                   AMP
      I.   Allegro moderato e grazioso
      II.  Adagio
      III. Allegro vivace

1931    *Suite for Oboe and Piano*                                     ECS
      I.   Prelude
      II.  Sarabande
      III. Minuetto
      IV. Nocturne
      V.  Gigue

1933    *Concerto for Orchestra*                                       AMP
      I.   Allegro moderato ma energico
      II.  Allegro vivace
      III. Adagio—Allegro moderato

1933    *String Quartet No. 1*                                         AMP
      I.   Allegro
      II.  Adagio
      III. Allegro vivace

1934    *Prelude and Fugue for Orchestra*                              AMP

1935    *String Quartet No. 2*                                         GS
      I.   Lento—Allegro
      II.  Adagio molto e con espressione
      III. Allegro giusto

1935    *Trio No. 1 for Violin, Cello and Piano*                       AMP
      I.   Allegro
      II.  Adagio
      III. Allegro con brio
      IV. Allegro moderato

1937    *Concertino for Piano and Chamber Orchestra*                   AMP

1937    *Symphony No. 1*                                               AMP
      I.   Andantino quasi adagio—Allegro
      II.  Adagio
      III. Allegro con fuoco

1938    *Carnival Song for Men's Chorus and Brass Instruments*    AMP

1938    *The Incredible Flutist*                                       AMP

1939    *Suite from the Ballet "The Incredible Flutist"*               AMP

1939    *Sonata for Violin and Piano*                                  AMP
      I.   Moderato

II.   Andantino quasi adagio
III.  Allegro

| | | |
|---|---|---|
| 1939 | *Concerto No. 1 for Violin and Orchestra*<br>I.   Allegro energico<br>II.  Andantino molto tranquillo<br>III. Allegro con spirito | B&H |
| 1940 | *Chromatic Study on the Name of Bach for Organ* | HWG |
| 1941 | *Sinfonietta for Chamber Orchestra*<br>I.   Allegro grazioso<br>II.  Adagio<br>III. Allegro vivo | B&H |
| 1942 | *Fanfare for the Fighting French for Brass Instruments and Percussion* | B&H |
| 1942 | *Quintet for Flute and String Quartet*<br>I.   Allegro moderato e grazioso<br>II.  Andantino con espressione<br>III. Vivace e leggiero<br>IV.  Allegro non troppo | AMP |
| 1942 | *Interlude for Viola and Piano* | B&H |
| 1943 | *Prelude and Allegro for Organ and Strings* | AMP |
| 1943 | *Passacaglia for Piano* | TP |
| 1943 | *Symphony No. 2*<br>I.   Moderato<br>II.  Adagio<br>III. Allegro | AMP |
| 1944 | *Fugue on a Victory Tune for Orchestra* | Ms. (Library of Congress) |
| 1944 | *Partita for Violin, Viola and Organ*<br>I.   Prelude<br>II.  Sarabande<br>III. Variations<br>IV.  Burlesca | AMP |
| 1944 | "Variation on a Theme by Eugene Goossens for Orchestra" | Ms. (Library of Congress) |
| 1945 | *Improvisation for Piano* | DMC |
| 1945 | *Sonatina for Violin and Harpsichord*<br>I.   Allegro leggiero | B&H |

II.  Adagio espressivo
III. Allegro vivo

1946    *Divertimento for Nine Instruments*                     BMI
    I.   Allegro
    II.  Tranquillo
    III. Vivo

1947    *String Quartet No. 3*                                   B&H
    I.   Allegro
    II.  Lento
    III. Allegro

1947    *Symphony No. 3*                                         B&H
    I.   Andantino
    II.  Allegro
    III. Adagio
    IV.  Allegro

1948    *Second Suite for Orchestra*                             AMP
    I.   Prelude
    II.  Sarabande
    III. Intermezzo
    IV.  Passacaglia and Fugue

1948    *Toccata for Orchestra*                                  B&H

1949    *Quintet for Piano and String Quartet*                   AMP
    I.   Allegro comodo
    II.  Adagio
    III. Allegro vivo

1949    *Duo for Viola and Cello*                                AMP
    I.   Allegro risoluto
    II.  Andante sereno
    III. Allegro brillante

1950    *Tunbridge Fair: Intermezzo for Symphonic Band*         B&H

1950    *Symphony No. 4*                                         AMP
    I.   Piacevole
    II.  Ballando
    III. Contemplativo
    IV.  Energico

1951    *String Quartet No. 4*                                   AMP
    I.   Soave
    II.  Adagio
    III. Leggiero vivace
    IV.  Con fuoco

1952    *Fantasy for English Horn, Harp and Strings*                 AMP

1954    *Symphony No. 5*                                             AMP
    I.   Lento—Allegro con spirito
    II.  Adagio
    III. Allegro lieto

1955    *Symphony No. 6*                                             AMP
    I.   Fluendo espressivo
    II.  Leggerissimo vivace
    III. Adagio sereno
    IV. Allegro energico

1956    *Serenata for Orchestra*                                     AMP
    I.   Con allegrezza
    II.  Con sentimento
    III. Con spirito

1956    *Quintet for Wind Instruments*                               AMP
    I.   Animato
    II.  Con tenerezza
    III. Scherzando
    IV. Allegro comodo

1957    *Concerto for Viola and Orchestra*                           AMP
    I.   Con moto moderato e flessibile
    II.  Adagio con fantasia
    III. Allegro vivo

1958    *Psalm and Prayer of David for Mixed Chorus and Seven*       AMP
    *Instruments*

1959    *Three New England Sketches*                                 AMP
    I.   Seaside
    II.  Summer Evening
    III. Mountains

1959    *Concerto for Two Pianos and Orchestra*                      AMP
    I.   Allegro non troppo
    II.  Adagio
    III. Con spirito

1960    *Concerto No. 2 for Violin and Orchestra*                    AMP
    I.   Moderato
    II.  Adagio
    III. Allegro

1960    *Symphony No. 7*                                             AMP
    I.   Con moto

II.   Adagio pastorale
III.  Allegro festevole

| 1961 | *Symphonic Prelude for Orchestra* | AMP |

| 1962 | *Lincoln Center Festival Overture for Orchestra* | AMP |

1962  *String Quartet No. 5*                             AMP
    I.   Allegro
    II.  Adagio
    III. Allegro

| 1963 | *Variations on a Theme by E. B. Hill for Orchestra* | AMP |

| 1963 | *Capriccio for Harp and String Orchestra* | AMP |

1964  *Quartet for Violin, Viola, Cello and Piano*       AMP
    I.   Leggero e scorrevole
    II.  Adagio sostenuto
    III. Allegro vivo

1964  *Sextet for Stringed Instruments*                  AMP
    I.   Adagio espressivo
    II.  Leggerissimo e vivace assai
    III. Energico

1965  *Symphony No. 8*                                   AMP
    I.   Moderato mosso
    II.  Lento assai
    III. Allegro marcato

| 1965 | *Pine Tree Fantasy for Orchestra* | AMP |

1966  *Trio No. 2 for Violin, Cello and Piano*           AMP
    I.   Capriccioso
    II.  Adagio
    III. Sostenuto con vigore

| 1966 | *Variations for Cello and Orchestra* | AMP |

| 1967 | *Concerto for Clarinet and Orchestra* | AMP |

| 1967 | *Ricercare for Orchestra* | AMP |

| 1967 | *Souvenirs for Flute, Viola and Harp* | Ms (Boston Public Library) |

| 1969 | *Ceremonial Fanfare for Brass Instruments* | AMP |

| 1970 | *Fantasia for Violin and Orchestra* | AMP |

| | | |
|---|---|---|
| 1971 | *Concerto for Flute and Orchestra* | AMP |

1972    *Duo for Cello and Piano*                    Ms. (Boston
         I.    Calmo e ritenuto                     Public Library)
         II.    Animato
         III.   Grazioso con moto

1973    *Three Counterpoints for Violin, Viola and Cello*     AMP
         I.    Espressivo con moto
         II.    Adagio sereno
         III.   Allegro spiccato

1974    "Variation on Happy Birthday"              Ms. (RCA Records)

1975    *Bicentennial Fanfare for Orchestra*         Ms. (Boston
                                                  Public Library)

1976    *Concerto for String Quartet, Wind Instruments and*   AMP
         *Percussion*

## Arrangements for Orchestra

1936    Debussy, "Clair de lune"                    Ms. (Library of
                                                  Congress)

1945    Fauré, *Prométhée,* Act II, Scene I          Ms. (Library of
                                                  Congress)

undated   Beethoven, "Adagio," *Piano Sonata* Op. 24, No. 2   Ms. (Library of
                 ("Moonlight")                                   Congress)

## Legend for Publishers

| | |
|---|---|
| AMP | Associated Music Publishers, N.Y. |
| B&H | Boosey and Hawkes, N.Y. |
| BMI | Broadcast Music Inc., N.Y. |
| ECS | E. C. Schirmer, Boston |
| GS | G. Schirmer, N.Y. |
| HWG | H. W. Gray Co., N.Y. |
| TP | Theodore Presser, N.Y. |

# Appendix C

# Discography

Piston owned a record player for most of his career, and his last stereo set, which included a Philips 202 turntable, a Sansui 350A receiver, Advent speakers, and a reel-to-reel Sony TC 353D tape recorder, was a fine, expensive unit. But Piston never took much of an interest in recordings: he was very sensitive to their lack of sound fidelity. (This certainly could not have attracted him to writing music for film, let alone television.) Moreover, Piston was particularly intrigued by the uniqueness of every performance ("What can be more aleatoric," he once asked, "than the risk a composer takes by having one performer play it, then another performer play it?"). Early in his career, it is true, he played the piano for recordings of his *Suite for Oboe and Piano* and his *Sonata for Violin and Piano*, but in later years, he was indifferent to records to the point that if a record company or a performer neglected to send him a new recording of his music, he was not likely to hear it. Compared to his library of 1,340 musical scores and 745 books, Piston's collection of 85 records does indeed seem scanty, though it significantly contained music by Varèse, Boulez, Xenakis, Wolpe, and other avant-garde composers.

Despite the composer's relative uninvolvement, the Piston discography has grown, over the years, to substantial length. All eight symphonies, much of the chamber music, and many other works have now been recorded. Record companies, however, have unfortunately neglected Piston's music from the 1960s and 1970s; and it is especially regrettable that Zabaleta, Rostropovich, Accardo, Dwyer, and others have not, as yet, recorded the concertos that Piston wrote for them. On the other hand, these and other performances are preserved on tape and housed in various archives, most notably the Library of Congress, the New York Public Library, the Boston Public Library, and Dartmouth's Hopkins Center for the Performing Arts.

The following list, however, is limited to disc recordings, and, furthermore, to those that have been issued, with but a few exceptions, in the United States. Most of these recordings are no longer commercially available (some, indeed, never were), but can often be found in good college and public libraries. All recordings are entered alphabetically by composition title. Different recordings of the same work are in chronological sequence, as are variants and reissues of the same recording. Record numbers are italicized if the recording is in stereo, and in the case of mono and stereo releases of the same recording, only stereo numbers are given. The discography also makes use of the following abbreviations:

| | |
|---|---|
| 78 | 78 rpm |
| d.c. | different coupling (for reissues) |
| -2,-3,-4 | two, three, and four-record sets, respectively |
| ees | electronically-enhanced stereo |
| SQ | stereo/quadraphonic compatible |

In both format and content, this discography is very much indebted to William D. Curtis's excellent "Piston Discography," *American Record Guide*, July, 1977, pp. 38–39, with an addendum in the July, 1977, issue, p. 42.

*Carnival Song for Men's Chorus and Brass Instruments* (1938)

Harvard Glee Club; Brass Ensemble of the Boston Symphony Orchestra—G. Wallace Woodworth
RCA Victor 18013 (78)

Cornell University Glee Club; Rochester Symphonic Brass Ensemble—Thomas A. Sokol
Fleetwood 6001

*Chromatic Study on the Name of Bach* (1940)

Mildred Andrews, organ
University of Oklahoma Recording, No. 2

Käte van Tricht, organ
Psallite *PET 144-280574*

Robert Noehren, organ
Lyrichord *LLST 7191*

*Concertino for Piano and Chamber Orchestra* (1937)

Alexander Jenner, piano; Vienna State Academy Orchestra—William Strickland
Vox PL 7750

Marjorie Mitchell, pianist; Gëteborg Symphony Orchestra—William Strickland
CRI 180

Gary Steigerwalt, piano; Philharmonia Virtuosi of New York—Richard Kapp
Turnabout *TV 34733*

*Concerto For Orchestra* (1933)

Polish National Radio Orchestra—William Strickland
CRI *SD 254*

*Concerto for String Quartet, Wind Instruments and Percussion* (1976)

Emerson Quartet (Eugene Drucker, Philip Setzer, Lawrence Dutton, Eric Wilson); Juilliard Orchestra—Sixten Ehrling
CRI *SD 248 (78)* (The "78" refers to the record's year of publication, 1978.)

*Concerto for Viola and Orchestra* (1957)

Paul Doktor, viola; Louisville Orchestra—Robert Whitney
Louisville LOU 633

*Concerto No. 1 for Violin and Orchestra* (1939)

Hugo Kolberg, violin; Berlin Symphony Orchestra—Otto Matzerath
EMI Odeon O 80610
Mace MXX 9089

*Divertimento for Nine Instruments* (1946)

Boston Symphony Chamber Players (Doriot Anthony Dwyer, flute; Ralph Gomberg, oboe; Gino Cioffi, clarinet; Sherman Walt, bassoon; Joseph Silverstein, Alfred Krips, violins; Burton Fine, viola; Jules Erskin, cello; Georges Moleux, double bass)
RCA Victor set *LSC 6167* (-3)

*Duo for Viola and Cello* (1949)

Irving Ilmer, viola; Leopold Teraspulsky, cello
Coronet *LPS 1715*

*Improvisation for Piano* (1945)

Andor Földes, piano
Vox 16070, in set 174 (78, -4)

*The Incredible Flutist: complete ballet* (1938)

Louisville Orchestra—Jorge Mester
Louisville *LS 755*

*The Incredible Flutist: Suite* (1939)

Boston Pops Orchestra—Arthur Fiedler
RCA Victor set M or DM 621 (78, -2)
RCA Camden Cal 145 (here called the Boston Festival Concert Orchestra)

Berlin Radio Symphony Orchestra—Arthur Rother
Urania URLP 7902

Boston Pops Orchestra—Arthur Fiedler (new recording)
RCA Victor set LM 6113 (-3)
RCA Victor LM 2084 (d.c.)

Cleveland Pops Orchestra—Louis Lane
Epic *BC 1013*

Eastman-Rochester Symphony Orchestra—Howard Hanson
Mercury *SR 90206*
Mercury *SR 90423* (d.c.)
Mercury *SRI 75050* (d.c.)

New York Philharmonic—Leonard Bernstein
Columbia *MS 6943*
Columbia set *MG 31155* (d.c., -2)

M.I.T. Symphony Orchestra—David Epstein
Turnabout *QTV-S 34670* (SQ)

*Partita for Violin, Viola and Organ* (1944)

Samuel Thaviu, violin; Kras Malno, viola; V. W. Fillinger, organ
ASCAP PFCM CB 190 (noncommercial issue)

*Passacaglia for Piano* (1943)

Roger Shields, piano
Vox set *SVBX 5303* (-3)

*Prelude and Allegro for Organ and Strings* (1943)

E. Power Biggs, organ; Boston Symphony Orchestra—Serge Koussevitzky
RCA Victor 11-9262
Columbia set M4X-35180 (-4)

*Psalm and Prayer of David for Mixed Chorus and Seven Instruments* (1958)

Peabody Conservatory Concert Singers; instrumentalists unnamed—Gregg Smith
Vox set *SVBX-5353* (-3)

*Quintet for Piano and String Quartet* (1949)

Johana Harris, piano; New Music String Quartet (Broadus Erle, Matthew Raimondi,
Walter Trampler, Claus Adam)
ASCAP PFCM CB 159 (noncommercial issue)

Earl Wild, piano; Walden String Quartet (Homer Schmitt, Bernard Goodman, John
Garvey, Robert Swenson)
WCFM LP 14
McIntosh Music MM 109
Heliodor *HS 25027* (d.c., ees)

*Quintet for Wind Instruments* (1956)

Boston Woodwind Quintet (Doriot Anthony Dwyer, flute; Ralph Gomberg, oboe; Gino
Cioffi, clarinet; Sherman Walt, bassoon; James Stragliano, French horn)
Boston Records *BST 1005*

Boehm Quintette of New York (Susan Stewart, flute; Phyllis Bohl, oboe; Don Stewart,
clarinet; Richard Vrotney bassoon, Joseph Anderer, French horn)
Orion *ORS 75206*

*Serenata for Orchestra* (1956)

Louisville Orchestra—Robert Whitney
Louisville LOU 58-6

*Sonata for Flute and Piano* (1930)

Jean-Pierre Rampal, flute; Robert Veyron-Lacroix, piano
Felsted RL 89007

Doriot Anthony Dwyer, flute; Barbara Korn, piano
Claremont CR 1205

only the first movement, "Allegro moderato e grazioso"
Sarah Baird Flouse, flute; Cecilia Ewing, piano
Coronet 1245

Julius Baker, flute; Anthony Makas, piano
Westminster *Wst 17121*

Keith Bryan, flute; Karen Keys, piano
Orion *ORS 76242*

Laila Padorr, flute; Anita Swearengin, piano
Laurel *LP 14*

Ingrid Dingfelder, flute; Anita Gordon, piano
CRI *SD 394*

*Sonata for Violin and Piano* (1939)

Louis Krasner, violin; Walter Piston, piano
Columbia set MX 199 (78, -2)

Joseph Fuchs, violin; Arthus Balsam, piano
Decca DL 9541

*Sonatina for Violin and Harpsichord (or Piano)* (1945)

Alexander Schneider, violin; Ralph Kirkpatrick, harpsichord
Columbia ML 4495

Paul Zukofsky, violin; Gilbert Kalish, piano
Desto set *DC 6435-37* (-3)

*String Quartet No. 1* (1933)

Dorian String Quartet (Alexander Cores, Harry Friedman, David Mankovitz, Bernard
    Greenhouse)
Columbia set M or AM 388 (-3)

Juilliard String Quartet (Robert Mann, Robert Koff, Raphael Hillyer, Arthur Winograd)
ASCAP PFCM CB 157 (non-commercial issue)

*String Quartet No. 2* (1935)

Budapest Quartet (Josef Roisman, Edgar Ortenberg, Boris Kroyt, Mischa Schneider)
New Worlds Records NW 302

*String Quartet No. 5* (1962)

Kohon Quartet (Harold Kohon, Alvin Rogers, Eugenie Dengel, David Moore)
Vox set *SVBX 5305* (-3)

*Suite for Oboe and Piano* (1931)

Louis Speyer, oboe; Walter Piston, piano
Technichord T 1561 (78)

Wayne Rapier, oboe; John Perry, piano
Coronet *LPS 1409*

*Symphony No. 1* (1937)

Louisville Orchestra—Jorge Mester
Louisville *LS 766*

*Symphony No. 2* (1943)

Vienna Symphony Orchestra—Dean Dixon
American Recording Society ARS 1
American Recording Society ARS 112 (these two ARS releases credit this performance
  to the American Recording Society Orchestra)
Desto *DST 6410* (d.c., ees)

Boston Symphony Orchestra—Michael Tilson Thomas
Deutsche Grammophon *2530 103*

*Symphony No. 3* (1947)

Eastman-Rochester Orchestra—Howard Hanson
Mercury *MS 50077*
Mercury *MS 50083*
Mercury *SRI 75107*

*Symphony No. 4* (1950)

Philadelphia Orchestra—Eugene Ormandy
Columbia ML 4992
Columbia CML 4992

*Symphony No. 5* (1954)

Louisville Orchestra—Robert Whitney
Louisville *LS 653*

*Symphony No. 6* (1955)

Boston Symphony Orchestra—Charles Munch
RCA Victor LM 2083
New World Records NW 286 (d.c.)

Moscow Radio Symphony—Alexander Gauk
*S 0255056*

*Symphony No. 7* (1960)

Louisville Orchestra—Jorge Mester
Louisville *LS 746*

*Symphony No. 8* (1965)

Louisville Orchestra—Jorge Mester
Louisville *LS 746*

*Three Pieces for Flute, Clarinet and Bassoon* (1925)

Barrère Woodwind Ensemble (Georges Barrère, flute; Fred van Amburgh, clarinet;
  Angel del Busto, bassoon)
New Music Quarterly Recordings 1113 (78)

members of the New Art Wind Quintet (Andrew Lolya, flute; Irving Neidich, clarinet; Tina di Dario, bassoon)
Classic Editions set CE 2003(-2)

members of the Berkshire Woodwind Ensemble (James Pappoutsakis, flute; Pasquale Cardillo, clarinet; Ernst Panenka, bassoon)
Unicorn UNLP 1029

members of the Soni Ventorum Woodwind Quintet (Felix Skowronek, flute; William McColl, clarinet; Arthur Grossman, bassoon)
Lyrichord *LLST 7158*

Bennington Woodwind Trio (Sue Ann Kahn, flute; Gunnar Schonbeck, clarinet; Maurice Pachman, bassoon)
Golden Crest *CRS 4140*

*Trio No. 1 for Violin, Cello and Piano* (1935)

New York Trio (Rachmael Weinstock, violin; Otto Deri, cello; Fritz Jahoda, piano)
Persepctive PR 2004

Temple University Trio (Helen Kwalwasser, violin; Michael Haran, cello; Alexander Fiorillo, piano)
Golden Crest *CRS 4117* (SQ)

Western Arts Trio (Brian Hanly, violin; David Tomatz, cello; Werner Rose, piano)
Laurel *LR 104*

*Tunbridge Fair: Intermezzo for Symphonic Band* (1950)

Eastman Symphonic Wind Ensemble—Frederick Fennell
Mercury MG 40006
Mercury MG 50079
Mercury *SRI 75086* (ees)

# Notes

## Chapter 1

1. Elliott Carter, "Walter Piston," *Musical Quarterly* 32 (1946), p. 355. Carter also writes that the composer's father "only knew how to count up to five in the foreign language."

2. Carini's letters to Piston are in the Piston Collection in the Boston Public Library.

3. Virgil Thomson, *Virgil Thomson* (New York: Da Capo Press, 1966), p. 47. Thomson writes, "He had a good mind, too, and firm opinions. But, as for so many of Italian background, both life and art were grim, without free play." In a personal interview, 13 August 1977, Thomson stated, point-blank, Piston "was as wop as they come." Incidentally, authors of Italian-American culture, such as Ibrizzo and Mondello in The *Italian-Americans* (New York: Twayne Publishers, 1971), have included Piston in their surveys. This last named book is the source for the figure on Italian immigrants in Maine, p. 219.

4. Private tape of a 79th birthday interview on WGBH, Boston, 19 January 1973.

5. Personal interview with Flore Craig, Piston's niece, August, 1977.

6. George Bacon, *Rockland, Belfast and Vicinity* (Newark: Glenwood Publishing Co., 1892), p. 6.

7. This and other letters from Piston to Betty Thorndike are in the possession of Mrs. Thorndike.

8. Personal letter from Edward Piston, 19 August 1977.

9. E. Piston, letter.

10. Phone conversation with Ruth Naugler, 22 July 1979.

11. Personal interview with Margaret Nason, 29 August 1979.

12. Phone conversation with Jean Piston, Edward's wife, 19 July 1979.

13. Nason interview. Most other discussion of the Nasons is also based on this interview, and on two personal letters from Mrs. Nason, 26 July 1977, and 12 September 1977.

14. Paraphrased to me from memory by Margaret Nason.

15. William Trash, *The Reverand Elias Nason*, printed for private distribution (Boston: 1899).

16. Information on the Belmont circle is based on personal letters from Alison Coolidge, 17 February 1979 and 20 February 1979, and on personal interviews with Grace Reasoner Clark, 19 August 1979, and Nelson Chase, 21 August 1979.

17. Ruth Sutro, the daughter of Kathryn's first cousin, Frederick, lives in Needham, close to Belmont. In a letter to this author dated 29 January 1979, Mrs. Sutro writes: "Gertrude first attended Massachusetts Normal Art School and became a teacher of art in Billerica. Kathryn told me that she herself was prevented from entering the Normal Art School as early as she might have because Gertrude wanted Kathryn at home as a ready model. I own a 7˝ by 10˝ oil painting by Gertrude showing Kathryn in a profile reading in a rocking chair. She wears a long white dress (similar to the one in Whistler's 'Girl in White') and a pink necklace. Her bouffant auburn hair is tied back by an enormous pink bow. Gertrude married William Donahue and they lived in New York City, with a summer home in Connecticut (near which Tom and Margaret settled at Lyme later on). William D. painted in the style of Jackson Pollock. Gertrude painted country fairs, bright flowers, interiors featuring her cat, in a realistic style, with emphasis on brilliant color. I met her only once, near the end of her life and was greatly attracted to her.

    Kathryn painted more broadly, with a great tendency to depict landscapes. I enclose a copy of the program from a joint Nason show in Boston in 1945, which I attended. At that time, Kathryn's paintings were chiefly landscapes, many painted from the hilltop behind the Pistons' summer home in South Woodstock, Vt. Later, Kathryn painted more floral compositions and interior still lifes. The show of her work in Belmont in March 1976 which was scheduled before her death and which became a memorial show (see her obituary) contained many more still lifes and floral arrangements than landscapes. Her style grew more detailed and colorful, her later work more reminiscent of Gertrude's than before . . .

    Re modern non-representational art, I remember Kathryn's comment, to the effect that the painting is as subjective as dreams, and no one wants to hear about another person's dreams . . . In a rare comment about *her* painting, Kathryn stated that she would start to draw the subject in front of her—grasses, flowers, then look for repetitions of lines and directions to enhance the design of the composition."

18. Personal interview with John and Helen Groden, August 21, 1979.

19. Personal letter from Betty Thorndike, December 11, 1978. According to a photograph in the possession of Mrs. Thorndike, Amory and Walter may have travelled once more to Paris in 1928.

20. Letter to the State Department, April 6, 1959, Piston Collection.

21. Personal interview with Mary Aiken, 27 August 1979.

22. Piston Collection.

23. *The Collected Novels of Conrad Aiken* (New York: Holt, Rinehart and Winston, 1964), p. 195.

24. Aiken. *The Collected Poems*, 2nd edition (New York: Oxford University Press, 1970), p. 942.

25. Personal letter from Fidelia Crane, 29 July 1977. In a personal interview on 18 July 1981, Mrs. Crane told this author that Piston was "like common folk" and a good Republican like herself. She approved of his preference for Mr. over Professor or Dr., but had little appreciation for his music.

26. "Three Nasons in One Art Show," *Christian Science Monitor* (5 December 1945).

27. "Composer and Artist Wife Honored at Symphony Hall," *Boston Traveler* (17 April 1944).

28. WGBH interview, 19 January 1973.

29. Personal interview with David Diamond, 2 August 1979.

30. Personal interview with George Humphrey, 19 August 1979. Humphrey told me that the distortion of sound caused by hearing aids discouraged Piston from wearing one.

**Chapter 2**

1. George Henry Lovett Smith, "Walter Piston: American Composer," *Magazine of Art* 33 (1940), p. 99.

2. See Chapter 1, p. 5. As evidenced by his friendship with Nelson Chase and Conrad Aiken, Piston remained something of a bohemian, at least until the 1940s. How many of his Harvard students would have guessed that in the class books that recorded their names and grades, Piston kept a list of wines with letter grades as well?

3. Peter Westergaard, "Conversation with Walter Piston," in *Perspectives on American Composers*, edited by Boretz and Cone (New York: W. W. Norton and Co., 1971), p. 156.

4. The town of Rockland wrote to Piston that they thought they found a flute that had belonged to his grandfather. Piston Collection.

5. Margaret Fairbanks, Interview with Walter Piston, Rodgers and Hammerstein Archive, New York Public Library, ca. 1967.

6. Personal letter from Edward Piston, 15 October 1977.

7. Phone conversation with Ruth Naugler, 22 July 1979.

8. Westergaard, "Conversation with Walter Piston," p. 156.

9. Madeleine Goss, *Modern Music-Makers* (New York: E. P. Dutton and Co., 1952), p. 168.

10. Ibid.

11. WGBH interview, 19 January 1973.

12. Westergaard, "Conversation with Walter Piston," p. 157.

13. Ibid.

14. Quoted by Eric Salzman in "Piston: Ex-Teacher," *New York Times* 31 January 1954, p. 7.

15. See the Westergaard interview (p. 158) and, in the same book, Edward Cone's "Conversation with Roger Sessions," p. 91.

16. Virgil Thomson, *Virgil Thomson* (New York: Da Capo Press, 1966), p. 45.

17. The lineage, traced by Alan Kendall in *The Tender Tyrant* (Wilton, Connecticut: Lyceum Books, 1977), is Widor, Lemmens, Hesse, Forkel, C. P. E. Bach, J. S. Bach.

18. Edward Ballantine, liner notes to the *Variations*, played by the composer, Festival Recordings, FLP 70–201.

19. Thomson, *Virgil Thomson*, p. 51.

20. See Chapter 9, p. 000.

21. Walter Raymond Spalding, *Music: An Art and A Language* (New York: Arthur P. Schmidt, Co., 1920), p. 338.

22. Walter Raymond Spalding, *Music at Harvard. A Historical Review of Men and Events* (New York: Coward-McCann, 1935), pp. 161, 202.

23. Thomson, *Virgil Thomson*, p. 46.

24. William Austin, *Music in the 20th Century* (New York: W. W. Norton, 1966), p. 61.

25. Edward Burlingame Hill, *Modern French Music* (New York: Houghton Mifflin, 1924: reprinted Da Capo Press, 1969), p. 2.

26. Virgil Thomson, *American Music Since 1910* (New York: Holt, Rinehart and Winston, 1970), p. 151.

27. Quoted by John A. Hammerton in *Stevensonia*, revised edition (Edinburgh: John Grant, 1910), pp. 236–37.

28. George Smith, "Edward Burlingame Hill," *Modern Music* 16 (1939), p. 13 (hereafter cited as *MM*).

29. David Ross Baskerville, *Jazz Influence on Art Music to Mid-Century* (Ph.D., University of California—Los Angeles, 1965), p. 335.

30. Thomson, *Virgil Thomson*, p. 65.

31. Smith, "Hill," p. 13.

32. Anonymous liner notes to Hill's *Sextet for Wind Instruments and Piano*, Op. 39, Columbia ML 4846.

33. Personal interview with Mary Aiken, 27 August 1979; also cited in a letter from Aiken to Edward Burra, 2 October 1952, *Selected Letters*, p. 301.

34. Westergaard, "Conversation with Walter Piston," p. 157.

35. Phone conversation with Theodore Ruggles, manager and trombonist for the Pierian Sodality during Piston's tenure, 22 July 1979.

36. Both reviews are quoted in a Publicity Pamphlet for the Pierian Sodality Orchestra, Harvard University Archives.

37. Spalding, *Harvard*, p. 97. The other notable regimes were those of Walter Forcheimer (1884–1887), Philip Clapp (1907–1909), and Chalmers Clifton (1909–1911).

38. Westergaard, "Conversation with Walter Piston," p. 158.

39. Ibid., p. 159. Piston dedicated his *Third Quartet* to Alexanian.

40. Piston collection.

41. Austin, *Music*, p. 393.

42. Personal interview with Thomson, August 13, 1977.

43. Thomson, *Virgil Thomson*, p. 206.

44. Paul Dukas, "Les tendencies de la musique contemporaine," *Courrier Musical*, January 1924, reprinted in *Ecrits sur la musique* (Paris: SEFI, 1948), p. 668, unpublished translation by William Austin.

45. "Stravinsky's Rediscoveries," in *Stravinsky in the Theatre*, edited with an introduction by Minna Lederman (New York: Farrar, Straus and Giroux, 1949; reprint ed., New York: Da Capo Press, 1975), p. 130.

46. Westergaard, "Conversation with Walter Piston," p. 158.

47. Archibald T. Davison, *Music Education in America* (New York: Harper and Brothers, 1926), p. 141.

48. Quoted by Daniel Gregory Mason in *Music In My Time and Other Reminiscenses* (New York: MacMillan and Co., 1938), p. 389.

49. Quoted by Kendall, *The Tender Tyrant*, pp. 58-59.

50. Westergaard, "Conversation with Walter Piston," p. 159.

51. Kendall, *The Tender Tyrant*, p. 58.

52. Westergaard, "Conversation with Walter Piston," p. 159.

53. Thomson, *Virgil Thomson*, pp. 57–58.

**Chapter 3**

1. Peter Westergaard, "Conversation with Walter Piston," in *Perspectives on American Composers*, edited by Boretz and Cone (New York: W. W. Norton and Co., 1971), p. 160.

2. Private tape of an 80th birthday interview on WGBH, Boston, 19 January 1974.

3. Piston, liner notes to *American Woodwind Symposium*, by the New Art Wind Quintet, Classic Editions Recordings CE 2003.

4. Virgil Thomson, *Virgil Thomson* (New York: Da Capo Press, 1966), p. 79.

5. Roger Sessions, "An American Evening Abroad," *MM* 44 (1926), p. 33.

6. Raymond Petit, "Musique d'Amérique du Nord," *Revue Musicale* 7 (1925–26), pp. 299–300.

7. E. B. Hill, *The Radcliffe News*, Vol. XV, No. 23, Cambridge, Mass., 15 April 1927, p. 1.

8. Israel Citkowitz, review of Piston's *Oboe Suite*, *MM* 12 (1935), pp. 190–91.

9. From the private correspondence of Rebecca Kelly.

10. Colin McPhee, review of Piston's *Concerto for Orchestra*, *MM* 13 (1936), p. 43. McPhee mistakenly refers to the work as a "symphony." Hugo Leichtentritt, in *Serge Kous-*

*sevitzky* (Cambridge: Harvard University Press, 1947), p. 115, writes, in a discussion of the *First Symphony*, "Though called a symphony, this score might just as well have been entitled a concerto, and conversely, Piston's older concerto for orchestra might be termed a symphony. The style in the two works is not greatly differentiated." Both McPhee and Leichtentritt show less concern for genre titles than is suggested by Piston's music.

11. Henry Pleasants, "First-Time Fever," *MM* 16 (1939), p. 83; Aaron Copland, "From the '20s to the '40s and Beyond," *MM* 20 (1942–43), p. 81; Ingolf Dahl, "Neglected Works: A Symposium," *MM* (1946), p. 12.

12. Bruno Walter, *Of Music and Music Making*, translated by Paul Hamburger (London: Faber and Faber, 1957), p. 205.

13. Sister Gregory Joseph, *Twentieth Century Composers on Fugue* (Chicago: School of Music, De Paul University, 1966), pp. 2, 37. Of the other forty-two responses, William Schuman's is perhaps closest to Piston's: "Fugue is not a form but a procedure—a principle. As a principle, its potential is everlasting" (p. 43). Ingolf Dahl, Gail Kubik, and Harold Shapero cite Piston in their answers.

14. Theodore Chanler, review of Piston's *First String Quartet, MM* 11 (1934), p. 142.

15. Aaron Copland, *The New Music 1900–1960*, revised edition (New York: W. W. Norton, 1941, 1968), p. 132.

16. Elliott Carter, "Walter Piston," *Musical Quarterly* 32 (1946), p. 367 (hereafter cited as *MQ*).

17. Robert Donahue, "A Comparative Analysis of Phrase Structure in Selected Movements of the String Quartets of Béla Bartók and Walter Piston," D.M.A. Thesis, Cornell University, 1964.

18. Virgil Thomson, *American Music Since 1910* (New York: Holt, Rinehard and Winston, 1970), p. 62.

19. Goddard Lieberson, "Over the Air," *MM* 15 (1937), p. 54.

20. Piston Collection.

21. L. A. Sloper, review of Piston's *First Symphony, Christian Science Monitor* (9 April 1938), p. 10.

22. Moses Smith, "Boston News," *MM* 16 (1938–39), p. 116.

23. Moses Smith, *Koussevitzky* (New York: Allen, Towe and Heath, Inc., 1947), p. 267.

24. Elliott Carter, "Season of Hindemith and Americans," *MM* 16 (1938–39), p. 251.

25. Leonard Bernstein, "Boston Carries On," *MM* 15 (1937–38), p. 240.

26. Arthur Berger, "Scores and Records," *MM* 23 (1946), p. 134.

27. Peter Davis, "Some Contemporary Labors of Love," *New York Times* (16 September 1979), p. 24.

28. Israel Citkowitz, "Walter Piston—Classicist," *MM* 13 (1936), pp. 3–10.

29. Arnold Hauser, *The Social History of Art*, Vol. I (New York: Alfred A. Knopf, 1952); *Mannerism* (New York: Alfred A. Knopf, 1965).

30. Arnold Hauser, *Social History*, p. 356.

31. The politics of mannerism is also discussed in Cyrus Hoy's "Jacobean Tragedy and the Mannerist Style," *Shakespeare Study 26*, edited by Kenneth Mur (Cambridge: University Press, 1973), pp. 49–69. It is interesting to note that Hindemith's 1934 opera, *Mathis der Maler*, concerns a mannerist painter, Grünewald, who decides against participation in the sixteenth-century Peasants' War.

32. Hauser, *Mannerism*, pp. 371, 372.

33. Personal interview with David Diamond, 10 August 1979.

34. Perhaps the same could also be said of Hindemith and others. Picasso is a figure already often discussed in the context of both surrealism and neoclassicism. The Italian painter Chirico is even more obviously related to both currents.

**Chapter 4**

1. WGBH interview, 19 January 1974.

2. "Jan Veen Dies," *Dance Magazine* 41 (July, 1967), p. 4.

3. Grant Code, "Hans Wiener Begins a New Career," *Dance Observer* 8 (March, 1941), p. 1.

4. John Martin, "Veen-Thirney in Recital," *New York Times* (December 9, 1941).

5. Aaron Copland, *The New Music* 1900–1960 (New York: W. W. Norton, 1968) pp. 161–62.

6. M. A. DeWolfe Howe, *The Boston Symphony Orchestra 1881–1931* (New York: Houghton Mifflin Co., 1931), p. 166.

7. David Diamond, for instance, thought a classical tale from antiquity would have better suited Piston, according to a personal interview, 10 August 1979.

8. WGBH interview, 19 January 1974.

9. In the four-hand arrangement, some of the names of the dances are different. The "Dance of the Trainer and Monkeys" is the "Dance of the Poodles;" the "Dance of the Crystal Gazer" is the "Dance of the Astrologer;" and the "Dance of the Jugglers" is the "Dance of the Tumblers."

10. WGBH interview, 19 January 1974.

11. Booth's poem is in the Piston Collection, and was also published in the April, 1959 issue of *Fine Arts Magazine* at the University of Connecticut.

12. As printed in liner notes to a recording of *Carnival Song* by the Cornell University Glee Club and the Rochester Symphony Brass, conducted by Thomas Sokol, Fleetwood Records FLP 6001.

13. Quoted in the *Boston Symphony Orchestra Programmes 1956–1957*, p. 147.

14. Copland, *The New Music*, p. 131. Copland may also have been thinking of Britten (see p. 208 n 8).

15. Virgil Thomson, *The State of Music* (New York: William Morrow and Company, 1939), p. 98.

16. Ibid., p. 102

17. Quoted by George Smith, "Walter Piston: American Composer," *Magazine of Art* 33 (1940), p. 128. Twenty years later Piston echoed these sentiments in an article, "Can Music be Nationalistic?" *The Music Journal* 19 (Oct., 1961), p. 86.

18. Personal letter from Siegmeister, 15 April 1979.

**Chapter 5**

1. Virgil Thomson, *American Music Since 1910* (New York: Holt, Rinehart and Winston, 1970), p. 82.

2. Hugo Leichtentritt, *Serge Koussevitzky* (Cambridge: Harvard University Press, 1947), p. 118.

3. Elliott Carter, "Walter Piston," *MQ* 32 (1946), p. 369.

4. Walter Piston, "The Music Criticism Racket," *MM* 22 (1945), p. 285.

5. Virgil Thomson, *Virgil Thomson* (New York: Alfred A. Knopf, 1966), p. 141.

6. Igor Stravinsky, *Poetics of Music*, translated by Arthur Knodel and Ingolf Dahl (Cambridge: Harvard University Press, 1942), p. 94.

7. Stravinsky, *Poetics*, p. 97.

8. Harold Shapero, "Neglected Works: A Symposium," *MM* 23 (1946), p. 8; reaffirmed in a personal interview on 1 December 1978. Britten told Copland at the work's premiere "that there was no composer in England of Piston's age who could turn out anything so expert." Copland, letter to Elliott Carter, 11 August 1940, Carter Collection, New York Public Library.

9. Igor Stravinsky, *Themes and Conclusions* (London: Faber and Faber, 1972), p. 50.

10. Stravinsky, *Themes*, p. 49.

11. John N. Burk, "Symphony in C Major," *Boston Symphony Orchestra Programmes* (17 January 1941), p. 549.

12. Shapero, interview.

13. Michael Steinberg, "Composer turned from painting to music," *Boston Globe* (January 19, 1969), A24.

14. Ross Lee Finney, "Piston's Violin Sonata," *MM* 17 (1939–1940), p. 211.

15. *Letters of Composers. An Anthology 1603–1945*, Norman Gertrude and Miriam Lubell Shrifte, editors (New York: Alfred Knopf, 1946), p. 367.

16. Personal interview with Mario di Bonaventura, 17 August 1977.

17. Goossens, letter to Walter Piston, 30 August 1942, Library of Congress, Music Division, Washington, D.C.

18. Claire R. Reis, *Composers, Conductors and Critics* (New York: Oxford University Press, 1955), p. 165.

19. Lou Harrison, "First-Time Fashions, New York, 1944," *MM* 22 (1944–1945), p. 32.

20. Arthur Berger, "Scores and Records," *MM* 23 (1946), p. 308.

21. WGBH interview, 19 January 1973. Daniel Pinkham's anecdote is also transcribed from this broadcast.

22. Leichtentritt, *Serge Koussevitzky*, p. 122.

23. WGBH interview, 19 January 1973.

24. Carl Sandburg, *The People, Yes* (New York: Harcourt, Brace and Company, 1936), p. 44.

25. S. L. M. Barlow, "Mrs. Coolidge's Birthday Party," *MM* 22 (1945), p. 41. Barlow also suggests an affinity with the American painter, Albert Ryder.

26. WGBH interview, 19 January 1973.

27. Hans Kindler, Letter to Walter Piston, 6 March 1944, Library of Congress, Music Division, Washington, D.C.

28. Leinsdorf, letter to Walter Piston, 1 March 1946, Library of Congress, Music Division, Washington, D.C.

29. Ray Brown, "Piston's New Symphony in Washington," *MM* 21 (1943–1944), p. 179; Moses Smith, "Americans and Shostakovich in Boston," *MM* 21 (1943–1944), p. 253; Charles Mills, "Over the Air," *MM* 21 (1943–1944), p. 269; Colin McPhee, "Scores and Records," *MM* 22 (1944–1945), p. 129; Donald Fuller, "Forecast and Review," *MM* 23 (1946), p. 48.

30. McPhee, "Scores and Records," *MM* 21 (1943–1944), p. 112. McPhee writes: "A brief Passacaglia for piano by Walter Piston is more a tribute to the erudite Hindemith style than the expression of any personal emotion." And in "Scores and Records," *MM* 22 (1945), p. 130, McPhee says: "Arrow also gives us Piston's Prelude and Allegro for Organ and Strings, but such rapid, skipping-all-over passage work for the organ which runs through the allegro never seems to do more for my ears than accentuate the ridiculous and macabre tone of the organ."

31. Fuller, "Stravinsky Full-Length Portrait," *MM* 23 (1946), p. 48. Fuller writes: "The Sonatina for violin and harpsichord, on a first performance by Alexander Schneider and Ralph Kirkpatrick, shows Piston reverting to his straitjacketed neoclassicism. The results are of course expert, yet not often moving."

32. Donald Fuller and Moses Smith; see note 29.

## Chapter 6

1. Program notes for a concert of The Civic Symphony Orchestra of Boston, Paul Cherkassy, conductor, 18 April 1945.

2. Virgil Thomson, *American Music Since 1910* (New York: Holt, Rinehart and Winston, 1970), p. 62.

3. Elliott Carter, "Walter Piston," *Musical Quarterly* 32 (1946), p. 373.

4. Ibid., p. 362.

5. Ibid., p. 363.

6. Ibid., p. 372.

7. Donald Fuller, "Stravinsky Full-Length Portrait," *MM* 23 (1946), p. 48.

8. Peter Ustinov, from a recorded discussion on chamber music in an anthology entitled

The *Boston Symphony Chamber Players*, RCA LSC–6167, that includes performances of the Piston and Carter works.

9. WGBH interview, 19 January 1974.

10. WGBH interview, 19 January 1974.

11. Carter, "Walter Piston," p. 372.

12. William Bergsma, "Music Reviews," *Notes* 7 (1949–1950), p. 132.

13. In program notes to the work, Piston writes that the second theme is "played by the bassoon, clarinets and English horn." I assume that this is an oversight and Piston means the theme played by the *horn*, clarinets and English horn at measure 21. The first and third themes are, respectively, for oboe (m. 4) and for brass (m. 39).

14. Quoted by Steinberg in "Happy 80th Birthday, Walter Piston," *Boston Sunday Globe* 20 January 1974, A–9.

15. If Piston's finale is untypically bombastic, this can be ascribed to the influence of the Copland work, although Piston (characteristically) has his own amusing explanation, as reported by Madeleine Goss in *Modern Music-Makers* (New York: E. P. Dutton and Co., 1952), p. 174: "It was written during the summer when an artesian well was being dug outside my window, and I had to write music loud enough to overcome the noise."

16. "Stravinsky—Darling of Moderns Lauds 2 Americans: Copland and Piston," *New York World Telegram* (February 10, 1945).

17. WGBH interview, 19 January 1974.

18. WGBH interview, 19 January 1974.

19. Jay S. Harrison, "Munch and Music: His Current Views," *New York Herald Tribune* (Sunday, 6 March 1960).

20. David Hall, liner notes to *American Concert Band Masterpieces*, Frederick Fennell and the Eastman Wind Ensemble, Mercury SRI 75086.

21. Ray Bearse, editor, *Vermont. A Guide to the Green Mountain State*, third edition (Boston: Houghton Mifflin Co., 1938), p. 374.

22. "The World's Fair," *The Vermonter* 35 (September, 1930), p. 206.

23. Walter Piston, program notes for the *Toccata, Boston Symphony Orchestra Programmes* (17 January 1974).

24. Mark DeVoto, "In Memoriam: Walter Piston (1894–1976)," *Perspectives of New Music* (1977), pp. 243–44.

25. Lawrence Morton, "Reviews of Records," *Musical Quarterly* 39 (1953), p. 659.

26. Personal interview with Virgil Thomson, 13 August 1977.

27. Otto Deri, *Exploring Twentieth-Century Music* (New York: Holt, Rinehart and Winston, 1968), p. 478.

28. Personal letter from George Humphrey, 1 August 1977.

29. Fairbanks interview, ca. 1967.

30. Piston, letter to Ruth Watanabe, 5 April 1958, Watanabe Correspondence, Sibley Library, Eastman School, Rochester, New York.

31. William Austin, "Piston's Fourth Symphony," *Music Review* 16 (May, 1955), pp. 120–37.

32. Quoted by Ferguson in *Masterworks of the Orchestral Repertory* (Minneapolis: University of Minnesota Press, 1954), p. 419.

33. Quoted by Roy in "Walter Piston," *Stereo Review* 24 (April, 1970), p. 63.

**Chapter 7**

1. Walter Piston, "Fantasy for English Horn, Harp and Strings," *Boston Symphony Orchestra Programmes* 74 (1953–1954), p. 498.

2. Walter Piston, "The Sixth Symphony," *Boston Symphony Orchestra Programmes* 76 (1955–1956), p. 284.

3. Wilfred Mellers, *Music in a New Found Land* (New York: Alfred A. Knopf, 1965), p. 34. Further, Mellers's statement, "The Teutonic origins of this academicism are, however, modified by prolonged residence in Paris," is mistaken on two counts. First, it overlooks the French background of Piston's education at Harvard; and second, it exaggerates the two years Piston spent in Paris.

4. Mellers, *Music*, pp. 35–36.

5. Dimitri Kabalevsky, *Pravda* (14 September 1956); quoted in *Boston Symphony Orchestra Programmes* 1956–1957, p. 147.

6. Vernon Duke, *Listen Here!* (New York: Ivan Obolensky, Inc., 1963), p. 68.

7. Peter Jona Korn, "The Symphony in America," in *The Symphony, Vol. II. Elgar to the Present Day*, edited by Robert Simpson (Baltimore: Penguin Books, 1967), pp. 255–56. Korn is perhaps thinking of Mellers when he writes, "Something that is often said—incorrectly—of Walter Piston is true for William Schuman: he is the prototype of an academic composer" (p. 256). Korn might have been thinking of Thomson and Chase as well. He also anticipates a comment by Robert Layton in an article entitled "U.S.A." in *Twentieth Century Music*, edited by Rollo Myers (New York: Orion Press, 1968); Layton writes, "Piston is the scholarly and academic composer of his generation" (p. 234).

8. The *Sinfonietta* does not use any trumpets, timpani, or harp, and uses only two horns.

9. Walter Piston, record liner notes for the *Quintet for Woodwind Instruments*, the Boehm Quintette, Orion ORS 75206.

10. William Flanagan, "Record Reviews," *Musical Quarterly* 44 (1958), pp. 551–53.

11. Walter Piston, "Viola and Orchestra," *Boston Symphony Orchestra Programmes* 78 (1957–1958), pp. 1136–42.

12. Irving Kolodin, "Music to my Ears," *Saturday Review* 41 (5 April 1958), p. 22. "Primrose" is a pun on the violist William Primrose.

13. Jaroslav Karlovsky, letter to Piston, 9 January 1965, Piston Collection. The Czech "thaw," it seems, witnessed a lively interest in Piston's music. On 10 April 1965, some months after Karlovsky's letter, a letter from the Czech Wind Quintet told Piston of their recording of the *Wind Quintet*, praised his "wonderful" *Sixth Symphony*, and expressed interest in his other music.

14. Piston, "Viola and Orchestra," pp. 1138–40.

15. Walter Piston, from an untitled article in the Piston Collection.

16. Melvin Stecher and Norman Horowitz, undated letter to Piston, Piston Collection.

17. Robert Newall, "Traveling Pianists Talk About Travels, School," *Bangor Daily News* (20 February 1969).

18. Michael Steinberg, "Exhumed Symphony very much alive," *Boston Globe* (2 November 1968).

19. Personal interview with Fuchs, 10 March 1979. Fuchs is still a staunch admirer of Piston's music, and comments, "Nowadays everyone just wants to hear Mahler, but Piston is one of the great classic American composers."

20. Harold Schoenberg, "Music: Season's End for Philharmonic," *New York Times* (Saturday, 19 May 1962).

21. Paul Henry Lang, "New York Philharmonic," *New York Herald Tribune* (19 May 1962).

22. Piston also made charitable contributions to, above all, the Audubon Society and other wildlife organizations, the Boston Dance Theatre, the Greater Boston Youth Symphony, the Boston Symphony Orchestra, the Longy School of Music, the Museum of Fine Arts, the Boston Public Library, Harvard, Planned Parenthood and other health centers, and other organizations.

23. Personal interview with Margaret Nason, 29 August 1979.

24. Robert Dumm thought the *Three Sketches* the most "engaging" of the Festival's many commissions, "Worcester Fete Marks Centenary," *Musical Courier* 1959–1960 (December, 1959), p. 6.

25. Walter Piston, "Three New England Sketches," *Boston Symphony Orchestra Programmes* 80 (1960–1961), p. 84.

26. Walter Piston, "Can Music be Nationalistic?" *Music Journal* 19 (October, 1961), p. 86.

27. A critical note is sounded in a 1958 article, "More Views on Serialism," *The Score* 23 (July, 1958), in which Piston writes, "Now that we find ourselves surrounded by the forces of total organization, in and out of music. . . ." (p. 46). Is Piston alluding to foreign Communist states, or domestic trends, or both? Furthermore, Piston was not an uncritical Republican. Richard French remembers that Piston thought Ronald Reagan "a joke."

### Chapter 8

1. Personal interview with Grace Reasoner Clark, 19 August 1979.

2. Personal interview with Mario di Bonaventura, 17 August 1977, and Richard French, 4 January 1978.

3. Fairbanks interview, ca. 1967.

4. Peter Westergaard, "Conversation with Walter Piston," in *Perspectives on American Composers*, edited by Benjamin Boretz and Edward Cone (New York: W. W. Norton, 1971), p. 157.

5. See Appendix A.

6. Walter Piston, *Cleveland Symphony Orchestra Programs* 43 (1960–1961), p. 774.

7. A holograph of the work survives in the Piston Collection, but published copies of the work, now out of print, are hard to obtain.

8. Betty Thorndike, personal letter to Walter and Kathryn Piston. Mrs. Thorndike writes, "I can't tell you how much I miss the wonderful excuse we used early in the year to put our minds to helping on the opera project and how much we miss it and still hope there may be some revival of it . . . We can't resist telling you that we got so enthusiastic about your opera with its Maine coastal setting that we even had a plan to take you on a lobster fishing boat to get some real coastal feeling. If any of these ideas tempt you, opera or no opera, just say the word."

9. WGBH interview, 19 January 1974.

10. Fairbanks interview, ca. 1967.

11. Rorem, record liner notes to *The American Art Song*, New World Records, NW 243.

12. Barber, record liner notes to *Songs of Samuel Barber and Ned Rorem*, New World Records, NW 229.

13. Personal letter from Peyton Hibbitt, 4 July 1980.

14. Piston, program notes, Piston file, BMI, Inc., New York, New York.

15. Donald Chittum, program notes to Piston's *String Quartet No. 5*, played by the Kohon Quartet, *American String Quartets Volume II: 1900–1950* (Piston's quartet, be it noted, was written in 1962).

16. Piston, *Boston Programmes* 84 (1964–65), p. 1183.

17. Michael Steinberg, "New Piston Symphony, Johannesen's Brahms," *The Boston Globe* (6 March 1965).

18. Personal interview with Shapero, 1 December 1978.

19. Louis Biancolli, "Piston, Boston Symphony Shine," *New York World Telegram and Sun* (1 April 1965).

20. David Hall, "Piston: Symphony No. 7, Symphony No. 8," *Stereo Review* 36 (May, 1976), p. 120.

21. Harris Lindenfeld, "Three Symphonies of Walter Piston, An Analysis," DMA Thesis, Cornell University, June 1975.

22. Lindenfeld more or less correctly divides the first movement into four sections (This author would prefer mm. 1–38, 39–50, 51–62, 63–93 to Lindenfeld's mm. 1–35, 36–51, 51–83, 84–93, but the movement is essentially a through-composed arch), but his analysis of this second movement is more seriously flawed. We agree on the theme and the first two variations, but then Lindenfeld cites sections mm. 58–64, 65–69, and 70–105, as, respectively, the last two variations and the reprise. It is unlikely that Piston would write a seven and a five measure variation on a twenty-seven measure theme.

23. Personal interview with Herbert's widow, Jane Kibrick, 20 August 1979.

24. George Hill, letter to Piston, Piston Collection.

25. Piston, *Portland Symphony Orchestra Program Magazine* (16 November 1965), pp. 29–31.

26. Nadia Boulanger, letter to Piston, 31 January 1964, Piston Collection. In addition, a public 70th birthday greeting from Boulanger was published in a BMI catalogue of the composer's works. In this salute, Boulanger writes, "The great artist you are, all know! The eloquent, subtle and efficient professor you have been, many know too. The respect and affection which surrounds you show the man of great stature you are, is equally appreciated. But it might be that the building of this work, these books, this career, and this character, is not so well known. And it is a joy, I nearly say a duty, for one who has seen you grow year after year, to say, whatever shortly it has to be expressed here, what a superb example you gave and are giving of the making of oneself."

27. Westergaard, "Conversation with Walter Piston," p. 164.

28. Fairbanks interview.

29. Westergaard, "Conversation with Walter Piston," p. 164.

30. Fairbanks interview.

31. See the following extract from the Westergaard interview for the reason this section is identified as "Variation I" rather than as "Theme." Might the term "theme" also be inappropriate in discussing other variations by Piston?

32. Westergaard, "Conversation with Walter Piston," p. 166.

33. Howard Klein, "Rostropovich Adds Premiere to Series," *New York Times* (3 March 1967).

34. Fairbanks interview.

35. The other contributors were Babbitt, Bennett, Berio, Carter, Copland, Gerhard, Hanson, Harris, Kirchner, Myrow, Nabakov, Schuman, Sessions, Shchedrin, Stockhausen, Takemitsu, and Thomson; see Howard Shanet, *Philharmonic* (Garden City, New York: Doubleday and Co., Inc., 1975), p. 462.

36. Quoted by Michael Steinberg in "Happy 80th Birthday, Walter Piston," *The Boston Globe* (20 January 1974).

**Chapter 9**

1. See Chapter 1, p. 11.

2. Walter Piston, quoted in program notes, *Cincinnati Symphony Orchestra Programs* (14 November 1975).

3. Personal interview with Mario di Bonaventura, 17 August 1977. Bonaventura also mentions that Piston preferred the Italian pronounciation for "Fantasia."

4. Eric Leinsdorf, letter to Walter Piston, 21 February 1964, Piston Collection, Boston Public Library.

5. WGBH interview, 19 January 1973.

6. WGBH interview, 19 January 1973.

7. Walter Piston, quoted in "B.S.O. to premier Piston flute concerto" by Thomas Dotton, *Boston Globe* (22 September 1972).

8. Leighton Kramer, *The Village Voice* (27 December 1973).

9. Michael Steinberg, "Thomas conducts B.S.O.'s 92nd opening concert," *Boston Globe* (23 September 1972).

10. Personal letter from Doriot Anthony Dwyer, 12 July 1977.

11. Nicanor Zabaleta, letter to Walter Piston, Piston Collection.

12. Fairbanks Interview, ca. 1967.

13. Personal letter from Luis Leguia, 1 September 1977. Leguia's description of the work as a "joy" echoes Wendell Margrave's review, "Leguia with Joy," in the *Washington Star-News*, 14 December 1974. Writes Margrave, "The piece itself is a joy. It is mature Piston, with all his care in construction and with a wealth of beautiful sound. It is essentially a piece of chamber music, difficult, but in no sense a display piece."

14. Personal letter from George Humphrey, 1 August 1977.

15. WGBH interview, 19 January 1973.

16. The Vermel-Piston correspondence is in the Piston Collection. The "steady procession of frustrating and upsetting events" may have concerned his and his wife's health.

17. Quoted in "Program Notes" by Harold Brown, *Portland Symphony Orchestra Programs* 52 No. 1 (1976–77), p. 34.

18. Harold Brown, "Program Notes."

19. Mark DeVoto, "In Memoriam: Walter Piston (1894–1976)," *Perspectives of New Music* 15 (1977), pp. 243–44.

20. Brown, "Program Notes."

21. WGBH interview, 19 January 1974.

22. Walter Piston and G. Wallace Woodworth, "Fifty years of the American Symphony Orchestra: Personal Vignettes," in *The American Symphony Orchestra*, edited by Henry Swoboda (New York: Basic Books, Inc., 1967), p. 17.

23. Quoted by Clark T. Irwin, Jr., in "Piston's Work Impresses," *Portland, Maine, Evening Express* (27 October 1976).

24. John Thornton, "Piston. Composer's Work in World Premiere Here Tonight," *Portland, Maine, Evening Express* (26 October 1976).

**Chapter 10**

1. Review of *Guide to the Practical Study of Harmony* by Peter Ilyich Tchaikowsky, in *Notes* 27 (June 1971), p. 708.

2. Review of *Harmonic Practice* by Roger Sessions, in *Musical Quarterly* 38 (1952), p. 458.

3. Ibid.

4. Review of *Modus Novus: Studies in Reading Atonal Melodies* by Lars Edlund, in *Music Educator's Journal* Vol. 52, No. 5 (April–May 1966), p. 119.

5. Walter Piston, *Principles of Harmonic Analysis* (Boston: E. C. Schirmer, 1933), p. 50.

6. See Chapter 5, p. 72.

7. Piston was never satisfied with the term "nonharmonic tone," and liked Sessions's coinage of "accessory tone." See the review of *Harmonic Practice*.

8. Piston, *Principles*, p. 2.

9. Ross Lee Finney, "Piston's Manual of Harmonic Practice," *Modern Music* 19 (November–December 1941), p. 69.

10. Walter Piston, "The Composer Speaks," in *Book of Modern Composers*, edited by David Ewen, second edition, revised and enlarged (New York: Alfred A. Knopf, 1950), p. 497.

11. See Chapter 2, p. 20.

12. Walter Piston, *Harmony*, third edition (New York: W. W. Norton, 1962), p. 369.

13. Review of *Harmonic Practice*.

14. Walter Piston, "The Music Criticism Racket," *Modern Music* 22 (1945), pp. 282–83.

15. Review of *Questions About Music* by Roger Sessions, *Notes* 27 (June 1971), pp. 705–7.

16. Walter Piston, *Counterpoint* (New York: W. W. Norton, 1947), p. 11.

17. Review of *Harmonic Practice*, p. 458.

18. These are found in the Piston Collection.

19. Walter Piston, "What is Good Music?" *New York Herald Tribune* (11 April 1961), p. 30.

20. Personal interview with John Groden, 21 August 1979; personal letter from Mark DeVoto, 24 July 1980; letters from Walter Piston to Betty Thorndike.

21. DeVoto, letter.

22. Walter Piston, "Thoughts on the Chordal Concept," *Essays on Music in Honor of Archibald Thompson Davison* (Cambridge: Harvard University Press, 1957), pp. 273–79.

23. Walter Piston, "Problems of Intonation in the Performance of Contemporary Music," in *Instrumental Music*, edited by David G. Hughes (Cambridge: Harvard University Press, 1959), pp. 70–79.

24. Walter Piston, "More Views on Serialism," *The Score* 23 (July 1958), pp. 46–49.

25. Personal interview with David Diamond, 2 August 1979.

26. Piston, *Harmony*, p. 335.

27. Piston, *Principles*, p. 1.

28. Piston, "Thoughts," p. 278.

29. Peter Stadlen, "Serialism Reconsidered," *The Score* 22 (February 1958), pp. 12–27.

30. Roger Sessions, "To the Editor," *The Score* 23 (July 1958), pp. 58–64.

31. Roberto Gerhard, "Apropos Mr. Stadlen," *The Score* 23 (July 1958), pp. 50–57.

32. Piston, "More Views," p. 46.

33. Ibid., p. 48.

34. Walter Piston, "Can Music be Nationalistic?" *Music Journal* 19 (October 1961), pp. 25, 86.

35. Ibid., p. 86.

36. Quoted by Russell Kerr in "Piston Pulitzer—The Winner Speaks," *Musical Courier* 163 (June 1961), p. 6.

37. Fairbanks interview.

38. Piston "More Views," p. 47.

39. Piston, *Orchestration*, pp. 176–77.

40. See Chapter 5, p. 72.

41. Walter Piston, "Stravinsky as Psalmist—1931," *Modern Music* 8 (January–February 1931), p. 43.

42. Walter Piston, "Stravinsky's Rediscoveries," in *Stravinsky in the Theatre*, edited with an introduction by Minna Lederman (New York: Farrar, Straus and Giroux, 1949; reprint ed., New York: Da Capo Press, 1975), pp. 130–31.

43. Eric White, "Stravinsky," in *Music in the Modern Age*, edited by F. W. Sternfeld (New York: Praeger, 1973), pp. 91–92.

44. Walter Piston "A Reminiscence," *Perspectives of New Music* 9–10 (1971), pp. 6–7.

45. Walter Piston, "Roy Harris," *Modern Music* 11 (1934), pp. 73–82.

46. Ibid., p. 80.

47. Quoted by Ellen Pfeifer in "Walter Piston musician of the month," *High Fidelity/Musical America* 24 (August 1974), pp. MA 4–5.

48. Piston, "The Composer Speaks," p. 497.

49. Personal interviews with David Diamond, 2 August 1979, and Richard French, 4 January 1978.

50. Interview with French.

51. Virgil Thomson, *Virgil Thomson* (New York: Da Capo Press, 1966), p. 141.

52. Piston, "The Music Criticism Racket," p. 283.

53. Personal interview with Virgil Thomson, 13 August 1977.

54. Minna Lederman, letter to Walter Piston, 28 April 1945, Piston Collection, Music Division, Library of Congress, Washington, D.C.

55. Piston, letter to Minna Lederman, 1 May 1945.

56. Piston, "The Music Criticism Racket," p. 282.

57. Ibid., p. 283.

58. Walter Piston, "Music in the Setting of World History," *Modern Music* 19 (November–December 1941), p. 64.

59. Personal interview with Harold Shapero, 1 December 1978.

60. Piston, letter to Chris Rouse, 22 February 1965, in the possession of Rouse.

61. Interview with French.

62. Interview with Diamond.

63. Piston, letter to Mr. Dana, 9 August 1948, Elliott Carter Letters, Music Division, New York Public Library. In the same letter, Piston requests that Dana send him Bowles's *Six Preludes*, David Diamond's *Sonatina*, and Krenek's *Eight Pieces*, all for piano.

64. Pfeifer, "Walter Piston," MA 5.

65. Pfeifer, "Walter Piston, Belmont, noted composer, author, teacher," *Boston Herald* (13 November 1976).

66. Pfeifer, "Walter Piston," MA 5.

67. Personal interview with Mario di Bonaventura, 17 August 1977.

68. Quoted by Louis Chapin in "Walter Piston at 70," *Musical America* 83 (December 1963), p. 34.

69. Interview with Shapero.

70. Piston, "Can Music," p. 86.

71. Walter Piston, "Teaching as a Composer's Craft," *Composer's News-Record* 9 (1949), pp. 1–2.

72. Walter Piston, "What a Young Composer Should Know," *Boston Symphony Orchestra Programmes* 72 (1952–1953), pp. 70–76.

73. Walter Piston, "The Composer Must Stay Individual," *Christian Science Monitor* (18 October 1958).

# Bibliography

This bibliography includes neither the large collections of unpublished Pistoniana in the Library of Congress and the Boston Public Library, nor the few unpublished items in the Carter Collection of the New York Public Library, the Watanabe Collection of the Sibley Music Library, and in private hands. Except for theses, taped interviews, personal interviews, and personal letters, all the material in this bibliography is published. Sources are listed alphabetically by author within the following classifications.

1. On Piston's Artistic and Intellectual Background
2. On Piston's Music: Background Sources
3. General Sources that Discuss Piston
4. On Piston
5. On Specific Works by Piston
6. On Piston's Family
7. Piston's Writings
8. Unpublished Taped Interviews
9. Unpublished Personal Interviews
10. Personal Letters

Section 5 is further subdivided alphabetically by composition title. It should be noted that sources in Sections 3 and 4 which touch upon specific works are not listed in Section 5. On the other hand, sources within Section 5 are repeated if they discuss more than one work.

## 1. On Piston's Artistic and Intellectual Background

Acquavella Galleries, Inc. *Amedeo Modigliani*. New York: Acquavella Galleries, Inc., 1971.
Aiken, Conrad. *The Collected Novels of Conrad Aiken*. New York: Holt, Rinehart and Winston, 1964.
─────── . *The Collected Poems*. 2nd ed. New York: Oxford University Press, 1970.
─────── . *Collected Short Stories*. Cleveland: World Publishing Co., 1960.
─────── . *Selected Letters of Conrad Aiken*. Edited by Joseph Killorin. New Haven: Yale University Press, 1978.
Atkins, Elizabeth. *Edna St. Vincent Millay and Her Times*. Chicago: University of Chicago Press, 1936.
Babbitt, Irving. *Rousseau and Romanticism*. Boston: Houghton Mifflin, 1919.
Bainbridge, John. *Garbo*. New York: Holt, Rinehart and Winston, 1955.
Barnard, Ellsworth. *Edwin Arlington Robinson. A Critical Study*. New York: MacMillan, 1952.

Barnes, Albert C., and de Mazia, Violette. *The Art of Henri-Matisse*. Marion, Pennsylvania: Barnes Foundation Press, 1933.

Bean, Philip C. *Winslow Homer at Prout's Neck*. Boston: Little, Brown and Company, 1966.

Bergson, Henri. *Creative Evolution*. Translated by Arthur Mitchell. New York: Modern Library, 1944.

Breé, Germaine. *Camus and Sartre*. New York: Delacorte Press, 1972.

Britten, Norman A. *Edna St. Vincent Millay*. New York: Twayne Publishers, 1967.

Burbank, Rex. *Thornton Wilder*. Boston: Twayne Publishers, 1961.

Burr, John I. H. *Revolution and Tradition in Modern American Art*. Cambridge: Harvard University Press, 1951.

Camus, Albert. *The Rebel*. Translated by Anthony Bower. New York: Alfred A. Knopf, 1956.

Corn, Wanda M., ed. *The Art of Andrew Wyeth*. Greenwich, New York: Graphic Society, 1973.

Cowley, Malcolm. *Exile's Return*. New York: Viking Press, 1934.

Coxe, Louis. *Edward Arlington Robinson*. New York: Pegasus, 1969.

Cozzens, James Gould. *By Love Possessed*. New York: Harcourt, Brace and World, 1957.

_____. *Morning, Noon and Night*. New York: Harcourt, Brace and World, 1968.

Domit, Moussa. *American Impressionist Painting*. Washington: National Gallery of Art, 1973.

Eliot, T. S. *The Complete Poems and Plays 1909–1950*. New York: Harcourt, Brace and World, 1962.

_____. *Selected Prose*. Edited with an Introduction by Frank Kermode. New York: Farrar, Straus and Giroux, 1975.

Fitch, James Marston. *Walter Gropius*. New York: Geroge Braziller, Inc., 1960.

Fitts, Dudley. *Poems 1929–1936*. Norfolk, Connecticut: New Directions, 1937.

Frost, Robert. *The Poetry of Robert Frost*. Edited by Edward Connery Lathem. New York: Holt, Rinehart and Winston, 1969.

Gide, André. *The Counterfeiters*. Translated by Dorothy Bussy. New York: Vintage Books, 1973.

Gould, Jean. *The Poet and Her Book*. New York: Dodd, Mean and Co., 1969.

Hammerton, John A. *Stevensonia*. Revised edition. Edinburgh: John Grant, 1910.

Harmer, J. B. *Victory in Limbo. Imagism 1908–1917*. New York: St. Martin's Press, 1975.

Hauser, Arnold. *Mannerism*. New York: Alfred A. Knopf, 1965.

_____. *The Social History of Art*. New York: Vintage Books, 1951.

Hemingway, Ernest. *The Sun Also Rises*. New York: Charles Scribner's Sons, 1926.

Howgate, George W. *George Santayana*. New York: A. S. Barnes and Co., Inc., 1961.

Hyans, Joe. *Bogie. The Biography of Humphrey Bogart*. New York: New American Library, 1966.

Iorizzo, Luciano and Salvatore Mandello. *The Italian-Americans*. New York: Twayne Publishers, 1971.

James, Henry. *The Ambassadors*. Edited by S. P. Rosenbaum. New York: W. W. Norton, 1964.

James, William. *The Will to Believe and Other Essays in Popular Philosophy*. New York: Dover Publications, Inc., 1956.

Kramer, Hilton. *The Age of the Avant-Garde*. New York: Farrar, Straus and Giroux, 1973.

Lamont, Corliss. *Humanism as a Philosophy*. New York: Philosophical Library, 1949.

MacKown, Diana. *Dawns + Dusks. Louise Nevelson*. New York: Charles Scribner's Sons, 1976.

MacLeish, Archibald. *J.B.* Boston: Houghton Mifflin, 1956.
Marquand, John P. *The Late George Apley.* Boston: Little, Brown and Co., Inc., 1937.
_____. *Women and Thomas Harrow.* Boston: Little, Brown and Co., 1958.
Millay, Edna St. Vincent. *Collected Poems.* Edited by Norma Millay. New York: Harper and Row, 1956.
Mooney, Harry John, Jr. *James Gould Cozzens. Novelist of Intellect.* Pittsburgh: University of Pittsburgh Press, 1963.
Moravia, Alberto. *The Lie.* Translated by Angus Davidson. New York: Farrar, Straus and Giroux, 1966.
_____. *Man As An End. A Defense of Humanism.* Translated by Bernard Wall. New York: Farrar, Straus and Giroux, 1965.
Nash, George H. *The Conservative Intellectual Movement in America Since 1945.* New York: Basic Books, 1976.
National Collection of Fine Arts. *Milton Avery.* Introduction by Adelyn Breeskin. Greenwich, Connecticut: National Collection of Fine Arts, 1969.
O'Hara, John. *The Horse Knows the Way.* New York: Random House, 1963.
Pirandello, Luigi. *As You Desire Me.* Translated by Samuel Putnam. New York: E. P. Dutton and Co., Inc., 1931.
Placzek, Adolf K., gen. ed. *Architecture and Decorative Art.* Vol. 37. *Four Great Makers of Modern Architecture. Gropius. Le Corbusier. Mies van der Rohe. Wright.* New York: Da Capo, 1970.
Read, Herbert. *Art and Society.* New York: Schocken, 1966.
_____. *To Hell with Culture and Other Essays on Art and Society.* New York: Schocken, 1963.
Rexroth, Kenneth. *American Poetry in the Twentieth Century.* New York: Seabury Press, 1971.
Richardson, E. P. *A Short History of Painting in America.* New York: Thomas Y. Crowell, Co., 1956.
Robinson, Edward Arlington. *Selected Poems.* Edited by Morton Zabel. New York: MacMillan, 1965.
Rose, Barbara. *American Art Since 1900.* Revised and expanded edition. New York: Praeger Publishers, 1975.
Santayana, George. *The Last Puritan.* New York: Charles Scribner's Sons, 1936.
Schiff, Gert, ed. *Picasso in Perspective.* Englewood, New Jersey: Prentice-Hall, Inc., 1976.
Stein, Gertrude. *Paris France.* New York: Charles Scribner's Sons, 1940.
Valéry, Paul. *Selected Writings.* Edited by Anthony Bower and J. Laughlin. New York: New Directions, 1950.
Veblen, Thorstein. *The Theory of the Leisure Class.* New York: MacMillan, 1899.
Wheelwright, John. *Collected Poems.* Edited by Alvin H. Rosenfeld. New York: New Directions, 1971.
Wilder, Thornton. *The Bridge of San Luis Rey.* New York: Washington Square Press, 1939.
_____. *Our Town.* New York: Harper and Row, 1938.
Wilkies, George. *Americans in Paris.* New York: Doubleday and Co., 1969.
Yu-tang, Lin. *The Importance of Living.* New York: Reynal and Hitchcock, 1937.

**2. On Piston's Music: Background Sources**

Austin, William. "Harmonic Rhythm in 20th-Century Music." Ph.D. dissertation, Harvard University, 1950.
Bacon, George F. *Rockland, Belfast and Vicinity.* Newark, New Jersey: Glenwood Publishing Co., 1892.

Ballantine, Edward. Liner notes to his *Variations for Piano on "Mary Had a Little Lamb"*. Played by the composer. Festival Recording FLP 70-201.

Baskerville, David Ross. "Jazz Influence on Art Music to Mid-Century." Ph.D. dissertation, University of California—Los Angeles, 1965.

Berger, Arthur. "Stravinsky and the Younger American Composer." *The Score* 12 (June 1955): 38–46.

*Boston Symphony Orchestra Programmes*. 1904–1976.

Boulanger, Nadia. "Lecures on Modern Music." *Rice Institute Pamphlet* 13 (April 1926): 113–95.

Boyd, Everett Vernon, Jr. "Paul Dukas and the Impressionist Milieu: Stylistic Assimilation in Three Orchestral Works." Ph.D. dissertation, University of Rochester, 1980.

Brush, Gerome. *Boston Symphony Orchestra. Charcoal Drawings of its Members with Biographical Sketches*. Boston: Merrymount Press, 1936.

Carter, Elliott. "The Rhythmic Basis of American Music." *The Score* 12 (1955): 27–32.

Cone, Edward T. "Conversation with Roger Sessions." *Perspectives of New Music* 4 (1966): 29–46.

Copland, Aaron. "Serge Koussevitzky and the American Composer." *Musical Quarterly* 30 (1944): 255–69.

Davison, Archibald T. *Music Education in America*. New York: Harper and Brothers, 1926.

Dukas, Paul. "Les tendencies de la musique contemporaine." *Courier Musical*, January 1924. Reprinted in *Ecrits sur la musique*. Paris: SEFI, 1948. Unpublished translation by William Austin.

Eaton, Cyrus. *History of Thomaston, Rockland and South Thomaston Maine*. Hallowell: Masters, Smith and Co., 1865.

Edwards, George Thornton. *Music and Musicians of Maine*. Portland: Southworth Press, 1928.

*Fontainebleau School of Music Catalog*. 1921, 1928.

Foote, Arthur and Walter Spalding. *Modern Harmony in its Theory and Practice*. Boston: Arthur P. Schmidt, 1905.

Gerhard, Roberto. "Apropos Mr. Stadlen." *The Score* 23 (July 1958): 50–57.

*Harvard University Catalogs*. 1919–1960.

Hill, Edward Burlingame. *Modern French Music*. Boston: Houghton Mifflin, 1924.

Howe, M. A. DeWolfe. *The Boston Symphony Orchestra 1881–1931*. Boston: Houghton Mifflin, 1931.

Johnson, H. Earle. *Symphony Hall, Boston*. Boston: Little, Brown and Co., 1950.

*Longy School of Music Catalogs*. 1924–1938.

Lourie, Arthur. *Sergei Koussevitzky and His Epoch*. Translated by S. W. Pring. Freeport, New York: Books for Libraries Press, 1931.

Mangeot, August. "L'Ecole Normale de Musique." *Encyclopédie de la Musique et Dictionnaire de Conservatoire*. Series II, Vol. 6. Paris: Librairie Delagrave, 1931: 2626–27.

Marks, Edward. *They All Sang*. New York: Viking Press, 1934.

Mason, Daniel Gregory. *Music In My Time and Other Reminiscences*. New York: MacMillan, 1938.

―――――. *Tune In, America*. New York: Alfred A. Knopf, 1931.

Munch, Charles. *I Am a Conductor*. Translated by Leonard Burkat. New York: Oxford University Press, 1955.

Palmer, Christopher. *Impressionism in Music*. London: Hutchinson University Library, 1973.

Pound, Ezra. *Antheil and the Treatise on Harmony*. Chicago: Pascal Covici, 1927.

Rosenfeld, Paul. *An Hour with American Music*. Philadelphia: J. P. Lippincott, 1929.

Sessions, Roger. *Harmonic Practice*. New York: Harcourt, Brace and Co., 1951.

_____ . *The Musical Experience of Composer, Performer, Listener*. Princeton: Princeton University Press, 1950.

_____ . *Questions About Music*. Cambridge: Harvard University Press, 1970.

_____ . "To The Editor." *The Score* 23 (July 1958): 58–64.

Smith, George Henry Lovett. "Edward Burlingame Hill." *Modern Music* 16 (1939): 11–16.

Spalding, Walter. *Music: An Art and A Language*. New York: Arthur P. Schmidt, 1920.

Stadlen, Peter. "Serialism Reconsidered." *The Score* 22 (February 1958): 12–27.

Stravinsky, Igor. *Poetics of Music*. Translated by Arthur Knodel and Ingolf Dahl. Cambridge: Harvard University Press, 1942.

_____ . *Themes and Conclusions*. London: Faber and Faber, 1972.

Wyatt, Lucius Reynolds. "The Mid-Twentieth Century Orchestral Variation 1953–1963: An Analysis and Comparison of Selected Works." Ph.D. dissertation, University of Rochester, 1973.


**3.  General Sources that Discuss Piston**


Austin, William. *Music in the 20th Century*. New York: W. W. Norton, 1966.

Barber, Samuel. Liner notes to *Songs of Samuel Barber and Ned Rorem*. New World Records NW 229.

Briggs, John. *Leonard Bernstein*. New York: World Publishing Co., 1961.

Chase, Gilbert. *America's Music*. New York: McGraw Hill, 1955.

Copland, Aaron. *Copland on Music*. New York: W. W. Norton, 1944.

_____ . *The New Music 1900–1960*. Revised and enlarged edition. New York: W. W. Norton, 1968.

Coppock, Jane. "A Conversation with Arthur Berger." *Perspectives of New Music* 17 (1978): 40–67.

Deri, Otto. *Exploring Twentieth-Century Music*. New York: Holt, Rinehart and Winston, 1968.

Dickson, Harry Ellis. *"Gentlemen, More Dolce Please!" An Irreverant Memoir of Thirty Years in the Boston Symphony Orchestra*. Boston: Beacon Press, 1969.

Downes, Edward. "Musical Man of Letters." *The Music-Makers*. Edited by Deena Rosenberg and Bernard Rosenberg. New York: Columbia University Press, 1979: 96–113.

Drew, David. "American Chamber Music." *Chamber Music*. Edited by Alec Robertson. New York: Penguin Books, 1957: 321–28.

Duke, Vernon. *Listen Here!* New York: Ivan Obolensky, Inc., 1963.

Ewen, David. *Composers Since 1910*. New York: H. W. Wilson Co., 1969.

Fine, Irving. "Elementary Theory in the Music Curriculum at Harvard University." *Music Teachers National Association, Volume of Proceedings for 1948*. Pittsburgh: Association, 1950: 210–17.

Goss, Madeleine. *Modern Music-Makers*. New York: E. P. Dutton and Co., 1952.

Harden, Brian, ed. *Shore Village Story*. Rockland: Rockland Bicentennial Commission, 1976.

Harrison, Jay S. "Munch and Music: His Current Views." *New York Herald Tribune*, 6 March 1960.

Hitchcock, Wiley. *Music in the United States*. Second edition. Englewood, New Jersey: Prentice-Hall, 1974.

Hoover, Kathleen and John Cage. *Virgil Thomson. His Life and Music*. New York: Thomas Yoseloff, 1959.

Kendall, Alan. *The Tender Tyrant. Nadia Boulanger*. Wilton, Connecticut: Lyceum Books, 1977.

Korn, Peter Jona. "The Symphony in America." *The Symphony Vol. II. Elgar to the Present Day.* Edited by Robert Simpson. Baltimore: Penguin Books, 1967: 243–67.

Layton, Robert. "U.S.A." *Twentieth Century Music.* Revised edition. Edited by Rollo Myers. New York: Orion Press, 1968: 232–40.

Leichtentritt, Hugo. *Serge Koussevitzky. The Boston Symphony Orchestra and the New American Music.* Cambridge: Harvard University Press, 1947.

Machlis, Joseph. *Introduction to Contemporary Music.* New York: W. W. Norton, 1979.

McCorkle, Donald M., ed. "The Composer in Academia. Reflections on a Theme of Stravinsky." *College Music Symposium* 10 (1970): 57–98.

Mellers, Wilfred. *Music in a New Found Land.* London: Barrie and Rockliff, 1964.

"The reaction: It's unanimous (almost): they like Ozawa." *Boston Globe*, 3 February 1972.

Reis, Claire R. *Composers, Conductors and Critics.* New York: Oxford University Press, 1955.

Rorem, Ned. Liner notes to *The American Art Song.* New World Records NW 243.

Sacher, Abram L. *A Host at Last.* Boston: Little, Brown and Co., 1976.

Smith, Moses. *Koussevitzky.* New York: Allen, Towne, and Heath, Inc., 1947.

Spalding, Walter. *Music at Harvard.* New York: Coward-McCann, 1935.

"Stravinsky—Darling of Moderns Lauds 2 Americans: Copland and Piston." *New York World Telegram*, 10 February 1945.

Thomson, Virgil. *American Music Since 1910.* New York: Holt, Rinehart and Winston, 1970.

————. *Music Reviewed 1940–1954.* New York: Vintage Books, 1967.

————. *The Musical Scene.* New York: Greenwood Press, 1968.

————. *The State of Music.* New York: William Morrow and Co., 1939.

————. *Virgil Thomson.* New York: Alfred A. Knopf, 1966.

Ulrich, Homer. *Chamber Music.* Second edition. New York: Columbia University Press, 1966.

Willis, Wayne Carr. "A Fanfare for the Common Man: Nationalism and Democracy in the Arts of the American 1930's." Ph.D. dissertation, Brandeis University, 1977.

**4.  On Piston**

Archibald, Bruce. "Walter Piston." *The New Grove Dictionary of Music.* Vol. 14. Edited by Stanley Sadie, London: MacMillan, 1980.

Beck, Marial. "Classified Chronological Catalog of Works by United States Composer Walter Piston." *Boletín Interamericano de Música* 9–10 (January–March 1959): 59–65.

Berger, Arthur. "Walter Piston." *Trend*, January–February 1935: 210–12.

Carter, Elliott. "Walter Piston." *Musical Quarterly* 32 (1946): 354–75.

Chapin, Louis. "Walter Piston at 70." *Musical America* 83 (December 1963): 34.

Citkowitz, Israel. "Walter Piston—Classicist." *Modern Music* 13 (1936): 3–11.

Curtis, William D. "A Piston Discography." *American Record Guide*, June 1977: 38–39; addendum in the July 1977 issue: 42.

Daniel, Olivier, ed. *Walter Piston.* New York: Broadcast Music Industry, Inc., 1964.

DeVoto, Mark. "In Memoriam: Walter Piston (1894–1976)." *Perspectives of New Music* 15 (1977): 243–44.

Driscoll, Edgar J., Jr. "Walter Piston, composer and Harvard Professor." *Boston Globe*, 13 November 1976.

Eyer, Ronald. "Composer's Showcase." *New York Herald Tribune*, 31 March 1961.

Forbes, Elliot, Merritt, A. Tillman and Vosgerchian, Louise. "Walter Hamor Piston. Memorial Minute Adopted by the Faculty of Arts and Sciences, Harvard University." *Harvard University Gazette* 74 no. 34, 25 May 1979.

Hudson, Edward. "Walter Piston Dies: Composer Won Two Pulitzers." *New York Times*, 13 November 1976.
Kerr, Russell. "Piston Pulitzer—The Winner Speaks." *Musical Courier* 163 (June 1961): 5–7.
Pfeifer, Ellen. "Walter Piston, Belmont, noted composer, author, teacher." *Boston Herald*, 13 November 1976.
————. "Walter Piston musician of the month." *High Fidelity Musical America* 24 (August 1974): MA 4–5.
Roy, Klaus George. "Walter Piston." *Stereo Review* 24 (April 1970): 57–67.
Salzman, Eric. "Piston Ex-Teacher." *New York Times*, 31 January 1954.
Sheridan, Wilbur. "Chamber Music of Walter Piston." M.M. thesis, University of Rochester, 1947.
Slonimsky, Nicolas. "Walter Piston." *American Composers on American Music*. Edited by Henry Cowell. New York: Frederick Ungar, 1933: 125–27.
Smith, George Henry Lovett. "Walter Piston: American Composer." *Magazine of Art* 33 (1940): 98–99, 126–28.
Steinberg, Michael. "Composer turned from painting to music." *Boston Globe*, 19 January 1969.
————. "Happy 80th Birthday, Walter Piston." *Boston Globe*, 20 January 1974.
Taubman, Howard. "Piston at Sixty." *New York Times*, 31 January 1954.
Taylor, Clifford. "Walter Piston for his Seventieth Birthday." *Perspectives of New Music* 2 (1964): 102–14. Reprinted in *Perspectives on American Composers*. Edited by Benjamin Boretz and Edward Cone. New York: W. W. Norton, 1971: 171–83.
Westergaard, Peter. "Conversation with Walter Piston." *Perspectives of New Music* 7 (1968): 3–17. Reprinted in *Perspectives on American Composers*. Edited by Benjamin Boretz and Edward Cone. New York: W. W. Norton, 1971: 156–70.
Woodworth, G. Wallace. "Walter Piston." *Dictionary of Modern Music*. Edited by John Vinton. New York: E. P. Dutton, 1971.

**5. On Specific Works by Piston**

*Bicentennial Fanfare* (1975)

Sagmaster, Joseph. "Bicentennial Fanfare for Orchestra by Walter Piston." *Cincinnati Symphony Orchestra Programs* 81 (1975–1976): 14 November 1975.

*Capriccio for Harp and String Orchestra* (1963)

Parmenter, Ross. "Spain to Stage Big Festival Featuring Composers of All the Americas." In the files of BMI, Inc., and dated November 1964.

*Carnival Song* (1938)

Ghisi, Federico. *I Canti Carnascialeschi*. Florence: Olschki, 1937.
Medici, Lorenzo de. "Trionofo d'Arianna e Bacco." Translated by Robert Hall, Jr. Liner notes to *Carnival Song*, performed by the Cornell University Glee Club and the Rochester Symphony Brass Ensemble, Thomas Sokol conducting. Fleetwood FLP 6001.
Reese, Gustave. *Music in the Renaissance*. New York: W. W. Norton and Co., 1954.

*Chromatic Study on the Name of Bach* (1940)

"Piston Retires After 30 Years on Harvard Staff." *The Diapason* 51 (July 1, 1960): 18.

*Concertino for Piano and Chamber Orchestra* (1937)

Hantz, Mary Jane. "Walter Piston's use of contrapuntal devices in his *Concertino for Piano and Orchestra*." M.M. thesis, University of Rochester, 1943.
Lieberson, Goddard. "Over the Air." *Modern Music* 15 (1937): 53–55.

*Concerto for Clarinet and Orchestra* (1967)

Archibald, Bruce. "Music Reveiws." *Notes* 25 (June 1969): 824–26.

*Concerto for Flute and Orchestra* (1972)

Archibald, Bruce. "Current Chronicle." *Musical Quarterly* 59 (1973): 121–25.
Dotton, Thomas. "BSO to premiere Piston flute concerto." *Boston Globe*, 22 September 1972.
Kramer, Leighton. *Village Voice*, 27 December 1973.
Piston, Walter and Klaus Roy. "Concerto for Flute and Orchestra by Walter Piston." *Boston Symphony Orchestra Programmes* 92 (1972–1973): 16–25.
Steinberg, Michael. "Thomas conducts BSO's 92nd opening concert." *Boston Globe*, 23 September 1972.

*Concerto for Orchestra* (1933)

Copland, Aaron. "From the '20s to the '40s and Beyond." *Modern Music* 20 (1942–1943): 78–82.
Dahl, Ingolf. "Neglected Works: A Symposium." *Modern Music* 23 (1946): 11–12.
McPhee, Colin. "New York—January, February, 1936." *Modern Music* 13 (1936): 41–46.
Pleasants, Henry. "First-Time Fever." *Modern Music* 16 (1939): 82–85.

*Concerto for String Quartet, Wind Instruments and Percussion* (1976)

Brown, Harold. "Concerto for String Quartet, Wind Instruments and Percussion by Walter Piston." *Portland Symphony Orchestra Programs* 52 No. 1 (1976–1977): 34.
Irwin, Clark T., Jr. "Piston's Work Impresses." *Portland, Maine, Evening Express*, 27 October 1976.
Thornton, John. "Piston. Composer's Work in World Premiere Here Tonight." *Portland, Maine, Evening Express*, 26 October 1976.

*Concerto for Two Piano and Orchestra* (1959)

Newall, Robert. "Traveling Pianists Talk About Travels, Schools." *Bangor Daily News*, 20 February 1969.
Steinberg, Michael. "Exhumed Symphony very much alive." *Boston Globe*, 2 November 1968.

*Concerto for Viola and Orchestra* (1957)

Archibald, Bruce. "Reviews of five works issued or reissued by the Louisville Orchestra."
*Musical Quarterly* 64 (1978): 263–68.
Kolodin, Irving. "Music to my Ears." *Saturday Review* 41 (April 5, 1958): 22.
Piston, Walter. "Viola and Orchestra." *Boston Symphony Orchestra Programmes* 77
(1957–1958): 1136–42.

*Concerto No. 1 for Violin and Orchestra* (1939)

Shapero, Harold. "Neglected Works: A Symposium." *Modern Music* 23 (1946): 8–9.

*Concerto No. 2 for Violin and Orchestra* (1960)

Biancolli, Louis. "Philharmonic Closes Season." *New York World-Telegram and Sun*, 19 May
1962.
Callaghan, J. Dorsey. "Paray Mixes Old and New." *Detroit Free Press*, 18 May 1960.
Goldberg, Albert. "National Origins Hard to Detect at Concert." *Los Angeles Times*. 5 June
1961.
Kastendieck, Miles. "Farewell Concerts Form Triple Tribute." *New York Journal-American*,
19 May 1962.
Lang, Paul Henry. "New York Philharmonic." *New York Herald Tribune*, 19 May 1962.
Schonberg, Harold C. "Music: Season's End for Philharmonic." *New York Times*, 19 May
1962.

*Duo for Cello and Piano* (1972)

Margrave, Wendell. "Leguia with Joy." *Washington Star-News*, 14 December 1974.

*Duo for Viola and Cello* (1949)

Epstein, David. "Orchestra and Chamber Works by Piston." *Musical America* 77 (December 1, 1957): 26.

*Fantasia for Violin and Orchestra* (1970)

Archibald, Bruce. "Current Chronicle." *Musical Quarterly* 59 (1973): 121–125.
Pirie, Peter J. "Reviews of Music." *Music Review* 40 (May 1979): 157–58.

*Fantasy for English Horn, Harp and Strings* (1952)

Burk, John. "Fantasy for Solo English Horn, with Strings and Harp by Walter Piston."
*Boston Symphony Orchestra Programmes* 74 (1953–1954): 498.

*Fugue on a Victory Tune for Orchestra* (1944)

Harrison, Lou. "First-Time Fashion, New York, 1944." *Modern Music* 22 (1944–1945):
30–35.

*Harmony* (1941)

Burke, James Robert. "A Study of Theories of Non-Chord Tones Pertaining to the Music of the Period c. 1650 to c. 1875." Ph.D. dissertation, Indiana University, 1963.
Colucci, Matthew Joseph. "A Comparative Study of Contemporary Musical Theories in Selected Writings by Piston, Krenek and Hindemith." Ph.D. dissertation, University of Pennsylvania, 1957.
Drabkin, William. "Book Reviews." *Musical Times* 120 (June 1979): 485–86.
Finney, Ross Lee. "Piston's Manual of Harmonic Practice." *Modern Music* (November–December 1941): 69–71.
Novak, Saul. "Recent Approaches to the Study of Harmony." *Perspectives of New Music* 2 (1964): 150–58.
Salmenhaara, Erkki. *Soinnutus* [Harmony]. Helsinki: Otava, 1970.
————. *Sointuanalyysi* [Harmonic Analysis]. Helsinki: Otava, 1968.

*The Incredible Flutist* (1938)

Archibald, Bruce. "Reviews of five works issued or reissued by the Louisville Orchestra." *Musical Quarterly* 64 (1978): 263–68.
Booth, Philip. "The Incredible Flutist." *Fine Arts Magazine of the University of Connecticut*, April 1959.
Cannell, Kathleen. "Piston's 'Incredible Flutist' Revived." *Christian Science Monitor*, 20 April 1963.
Code, Grant. "Hans Wiener Begins a New Career." *Dance Observer* 8 (March 1941): 1.
Curtis, William D. "Fitting Memorial." *American Record Guide*, July 1977: 36–38.
H. K. A. "Modern Dance in the Making," *Boston Transcript*, 22 January 1938.
"The Incredible Flutist." *Dance* 4 (August 1938): 10.
"Jan Veen Dies." *Dance Magazine* 41 (July 1967): 4–5.
Kabalevsky, Dimitri. "An Opinion from Moscow." *Boston Symphony Orchestra Programmes* 76 (1956–1957): 116–17, 147. Originally in *Pravda*, 14 September 1956.
Lawrence, Robert. *Ballet and Ballet Music*. New York: Simon and Schuster, 1950.
Little, Barbara L. "Piston's humor displayed in his music at Fulton." *Daily Intelligence Journal, Lancaster*, 28 March 1966.
Martin, John. "Veen-Thimey in Recital," *New York Times*, 9 December 1941.
Moore, Robin. *Fiedler*. Boston: Little, Brown and Co., 1968.
Wiener, Hans. *Boston Transcript*, 22 January 1938.
Wilson, Carol Green. *Arthur Fiedler*. New York: Evans Publishing Co., 1968.

*Interlude for Viola and Piano* (1942)

K., I. "Reviews of Music." *Music and Letters* 34 (1953): 175.

*Lincoln Center Festival Overture* (1962)

Crowder, Charles. "Ormandy and His Men Back." *Washington Post*, 3 October 1962.

*Minuetto in Stile Vecchio for String Quartet* (1927)

Hill, E. B. *The Radcliffe News*. Vol. 15, No. 23, 15 April 1927.

*Partita for Violin, Viola and Organ* (1944)

Barlow, S. M. "Mrs. Coolidge's Birthday Party." *Modern Music* 22 (November 1944): 41.
MacLeish, Archibald. *A Time to Speak*. Boston: Houghton Mifflin, 1940.
Sandburg, Carl. *The People, Yes*. New York: Harcourt, Brace and Co., 1936.

*Passacaglia for Piano* (1943)

Agay, Denes, ed. *An Anthology of Piano Music. Vol. IV. The Twentieth Century*. Introduction by Louis L. Crowder. New York: Yorktown Music Press, 1971.
Gillespie, John. *Five Centuries of Keyboard Music*. New York: Dover, 1972.
McPhee, Colin. "Scores and Records." *Modern Music* 21 (1943–1944): 112–13.
Stevens, Elizabeth Mruk. "The Influence of Nadia Boulanger on Composition in the United States: A Study of Piano Solo Works by Her American Students." Mus. M.D. thesis, Boston University, 1975.

*Piano Sonata* (1926)

Petit, Raymond. "Musique d'Amérique du Nord." *Revue Musicale* 7 (1925–1926): 299–300.
Sessions, Roger. "An American Evening Abroad." *Modern Music* 4 (November–December 1926): 33–36.

*Pine Tree Fantasy for Orchestra* (1965)

Archibald, Bruce. "Music Reviews." *Notes* 25 (March 1969): 596–97.
"Pine Tree Fantasy by Walter Piston." *Portland Symphony Orchestra Program Magazine* 40 (1965–1966): 29–31.

*Prelude and Allegro for Organ and Strings* (1943)

McPhee, Colin. "Scores and Records." *Modern Music* 22 (1945): 129–30.

*Prelude and Fugue for Orchestra* (1934)

Walter, Bruno. *Of Music and Music Making*. Translated by Paul Hamburger. London: Faber and Faber, 1957.

*Quartet for Violin, Viola, Cello and Piano* (1964)

Pirie, Peter J. "Reviews of Music." *Music Review* 40 (May 1979): 157–58.
Steinberg, Michael. "Piston Quartet Debut at 'Arts Congregation.' " *Boston Globe*, 3 July 1964.
Strongin, Theodore. "American Music Sampled at N.Y.U." *New York Times*, 5 April 1967.

*Quintet for Flute and String Quartet* (1942)

Berger, Arthur. "Scores and Records." *Modern Music* 23 (1946): 306–9.
Re Pass, Richard. "New York Events." *Canon* 7 (1953–1954): 332.

*Quintet for Piano and String Quartet* (1949)

Morton, Lawrence. "Reviews of Records." *Musical Quarterly* 39 (1953): 657–59.

*Quintet for Wind Instruments* (1956)

Flanagan, William. "Record Reviews." *Musical Quarterly* 44 (1958): 551–53.
Piston, Walter. Liner notes to his *Quintet for Woodwind Instruments*. Played by the Boehm Quintette. Orion ORS 75206.

*Ricercare for Orchestra* (1967)

Archibald, Bruce. "Music Reveiws." *Notes* 25 (June 1969): 824–26.
Downes, Edward. "Ricercare for Orchestra by Walter Piston." *New York Philharmonic Program Notes* 126 (1967–1968): 7 March 1968.
Shanet, Howard. *Philharmonic*. Garden City, New York: Doubleday and Co., 1975.

*Second Suite for Orchestra* (1948)

Epstein, David. "Orchestra and Chamber Works by Piston." *Musical America* 77 (December 1, 1957): 26.

*Sinfonietta for Chamber Orchestra* (1941)

Burk, John N. "Symphony in C Major by Stravinsky." *Boston Symphony Orchestra Programmes* 60 (1940–1941): 548–56.

*Sonata for Flute and Piano* (1930)

*Commemorative Record of the One Hundred Concerts given by the Boston Flute Players' Club 1921–1940*
Meyer, Alfred H. "Yaddo—A May Festival." *Modern Music* 9 (1932): 172–76.
Smith, Carleton Sprague. "The I.S.C.M. Meets at Barcelona." *Modern Music* 13 (1936): 30–34.

*Sonata for Violin and Piano* (1939)

Finney, Ross Lee. "Piston's Violin Sonata." *Modern Music* 17 (1939–1940): 210–13.
Kennedy, Helen Louise. "Analysis of the Walter Piston Sonata for Violin and Piano." M.A. thesis, University of Rochester, 1956.

*Sonatina for Violin and Harpsichord* (1945)

Fuller, Donald. "Stravinsky Full-Length Portrait." *Modern Music* 23 (1946): 45–50.

*String Quartet No. 1* (1933)

Chanler, Theodore. "New York, 1934" *Modern Music* 11 (1934): 142–47.
Goldberg, Albert. "Kroll Quartet Gives Satisfying Concert." *Los Angeles Times*, 30 March 1962.

*String Quartet No. 2* (1935)

Donahue, Robert Lawrence. "A Comparative Analysis of Phrase Structure in Selected Movements of the String Quartets of Béla Bartók and Walter Piston." D.M.A. Thesis, Cornell University, 1964.

*String Quartet No. 3* (1947)

Bergsma, William. "Music Reviews." *Notes* 7 (1949–1950): 131–32.

*String Quartet No. 4* (1951)

Donahue, Robert Lawrence. "A Comparative Analysis of Phrase Structure in Selected Movements of the String Quartets of Béla Bartók and Walter Piston." D.M.A. thesis, Cornell University, 1964.
Sabin, Robert. "New Music Reviews." *Musical America* 74 (1954): 36.

*String Quartet No. 5* (1962)

Chittum, Donald. Liner notes to Piston's *String Quartet No. 5*. Played by the Kohon String Quartet, Vox SVBX 5305.

*Suite for Oboe and Piano* (1931)

Citkowitz, Israel. "Symphonic and Chamber Music, New York." *Modern Music* 12 (1935): 187–92.
*Commemorative Record of the One Hundred Concerts given by the Boston Flute Players' Club 1921–1940*

*Symphonic Prelude for Orchestra* (1961)

Roy, Klaus George. "Symphonic Prelude by Walter Piston." *Cleveland Symphony Orchestra Programmes* 43 (1960–1961): 771–79.

*Symphony No. 1* (1937)

Berger, Arthur. "Scores and Records." *Modern Music* 23 (1946): 134–37.
Bernstein, Leonard. "Boston Carries On." *Modern Music* 15 (1937–1938): 239–41.
Carter, Elliott. "Season of Hindemith and Americans." *Modern Music* 16 (1938–1939): 249–54.
Danner, Gregory Guy. "An Analysis of the slow movements of selected Piston symphonies" M.A. thesis, University of Rochester, 1981.
Davis, Peter. "Some Contemporary Labors of Love." *New York Times*, 16 September 1979.
Gaburo, Kenneth. "Studies in Pitch Symmetry in Twentieth Century Music." D.M.A. thesis, University of Illinois, 1962.
Sloper, L. A. "Boston Symphony." *Christian Science Monitor*, 9 April 1938.
Smith, Moses. "Boston News." *Modern Music* 16 (1938–1939): 114–16.

*Symphony No. 2* (1943)

Brown, Ray. "Piston's New Symphony in Washington." *Modern Music* 21 (1943–1944): 179–80.

Danner, Gregory Guy. "An Analysis of the slow movements of selected Piston symphonies." M.A. thesis, University of Rochester, 1981.

Fuller, Donald. "Stravinsky Full-Length Portrait." *Modern Music* 23 (1946): 45–50.

Lindenfeld, Harris Nelson. "Three Symphonies of Walter Piston. An Analysis." D.M.A. thesis, Cornell University, 1975.

McPhee, Colin. "Scores and Records." *Modern Music* 22 (1944–1945): 129–30.

Mills, Charles. "Over the Air." *Modern Music* 21 (1943–1944): 268–70.

Smith, Moses. "Americans and Shostakovich in Boston." *Modern Music* 21 (1943–1944): 251–53.


*Symphony No. 4 (1950)*


Austin, William. "Piston's Fourth Symphony. An Analysis." *Music Review* 16 (1955): 120–37.

Ferguson, Donald. "Piston." *Masterworks in the Orchestral Repertory*. Minneapolis: University of Minnesota Press, 1954: 418–21.


*Symphony No. 5 (1953)*


Archibald, Bruce. "Reviews of five works issued or reissued by the Louisville Orchestra." *Musical Quarterly* 64 (1978): 263–68.

Burk, John. "Symphony No. 5 by Walter Piston." *Boston Symphony Orchestra Programmes* 76 (1956–1957): 138–40.

Danner, Gregory Guy. "An Analysis of the slow movements of selected Piston symphonies." M.A. thesis, University of Rochester, 1981.


*Symphony No. 6 (1954)*


Burk, John. "Symphony No. 6 by Walter Piston." *Boston Symphony Orchestra Programmes* 75 (1955–1956): 282–88.

Kabalevsky, Dimitri. "An Opinion from Moscow." *Boston Symphony Orchestra Programmes* 76 (1956–1957): 116–17, 147. Originally in *Pravda*, 14 September 1956.

Lindenfeld, Harris Nelson. "Three Symphonies of Walter Piston. An Analysis." D.M.A. thesis, Cornell University, 1975.


*Symphony No. 7 (1960)*


Archibald, Bruce. "Music Reviews." *Notes* 25 (March 1969): 596–97.

————. "Reviews of five works issued or reissued by the Louisville Orchestra." *Musical Quarterly* 64 (1978): 263–68.

Burk, John. "Symphony No. 7 by Walter Piston." *Boston Symphony Orchestra Programmes* 82 (1962–1963): 22–28.

Danner, Gregory Guy. "An Analysis of slow movements of selected Piston symphonies." M.A. thesis, University of Rochester, 1981.

Eyer, Ronald. "Philadelphia Orchestra." *New York Herald Tribune*, 15 February 1961.

Halen, Walter John. "An Analysis and Comparison of Compositional Practices Used by Five Contemporary Composers in Works Titled 'Symphony.' " Ph.D. dissertation, Ohio State University, 1969.

Hall, David. "Piston Symphony No. 7; Symphony No. 8." *Stereo Review* 36 (May 1976): 120.
Lang, Paul Henry. "Boston Symphony." *New York Herald Tribune*, 25 October 1962.
"Piston Gets 5'G Commission from Philly Orch. Association." *The Cash Box*, 14 May 1960.

*Symphony No. 8* (1965)

Archibald, Bruce. "Reviews of five works issued or reissued by the Louisville Orchestra." *Musical Quarterly* 64 (1978): 263–68.
Biancolli, Louis. "Piston, Boston Symphony Shine." *New York World Telegram and Sun*, 1 April 1965.
Burk, John. "Symphony No. 8 by Walter Piston." *Boston Symphony Orchestra Programmes* 84 (1964–1965): 1183–90.
Danner, Gregory Guy. "An Analysis of slow movements of selected Piston symphonies." M.A. thesis, University of Rochester, 1981.
Hall, David. "Piston Symphony No. 7; Symphony No. 8." *Stereo Review* 36 (May 1976): 120.
Lindenfeld, Harris Nelson. "Three Symphonies of Walter Piston. An Analysis." D.M.A. thesis, Cornell University, 1975.
Steinberg, Michael. "New Piston Symphony; Johannesen's Brahms." *Boston Globe*, 6 March 1965.

*Three Counterpoints for Violin, Viola and Cello* (1973)

Pirie, Peter J. "Reviews of Music." *Music Review* 40 (May 1979): 157–58.

*Three New England Sketches for Orchestra* (1959)

Burk, John. "Three New England Sketches by Walter Piston." *Boston Symphony Orchestra Programmes* 80 (1960–1961): 80–84.
Dumm, Robert W. "Worcester Fete Marks Centenary." *Musical Courier* 160 (December 1959): 6.

*Three Pieces for Flute, Clarinet and Bassoon* (1925)

Piston, Walter. Liner notes to his *Three Pieces for Flute, Clarinet and Bassoon*. Played by members of the Art Wind Quintet. Classic Editions Recordings CE 2003.

*Toccata for Orchestra* (1948)

Piston, Walter. "Toccata for Orchestra." *Boston Symphony Orchestra Programmes* 93 (1973–1974): 625.

*Trio No. 2 for Violin, Cello and Piano* (1966)

Pirie, Peter J. "Reviews of Music" *Music Review* 40 (May 1979): 157–58.

*Tunbridge Fair: Intermezzo for Symphonic Band* (1950)

Bearse, Ray, ed. *Vermont. A Guide to the Green Mountain State*. Boston: Houghton Mifflin, 1938.

Goldman, Richard F. "Current Chronicle." *Musical Quarterly* 36 (1950): 592–95.

Hall, David. Liner notes to Piston's *Tunbridge Fair*. Played by Frederick Fennell and the Eastman Wind Ensemble. Mercury SRI 75086.

"The World's Fair." *The Vermonter* 35 (September 1930): 206.

*Variations for Cello and Orchestra* (1966)

Archibald, Bruce. "Music Reviews." *Notes* 25 (June 1969): 824–26.

Klein, Howard. "Rostropovich Adds Premiere to Series." *New York Times* 3 March 1967.

**6.   On Piston's Family**

"Art Association to honor Kathryn Nason Piston." *Belmont Citizen*, 26 February 1976.

Baum, Robert. "Quincy Tax Rate Only $13—(100 Years Ago)." *Patriot Ledger*, 7 December 1972.

"Composer and Artist Wife Honored at Symphony Hall." *Boston Traveler*, 17 April 1944.

Comstock, Francis Adams and William Dolan Fletcher. *The Work of Thomas Nason*. Boston: Boston Public Library, 1976.

Piston, Donald Stover. *Meteorlogy*. Philadelphia: P. Blakiston's Sons and Co., 1931. Second edition, 1941.

Renwick, Stephen Lee. "Thomas W. Nason. Poet Engraver of New England." *American Artist* 6 (November 1942).

Sutro, Ruth. "Reader Writes. Elias Nason Far From Obscure." *Patriot Ledger*, 26 December 1972.

————. "Thomas Nason: He Celebrated New England's Beauty." *Patriot Ledger*, 10 March 1976.

Trash, William Blake. *The Reverend Elias Nason, A.M.* Boston: Printed for Private Distribution, 1889.

**7.   Piston's Writings**

Piston, Walter. "Can Music be Nationalistic?" *Music Journal* 19 (October 1961): 25, 86.

————. "The Composer Speaks." *Book of Modern Composers*. Edited by David Ewen. Second edition, revised and enlarged. New York: Alfred A. Knopf, 1950: 496–97.

————. "The Composer Must Stay Individual." *Christian Science Monitor*, 18 October 1958.

————. *Counterpoint*. New York: W. W. Norton, 1947.

———— and Woodworth, G. Wallace. "Fifty years of the American Symphony Orchestra: Personal Vignettes." *The American Symphony Orchestra*. Edited by Henry Swoboda. New York: Basic Books, Inc., 1967: 10–20.

————. "Harmonic Rhythm." *Harvard Dictionary of Music*. Edited by Willi Apel. Cambridge: Harvard University Press, 1944.

————. *Harmony*. New York: W. W. Norton, 1941. Second edition, 1948. Third edition, 1962. Fourth edition, with Mark DeVoto, 1978.

————. "Letter to Arthur V. Berger." *Letters of Composers. An Anthology 1603–1945*. Compiled and edited by Gertrude Norman and Miriam Lubul Shrifte. New York: Alfred A. Knopf, 1946: 367.

————. "More Views on Serialism." *The Score* 23 (July 1958): 46–49.

_____ . "The Music Criticism Racket." *Modern Music* 22 (1945): 282–83.

_____ . "Music in the Setting of World History." *Modern Music* 19 (November–December 1941): 63–65.

_____ . *Orchestration*. New York: W. W. Norton, 1955.

_____ . *Principles of Harmonic Analysis*. Boston: E. C. Schirmer, 1933.

_____ . "Problems of Intonation in the Performance of Contemporary Music." *Instrumental Music*. Edited by David G. Hughes. Cambridge: Harvard University Press, 1959: 70–79.

_____ . "A Reminiscence." *Perspectives of New Music* 9–10 (1971): 6–7.

_____ . Review of *Harmonic Practice*, by Roger Sessions. *Musical Quarterly* 38 (1952): 457–68.

_____ . Review of *Modus Novus: Studies in Reading Atonal Melodies*, by Lars Edlund. *Music Educator's Journal* Vol. 52, No. 5 (April–May 1966): 119.

_____ . Review of *Questions About Music*, by Roger Sessions, and *Guide to the Practical Study of Harmony*, by Peter Ilyich Tchaikovsky. *Notes* 27 (June 1971): 705–8.

_____ . "Roy Harris." *Modern Music* 11 (1934): 73–82.

_____ . "Stravinsky as Psalmist—1931." *Modern Music* 8 (January–February 1931): 42–45.

_____ . "Stravinsky's Rediscoveries." *Stravinsky in the Theatre*. Edited with an Introduction by Minna Lederman. New York: Farrar, Straus and Giroux, 1949; reprint ed., New York: Da Capo Press, 1975: 130–31.

_____ . "Teaching as a Composer's Craft." *Composer's News-Record* 9 (1949): 1–2.

_____ . "Thoughts on the Chordal Concept." *Essays On Music in Honor of Archibald Thompson Davison*. Cambridge: Harvard University Press, 1957: 273–78.

_____ . "Walter Piston." *Twentieth Century Composers on Fugue*. Edited by Sister Gregory Joseph. Chicago: De Paul University, 1966: 37.

_____ . "What a Young Composer Should Know." *Boston Symphony Orchestra Programmes* 72 (1952–1953): 70–76.

_____ . "What is Good Music?" *New York Herald Tribune*, 11 April 1961: 30.

**8. Unpublished Taped Interviews**

Lazar, Joel. Fred Calland, "Options," National Public Radio. ca. 1976.

Piston, Walter. Margaret Fairbanks. Rodgers and Hammerstein Archive, New York Public Library, ca. 1967.

_____ . E. Power Biggs, Doriot Anthony Dwyer, and Daniel Pinkham. Robert Lurtsema, "Morning Pro Musica," WGBH Boston. 19 January 1973.

_____ . Robert Lurtsema, "Morning Pro Musica," WGBH Boston. 19 January 1974.

**9. Unpublished Personal Interviews**

Adler, Samuel. 14 March 1979.
Aiken, Mary. 27 August 1979.
Berger, Arthur. 1 December 1978.
Bonaventura, Mario di. 17 August 1977.
Chase, Nelson. 21 August 1979.
Clark, Grace Reasoner. 19 August 1979.
Copland, Aaron. 25 April 1979.
Craig, Flore. August 1977.
Diamond, David. 2 August 1979.

French, Richard F. 4 January 1978.
Fuchs, Joseph. 10 March 1979.
Groden, John and Helen Groden. 21 August 1979.
Hanson, Howard. September 1979.
Humphrey, George. 19 August 1979.
Kibrick, Jane. 20 August 1979.
Merritt, A. Tillman. 28 August 1979.
Nason, Margaret. 29 August 1979.
Naugler, Ruth. 22 July 1979.
Piston, Jean. 19 July 1979.
Reti, Marie-Christine. 21 August 1979.
Ruggles, Theodore. 22 July 1979.
Shapero, Harold. 1 December 1978.
Thompson, Randall. 21 August 1979.
Thomson, Virgil. 13 August 1977.

**10.  Personal Letters**

Aiken, Clarissa Lorenz. 26 April 1981.
Aiken, Mary. 18 February 1979; 8 June 1979.
Bernstein, Leonard. 5 October 1977.
Binkerd, Gordon. 23 November 1977.
Booth, Philip. 19 February 1980.
Boulanger, Nadia. 26 May 1977.
Coolidge, Alison. 17 February 1979; 19 February 1979.
Copland, Aaron. 5 August 1977.
Crane, Fidelia. 28 July 1977.
DeVoto, Mark. 24 July 1980.
Dwyer, Doriot Anthony. 12 July 1977.
Hibbitt, Peyton. 4 July 1980.
Hulbert, Alice. 31 October 1979.
Humphrey, George. 1 August 1977; 18 August 1977.
Kohs, Ellis. 14 October 1977.
Layton, Billy Jim. 8 October 1977.
Lee, Noel. 16 March 1978.
Leguia, Luis. 1 September 1977.
MacLeish, Archibald. 5 February 1981.
Moseley, Julia. 28 December 1978.
Nason, Margaret. 26 July 1977; 12 September 1977.
Piston, Edward. 19 August 1977; 15 October 1977.
Sapp, Allen. 23 September 1977.
Shackford, Charles. 12 November 1977.
Siegmeister, Elie. 15 April 1978.
Sutro, Ruth. 12 December 1978; 29 January 1979; 31 July 1979.
Thorndike, Betty. 11 December 1978; 19 February 1979; 1 March 1979; 21 October 1979.

# Index